How Novels Work

How Novels Work

John Mullan

OXFORD
UNIVERSITY PRESS

Great Clarendon Street, Oxford OX2 6DP

Oxford University Press is a department of the University of Oxford. It furthers the University's objective of excellence in research, scholarship, and education by publishing worldwide in

Oxford New York

Auckland Cape Town Dar es Salaam Hong Kong Karachi Kuala Lumpur Madrid Melbourne Mexico City Nairobi New Delhi Shanghai Taipei Toronto

With offices in

Argentina Austria Brazil Chile Czech Republic France Greece Guatemala Hungary Italy Japan Poland Portugal Singapore South Korea Switzerland Thailand Turkey Ukraine Vietnam

Published in the United States by Oxford University Press Inc., New York

First published 2006

British Library Cataloguing in Publication Data

Data available

Library of Congress Cataloging in Publication Data

Data available

Typeset by RefineCatch Limited, Bungay, Suffolk
Printed in Great Britain by
on acid-free paper by
Biddles Ltd., King's Lynn

ISBN 0-19-928177-7 (Hbk.) 978-0-19-928177-0 (Hbk.)

1

Acknowledgements

I would never have undertaken 'Elements of Fiction', my weekly articles for *The Guardian* on which this book is based, without the encouragement of Claire Armitstead and Giles Foden. Thanks also to Annalena McAfee, Susanna Rustin, Justine Jordan, and Pru Hone. Thanks for suggestions that they may now have forgotten making to Bas Aarts, Catherine Bennett, Kasia Boddy, Lindsay Duguid, Philip Horne, Danny Karlin, Gerry Nelson, Natasha Walter, and Sarah Wintell.

Charlotte Mitchell and John Sutherland, two colleagues from the English Department at University College London who are both far better read in the British Novel than I, were endlessly resourceful when I badgered them. Equally, my wife Harriet provided many fictional examples that she will find here masquerading as my own.

I am also grateful to those who wrote to me, or to *The Guardian*, with information, reflections, and descriptions of my errors. I have been indebted for particular points, now incorporated into this book, to Barry Ainslie, Sue Bridgwater, Seymour Chatman, Eric Dickens, Hugh Epstein, Mark Haddon, Alan Hollinghurst, Andy Holyer, Peter McDonald, Robin Milner-Gulland, Rod Prince, Elizabeth Roberts, Brian Robinson, Biljana Scott, Elaine Showalter, Alex Strick van Linschoten, and Uli Wienrich.

Finally, thanks to Sophie Goldsworthy and Andrew McNeillie at OUP for their encouragement, and to Laurien Berkeley and Andrew Hawkey for their editorial labours.

For Maud, Allegra, and William,
novel readers actual and future

Contents

References

ALL of the novels that I focus on in this book have been examined in my original 'Elements of Fiction' column in *The Guardian*. Quotations from these novels are referenced by page numbers, in parentheses, within the text. I give here the paperback editions that I have used, with the date of each novel's first publication.

The Select Bibliography at the back of this book details the editions of other novels that I have used. Quotations from these works too are referenced within the text. Though I have referred to widely available paperback editions, I provide, where possible, volume and chapter numbers as well as page numbers. Any reader with a different edition of, say, *Great Expectations* should still be able readily to find any passage cited. On the first occasion on which a given novel is mentioned I give, in parentheses, the date of its first publication.

Notes have been kept to a minimum and are reserved for references to non-fictional and foreign-language material.

Ali, Monica, *Brick Lane* (2003; Black Swan, 2004).

Amis, Martin, *Money* (1984; Penguin, 2000).

Atwood, Margaret, *The Blind Assassin* (2000; Virago, 2003).

Byatt, A. S., *Possession* (1990; Vintage, 1991).

Coe, Jonathan, *The Rotters' Club* (2001; Penguin, 2004).

Coetzee, J. M., *Disgrace* (1999; Vintage, 2000).

Cunningham, Michael, *The Hours* (1999; Fourth Estate, 1999).

DeLillo, Don, *Underworld* (1997; Picador, 1998).

Faber, Michel, *The Crimson Petal and the White* (2002; Canongate, 2003).

Fleming, Ian, *From Russia With Love* (1957; Penguin, 2004).
Franzen, Jonathan, *The Corrections* (2001; Fourth Estate, 2002).
Haddon, Mark, *The Curious Incident of the Dog in the Night-Time* (2003; Vintage, 2004).
Highsmith, Patricia, *Ripley Under Ground* (1974; Vintage, 1999).
Hollinghurst, Alan, *The Spell* (1998; Vintage, 1999).
Hornby, Nick, *How to Be Good* (2001; Penguin, 2002).
le Carré, John, *The Constant Gardener* (2001; Coronet, 2001).
Levy, Andrea, *Small Island* (2004; Review, 2004).
McEwan, Ian, *Atonement* (2001; Vintage, 2002).
Mitchell, David, *Cloud Atlas* (2004; Sceptre, 2004).
O'Hagan, Andrew, *Personality* (2003; Faber, 2004).
Pamuk, Orhan, *My Name Is Red* (2001; Faber, 2002).
Patchett, Ann, *Bel Canto* (2001; Fourth Estate, 2002).
Rendell, Ruth, *Adam and Eve and Pinch Me* (2001; Arrow, 2002).
Roth, Philip, *The Human Stain* (2000; Vintage, 2001).
Safran Foer, Jonathan, *Everything Is Illuminated* (2002; Penguin, 2003).
Shields, Carol, *Unless* (2002; Fourth Estate, 2003).
Smith, Zadie, *White Teeth* (2000; Penguin, 2002).
Spark, Muriel, *Aiding and Abetting* (2000; Penguin, 2001).
Swift, Graham, *Last Orders* (1996; Picador, 1996).
Tartt, Donna, *The Secret History* (1992; Penguin, 1993).
Trevor, William, *The Hill Bachelors* (2000; Penguin, 2001).
Yates, Richard, *Revolutionary Road* (1961; Methuen, 2001).

Introduction

SOME books we read once, but some we go back to. The literature we most value is what we revisit. For special kinds of writing, repetition can be the whole point. The intense pleasures of poetry are usually understood as coming from rereadings. Popular poetry anthologies and radio programmes enact these pleasures, reminding us of what we already knew as much as introducing us to what is yet unknown. In the ultimate example of being able to return to what we once read, we may even have poems or parts of poems by heart, in store. In rare cases, readers will have fragments of novels—resonant opening lines, perhaps—preserved in their memories. When the novelist William Thackeray first dined with Charlotte Brontë, he discomposed her by quoting from memory, as he smoked an after-dinner cigar, some cigar-smoke-inspired lines from *Jane Eyre* (1847)—lines that lead us to the heroine's meeting with Rochester in the garden of Thornfield, and to his first declaration of love for her. 'Sweet-briar and southernwood, jasmine, pink, and rose have long been yielding their evening sacrifice of incense: this new scent is neither of shrub nor flower; it is—I know it well—it is Mr Rochester's cigar' (vol. ii, ch. 8, 279).[1] Thackeray had been gripped by Brontë's novel, first reading it right through in a single day, and then returning to savour it.[2] Few readers will have extracts from their favourite novels seared on the memory like this, but all will know the gratification of coming again upon a passage that made some special impression on a previous reading.

Going back to a novel that you have read before marks it out.

The obvious definition of a 'classic' (a label still important to publishers of fiction) is a book that readers keep rereading. Given the sheer productivity of the fiction industry, it becomes more important than ever for any reader to possess a core of memorable novels. These are the books that have an afterlife, that can be gone back to. However, the process of returning to what has already been read, common enough in classrooms, is rarely imitated in most publicly accessible talk about novels. In newspapers, or on radio or television, analysing fiction most often takes the form of reviewing. This is necessarily a criticism of first impressions, largely aimed at potential rather than actual readers of any given novel. It is useful and often entertaining, but literary criticism should be something different. It should mean going back over a book you thought you knew, finding the patterns, or the inconsistencies, that you half-glimpsed before. Writing the newspaper articles on which this book is based, I was returning to novels that I had read. If the definition of a 'classic' is that it is a book that returns to life on every rereading, it seemed worth putting some contemporary fiction to this test, a test that a review cannot attempt.

Reviewers do at least write for the general reader. Many academic literary critics do not. There are kinds of literary scholarship that are valuable without having any wide appeal, yet there are also varieties of critical writing that are designedly inaccessible. Academic literary criticism, for the last two decades and more, has distinguished itself by its specialism and its obscurity. This has partly been thanks to the growth of literary theory, an avowedly more strenuous and certainly more hermetic way of talking about books. It made literary discourse forbidding not for its erudition or antiquarianism but for its style. Structuralism and then post-structuralism decreed that a special vocabulary was required to discuss texts (itself a term that was now de rigueur) in a properly analytical manner. Though a few of its phrases ('the death of the author', 'deconstruction') have escaped into the cultural bloodstream, its arguments have been designed to appeal only to an academic readership. Yet it is not just literary theory. There has been a more general tendency for the writing of literary academics to retreat into narrower and narrower specialisms. Articles and books are written to advance careers, to claim their spaces in university libraries, but not to find readers. There has always been a gap between academic literary criticism and the common reader; the great academic critics of the earlier twentieth century, like William Empson or F. R. Leavis, were no easy read. Equally, there have been excellent academic literary critics writing over the last couple of decades—John Carey, Frank Kermode, David Lodge, John Sutherland—who can all be read with enjoyment by anyone with an interest in the books they discuss. Yet it is undeniable that the discussion of literature in universities, and in the books and articles written by those employed there, became peculiarly sealed off from the rest of the world around the beginning of the 1980s.

This despite the growth of what might be thought of as popular forms of literary discussion. Apart from the ever-expanding world of reviewing, there are also enough literary festivals, readings, and public discussions of new writing to satisfy the most avid follower of current trends within fiction. The business of literary prizes, but especially prizes for fiction, fills newspaper pages and provides items on national television news. The rival merits of contemporary novelists become the stuff of public debate, however facile that debate might sometimes be. The best known, though not the richest, of these prizes, the Booker Prize, has lent itself as an adjective to characterize a certain kind of novel: 'Booker Prize fiction' is a species of ambitious literary writing that can still lay claim to a large readership. Since Salman Rushdie's *Midnight's Children* won the prize in 1981, and announced a new generation of novelists, this prize and others have regularly focused attention on serious recent fiction. And the talk is not just amongst readers. Never have authors, dispatched by their publishers on wearying tours to advertise their latest works, explained so often what their novels are about.

The Novel—its condition, its future, its new authors—has become a potential news item. Some of this is created by publicists and is mere hype, but it is not all commercial manipulation. The growth of reading groups, for instance, was not created by marketing departments. The extraordinary burgeoning of these groups suggests not just a hunger for reading, but—rather stranger—an appetite for critical discussion. The keen private delight given by a good book is not necessarily enough for many readers. They also want to talk about them and to test their impressions. Behind the reading group is what might be thought of as a tenet of literary criticism: that you do not necessarily know what you think of a book until you have heard what others think. Reading groups are everywhere. Publishers target them, newspapers survey them, broadcasters mimic them. There have been several novels based on reading groups and one droll television comedy series. Though reading groups may choose to talk about, say, books of history or biography, mostly they discuss novels.

This seems natural. We all share a sense that fiction has a unique capacity to live on in, even form, our imaginations. Critics in the earliest days of the English novel, in the eighteenth century, worried about this new kind of book exactly because it seemed to take possession of its readers. In their heated imaginations, though not in fact, these readers were mostly susceptible young women, who would become dangerously absorbed in these narratives. Unable, in the intensity of their reading, to distinguish beguiling fiction from reality, they would be misled into any number of follies or vices. 'Perhaps were it possible to effect the total extirpation of novels,' wrote Fanny Burney in her preface to *Evelina* (1778), 'our young ladies in general, and boarding-school damsels in particular, might profit from their annihilation' (8). However, 'since the distemper they have spread seems incurable', bidding defiance to 'the medicine of advice or reprehension', is it not just as well for the author to provide her own attempt at a novel 'which may be read, if not with advantage, at least without injury'? Burney's irony might just about have been read as proper modesty by contemporary moralists. We can laugh at their concerns more openly than Burney could. Yet the words we often use to praise a novel—*gripping, compelling, riveting*—confirm their belief that novels have a unique ability to seize their readers. 'I could not put it down' is a compliment almost invariably paid to a novel. With the power to absorb comes the possibility of critical judgement and critical argument. Each novel reader has an experience of the novel to describe, and even mere partisanship can generate a kind of critical analysis. Novels seem uniquely open to such analysis. They seem to invite it.

Reading groups provided the impetus for this book. It grew from a weekly column, 'Elements of Fiction', in the Review section of *The Guardian*. For four weeks in a row I would discuss aspects of a chosen novel. The aim was to see each week how some basic element of fiction—chapter titles, say, or characterization or dialogue—was used. I would try to illuminate the chosen novel by introducing comparable examples from other novels—usually from classic, sometimes from popular, fiction. The column was explicitly addressed to reading groups, and I made some effort to look at books they were likely to choose. All the novels were in paperback, and there was a leaning towards what is often called 'literary fiction'. The point was not to recommend the chosen novel (though I did not choose any books that I did not either like or admire); the point was to take a book that was in the public current of attention and to see what critical analysis could reveal about how it worked. The book came before the topics were chosen; the particular novel dictated the critical vocabulary that I explored. Though this meant that there were one or two critical terms that I would have liked to discuss and never did, I hope that it also meant that I did not come to the fiction with pre-formed analyses.

I have completely rewritten the original articles, but also rearranged them. They are not now grouped by the novels to which they are attached, but by the topics that they explore. I have written new introductions for the different chapters, making them, I hope, interesting whether or not the reader knows all the novels discussed. This book is addressed to anyone who is interested in the close analysis of fiction. I try to make a flexible critical vocabulary available to the general reader, to show that there is something between the rapid paraphrases and judgements of book reviews, on the one hand, and the recondite analyses of academic literary criticism on the other hand. It is striking how much of the talk about fiction that happens on radio or television, or at literary festivals, is talk about content. So often, a novel is discussable for what it is about. One emphasis that I have tried to carry over from academic literary criticism is the emphasis on form and technique. A novel absorbs us, I would say, not because of what it is about, but because of how it is written.

So this is a book about matters of form: how novels work rather than what they contain. It is here that a critic might have something to offer, apart from just another opinion. For criticism can make visible techniques and effects of which we are often only half-aware as we read.

Topics will sometimes appear familiar to most novel readers (plot, dialogue, location) and sometimes sound more technical (metanarrative, prolepsis, amplification). The vocabulary is less important than the patterns it can make visible. Equally, I think it is often revealing to put recent novels alongside novels from the past. So my hope has been to show not just how one particular novel is put together, but also how some knowledge of the history of fiction-making might make this clearer. When I discuss Nick Hornby's use of a female narrator I also explore Daniel Defoe's; I set Ian McEwan's use of weather against Austen's and Hardy's, and so on. Novelists themselves are often sharply aware of literary tradition and have been influenced by the novels they have read—or, indeed, studied, for a number of the novelists whose work I discuss turn out to have degrees in English Literature. Any historical perspective shows that novels do have recurrent preoccupations, and that even innovations and experiments often have their precedents. The analogies I draw with 'classic' fiction had to be brutally abbreviated in the original *Guardian* articles; I have expanded them in this book.

In my choice of novels I was happy to be influenced by popular taste and to take books that were, for some reason, in the public gaze. This might mean that I chose a novel that had just won a literary prize or unexpectedly appeared on best-seller lists. It might also mean that I looked at an earlier novel by an author who had just produced an admired or castigated new work of fiction. (Arguments between reviewers about Martin Amis's *Yellow Dog* (2003), for instance, prompted me to look at *Money*.) So there was often some sense of reappraising a writer's work in the light of later success (or failure). My practice of taking fiction that seemed of the moment led to some less predictable choices. The release of a new James Bond film made me think of examining one of Fleming's original novels (happily, just as it had been repackaged by Penguin as a 'Modern Classic'). I did consider removing such works from this book so that it would appear more clearly contemporary, but it would have been false to my own enthusiasms and also perhaps the miscellaneousness that characterizes the choices of reading groups.

I could not choose the latest novels because I took only works that were in print in paperback, aware that this is usually a criterion for reading groups. Though this began as a convenience, it had a useful critical consequence. It meant that, unlike a reviewer, I was often talking about a novel that had already been received, argued over, read, and reread. From the responses that I had from some of the readers of the newspaper, this meant that I was indeed sometimes looking at a book that they were talking about in a reading group. More generally, the point was to take a book that some of the readers of the column might have read, a book that had been in circulation. This was bringing to journalism an academic habit, the engagement with what is already known.

Journalism, especially when it involves the weekly fitting of an idea to a predetermined space, compels succinctness. This seems to me a blessed discipline: expatiation is certainly an academic vice. Only in one respect did I find that the discipline sometimes distorted, rather than merely restrained, what I had to say. The word limit meant that quotation was severely restricted. Yet the space for quotation is one of the necessary privileges of criticism. Quotation, generous where necessary, is at the heart of any worthwhile attempt to explore a literary work. From Coleridge to Christopher Ricks, some of the best of all English critics work from quotation, holding what has been written up to the light. I have wanted to catch particulars in the novels I was examining, and to do so by looking closely at characteristic extracts. So where I have expanded articles for this book, it is often by fuller quotation from the novels that I have discussed.

When I set out, I wanted my 'Elements of Fiction' articles to show that literary criticism could be intelligible without being glib. Literary criticism should be a way of rediscovering what makes a book live, and rereading the individual novels in order to write this book has often changed what I thought of them. Some of them were more responsive to the test of revisiting than others, and the reader will sometimes discern where I have found this. I have not avoided words of praise and dispraise: there are critical judgements in the book, but these are usually between more and less successful uses of fiction's elements. I am not trying to recommend a canon of contemporary fiction, but to show how a critical vocabulary can make our opinions lucid.

1
Beginning

THE Novel, that most accessible, democratic of literary forms, must establish its contract with its reader. It may be helped or hindered by all sorts of extraneous influences: cover design, encrustations of quotation from admiring reviewers, and the like. But it must also make its own way in the world. For the first half-century and more of its self-conscious existence, the Novel acknowledged its novelty as a type of writing. Samuel Richardson did this in anxious earnest, prefacing the first edition of his first novel, *Pamela* (1740), with a letter from an admirer declaring that the work that followed would 'infallibly be looked upon as the hitherto much-wanted Standard or Pattern for this Kind of Writing'.[1] In the preface to *Joseph Andrews* (1742), his contemporary and rival Henry Fielding announced with mock-solemnity the novelty of 'this Species of Writing, which I have affirmed to be hitherto unattempted in our Language' (8). This sense of unprecedentedness still lingers, even in a world where thousands of novels are published every year and where a novel seems the easiest kind of book for a literate person with a computer to write. One peculiarity of novels when they first arrived in the eighteenth century was that they told new stories rather than recomposing old ones. Their characters were, supposedly, singular; each novel had to introduce its readers to a new world. This has not changed.

The very permissiveness of those rules by which novels are written makes it necessary for a novelist to show a reader, in the beginning, what kind of thing he or she is reading, what he or she has signed up to. In his *Autobiography*, published posthumously in 1883, Anthony Trollope was characteristically straightforward about what he had learnt about being a novelist. 'It is the first necessity of his position that he make himself pleasant.'[2] He meant that a novelist who wanted to sell books should give pleasure, but also that he or she should be welcoming or accommodating. And this was partly a matter of how to begin, how to introduce your characters, and perhaps yourself, to your readers. Trollope's own novels usually commence with a self-conscious business of introduction—with explanations of what we need to know (capsule histories of leading characters, for instance) and reassurances about what we will later find out. Often, in a manner invented by Fielding, Trollope will begin by talking about the reader or readers of 'these pages' (*The Way We Live Now*, 1874–5, ch. i, p. 1) and making himself present to us as an arranger of his material.

This manner is now extremely rare in novels. Those that do not use framing devices (see below) are likely to thrust us straight into a story rather than introduce us to it. Trollope seems to have believed that the novelist owed the reader the courtesy of introducing his material. He was notably hostile to the so-called 'sensation novels' of his day (exemplified by works like Wilkie Collins's *The Woman in White*, 1859–60), and their habit of commencing with some startling incident. At the opening of his own novel *Is He Popenjoy?* (1878)—itself exploiting public interest in a sensational court case of the day—he explicitly deprecated this 'plan of jumping at once into the middle' (ch. i). For the conscientious novelist, 'the story must be made intelligible from the beginning, or the real novel readers will not like it'. 'Real novel readers' are presumably those who have long been dedicated to novel-reading, as opposed to those inexperienced consumers readily entertained by the tricks of sensation fiction.

While it is no longer common to meet a welcoming, gentlemanly author, ready with explanations, on the first page of a novel, we still need to be made acquainted with the tenets—the ground rules, as it were—of the fictional world into which we are entering. Our expectations are being shaped before we even read the novel's first sentence. Those introductory elements that usher us in to the main narrative are already guiding our habits of interpretation. Every novel will have at least a title to instruct us. Once titles, as given on title pages, were commonly lengthy and packed with information. The title page of Daniel Defoe's *Moll Flanders* (1721), for instance, informed the book's first readers that it contained

> The Fortunes and Misfortunes of the Famous Moll Flanders, &c. Who was Born in NEWGATE, and during a Life of continu'd Variety for Threescore Years, besides her Childhood, was Twelve Year a *Whore*, five times a *Wife* (whereof once to her own Brother), Twelve Year a *Thief*, Eight Year a Transported *Felon* in *Virginia*, at last grew *Rich*, liv'd *Honest*, and died a *Penitent*. *Written from her own* MEMORANDUMS.

This full title, with its pretence of documentary veracity as well as its sensationalism, is clearly part of the fiction (though there is no reason to think that it was composed by Defoe rather than his publisher). It encouraged eighteenth-century readers to associate Moll with notorious criminals and with the genre of criminal autobiographies that was already popular at the time. It also encouraged the reader to ask not 'What happens?' but 'How could all *this* happen?'

With its original title, Defoe's novel looks like something rather different from the literary classic that it has become. We might note that the original, purporting to be a version of the anti-heroine's own story, does not even have Defoe's name upon it. Its place on the library shelf was decided by publishers and readers long after its author's death. Few other novels have carried quite so much information on their title pages as this, but many originally had longer titles than those by which we now know them. Laurence Sterne's *Tristram Shandy* (1759–66) was in fact titled *The Life and Opinions of Tristram Shandy,*

Gentleman. This is a mock-title, suitably inflated for a narrator whose fate will be shown to have been made by 'small accidents' and apparently inconsequential events. The knowing reader will already be keyed to the novel's method of comic deflation. Later novels honed down titles, but commonly employed explanatory, occasionally teasing subtitles. Until the early nineteenth century, these had often composed a double title, with the second part being given as an alternative to the first: Samuel Richardson's *Pamela, or, Virtue Rewarded*, Fanny Burney's *Evelina, or, a Young Lady's Entrance into the World*, Mary Shelley's *Frankenstein, or, The Modern Prometheus* (1818). These seem to have avowed designs upon us. They prod us as to register the significance of the fictions on which we embark.

Without that commanding 'or' between the parts of a title, a subtitle becomes more reticent—a suggestion rather than a command. Such subtitles are fairly common in the nineteenth century: Thackeray's *Vanity Fair: A Novel Without a Hero* (1847–8); Elizabeth Gaskell's *Wives and Daughters: An Every-Day Story* (1864–6); George Eliot's *Middlemarch: A Study of Provincial Life* (1871–2). All these subtitles are calculated to nudge the readers and to communicate something of the novelist's deeper purposes. Most emphatic is perhaps Thomas Hardy's 'A Pure Woman' appended to the main title of *Tess of the d'Urbervilles* (1891). This steer to our interpretation is all the stronger given the notorious uncertainty of what happens to Tess when Alec d'Urberville takes advantage of her on that night in the Chase. Is she seduced? Or is it rape? Whatever our suppositions, she remains 'pure' in her author's mind, though tragically not in her husband's. Hardy's subtitle is defiant in the face of imagined censoriousness. Such once conventional control of our preconceptions is now rare.

In the eighteenth and nineteenth centuries almost any self-respecting novelist would next provide a preface, explaining and probably vindicating his or her purposes. For many decades these were commonly defensive, the novel being widely regarded as a 'low' or irresponsible genre. In her famous defence of novels and novel-reading in *Northanger Abbey* (1818), Austen refers wryly to 'that ungenerous and impolitic custom so common with novel writers, of degrading by their contemptuous censure the very performances, to the number of which they are themselves adding' (vol. i, ch. v, 21). She might have had in mind her successful contemporary Maria Edgeworth, whose novel *Belinda* (1801) she singles out for praise, for this began with a preface announcing, 'The following work is offered to the public as a Moral Tale—the author not wishing to acknowledge a Novel.' You might suspect irony, but the subsequent explanation—'so much folly, errour, and vice are disseminated in books classed under this denomination'—banishes that thought. Later prefaces were more confident. Dickens's *Oliver Twist* (1837–8) comes to many modern readers with an Author's Preface written for the third edition of 1841. It is an angry and righteous response to those critics who had taken exception to the novel's 'Newgate' subject matter.

> It is, it seems, a very coarse and shocking circumstance, that some of the characters in these pages are chosen from the most criminal and degraded of London's population; that Sikes is a thief, and Fagin a receiver of stolen goods; that the boys are pickpockets, and the girl is a prostitute.
>
> I confess I have yet to learn that a lesson of the purest good may not be drawn from the vilest evil. (p. xxv)

We are given a lengthy polemic unimaginable from a novelist now. When Dickens discusses his depiction of Nancy, who aids Oliver and is murdered for it by Sikes, he arrives at an assertion from which even other Victorian novelists might have flinched.

> It is useless to discuss whether the conduct and character of the girl seems natural or unnatural, probable or improbable, right or wrong. IT IS TRUE. (p. xxviii)

This was not to be the only time that Dickens composed a

preface to one of his novels as a rejoinder to his critics, and he was not the only novelist to do so. Frequently in the nineteenth century, as a novel was reprinted in subsequent editions, prefaces would be changed or supplemented, as an author mounted counter-attacks against critics or provided an antidote to misunderstanding. In some cases novelists' prefatory explanations after the event were elaborate. The prefaces to individual novels that Henry James composed for the New York edition of his fiction are substantial works of criticism. Conrad's, similarly composed for a collected edition of his fiction, are accounts of how the ideas for his books came to him. So in his Author's Note for *Nostromo* (1904), Conrad remembers how its germ was a 'vagrant anecdote' heard as a young sailor in the Gulf of Mexico, a story rediscovered 'twenty-six or twenty-seven years afterwards' in a 'shabby volume' in a second-hand bookshop (p. xl). It is as if, by showing how a novel originated, he can prove it to be, as he says in his 1920 Author's Note to *The Secret Agent* (1907), 'a perfectly genuine piece of work' (p. xxxvii).

A few novelists of the later twentieth century have acted in Conrad's manner. In the early 1970s Graham Greene composed introductions to the individual volumes of his collected works, published by Bodley Head. Reminiscing about the circumstances in which a novel was written, these made the personality of the author a dominant presence. Often they are droll: the 1974 Introduction to *Stamboul Train* (1932) tells us how its impecunious author could not at the time afford to travel beyond Cologne, explaining why, in the novel, there are 'more details on this first stretch of the line than I had the confidence to include later'.[3] Some of the Vintage paperback editions of Greene's novels currently available include the novelist's own introductions; others substitute introductions written by celebrity writers (Zadie Smith, Paul Theroux). Authorial prefaces have, however, largely died out, perhaps simply because the modern apparatus of publicity provides the author with many means of explaining his or her purposes and, if necessary, rebutting the gainsayers.

The title apart, the most common form of authorial guidance that is still sometimes provided at the beginning of a novel is the epigraph—the resonant quotation placed at the head of a narrative, often on its own page. With the epigraph the author seems directly to tell us of the novel's significance, of its essence. Or rather, not directly, for an epigraph is invariably a quotation, connecting a new novel with the already written. (In Chapter 10 I examine the use of quotations and epigrams scattered elsewhere in a novel.) Novelists who are more 'literary', we might think, are more likely to provide an opening epigraph, and more populist novelists not to do so. There is some truth in this: George Eliot usually had an epigraph, Dickens did not. But it is not always so. Some contemporary writers of thrillers or detective fiction—Minette Walters, Ian Rankin, and Colin Dexter, for instance—like to begin with apposite quotations. In these cases the epigraphs are more like amusing clues to the mysteries that follow than claims of literary allegiance. They do also advertise the erudition of the authors, suggesting that the novel of detection is, like Inspector Morse's crosswords, the light amusement of the intellectually sophisticated.

Once we are past these introductory guidelines, we may think we are to begin the story. But not necessarily so. Sometimes there are false beginnings, things that we have to be told before the true beginning. These are discussed in the sections below on the prologue and the framing device, both of them parts of a work of fiction rather than some imposition from outside it. Unlike the prefaces of old, they do not communicate the author's intentions. Prologues charge the novel with the significance of earlier events or later knowledge. Framing devices provide a fictional explanation of how the main story has come to us. Both ask us to see how much is already taken for granted in simply starting to narrate. Yet, by using either, the novelist loses the opportunity for what is discussed in the final part of this chapter: the arresting opening. This, especially if it is but a well-conceived sentence, can make the imagined world of a novel present in an instant. Most of the famous, quotable sentences from novels are such opening statements. The final part of this chapter therefore considers the special voltage of a novel's first sentence.

THE TITLE

Even the most common and unremarkable kind of title, the bare name of a novel's central character, will tell us something in advance about how to read. Jane Austen's *Emma* (1816) is about a singular and powerful individual, freed by wealth and lack of parental guidance, to exercise her sometimes imperious will. It is no accident that this is the only Austen novel to take its heroine's name as its title. To think of it another way, imagine that Henry James's *The Portrait of a Lady* (1881) were called *Isabel Archer*. This is not unimaginable, for Isabel is entirely the centre of the story, yet it would be to lose an important cue given us by James's title. However central are Isabel's experience, her consciousness, her choice of life, the title insists on a certain analytical distance. We watch her make her mistakes, we see the disastrous effects of her self-delusions. To give the novel its protagonist's name would be to encourage a sympathy that James seems to warn us off.

Unsurprisingly, both novelists and their publishers care very much about titles, knowing that they are the means by which a book first reaches out to its potential readers. Publishers have been known to put their novelists right in this matter. When Charles Monteith, editor at Faber and Faber, happened upon a novel by an unknown writer called William Golding that had been rejected by up to twenty other publishers, it was called *Strangers from Within*. Amongst other adjustments that Monteith suggested was the changing of the title to *Lord of the Flies*. One can hardly doubt that he was right. The phrase is used by the boys in the novel for the pig's head stuck on a pole to propitiate the 'beast' that supposedly haunts the island. It is a totem of savage fear. It is also the English version of a Hebrew name for the Devil, Beelzebub (see Matt. 12: 24). The title tells us, both more clearly and more subtly than Golding's earlier suggestion, how all that is fearful on the island comes from within the boys themselves.

What about the title that seems a guide to the reader? While it is common for a title to tell us who a novel is about (*David Copperfield* (1849–50), *Mrs Dalloway* (1925)) or where it is set (*Mansfield Park* (1814), *Washington Square* (1880)), it is more unusual, and more pointed, for the title to declare the book's theme. When he called his 1999 novel *Disgrace*, J. M. Coetzee joined other contemporary practising novelists who have announced their works with one-word abstractions. In recent years, there have been plenty. Salman Rushdie's *Shame* (1983) and *Fury* (2001), Peter Carey's *Bliss* (1981), Anita Brookner's *Providence* (1982), A. S. Byatt's *Possession*, Ian McEwan's *Atonement*. In each case the author appears to be pressing on the reader the significance, in the abstract, of the story that is to follow. These novels risk sounding as if they have theories in mind, each title being a nudge to the future undergraduate, a clue to the best focus of an essay. Perhaps such titles are particularly likely from novelists who themselves have had an academic training and have been taught to find the unifying ideas in narratives.

Novelists started using abstract-noun titles at the beginning of the nineteenth century for essentially didactic purposes. As well as those that came in pairs—Elizabeth Inchbald's *Nature and Art* (1796) or Jane Austen's *Sense and Sensibility* (1811)—there were novels like Mary Brunton's *Self-Control* (1811), Maria Edgeworth's *Patronage* (1814), and Susan Ferrier's *Marriage* (1818). The lessons of these were unswerving. Brunton's heroine discovers the joys of 'chastened affection' and 'tempered desires' (ch. xxxiv, 437). Edgeworth's novel displays in lengthy detail the evils of patronage. Ferrier diagrammatically contrasts the joys of a happy marriage with the pains of one undertaken foolishly. The one subtle early example is Austen's *Persuasion* (1818; a title decided by her brother Henry after her death, but probably in accordance with her wishes). This novel explores what persuades people not to follow their inclinations, but does not exactly recommend or condemn 'persuasion'. Later in the nineteenth century such titles became capacious rather than didactic: *War and Peace* (1863–9) is the obvious example. The title of Dostoevsky's *Crime and Punishment* (1866) sounds so straightforward—and does indeed sum up the inevitability of consequences in the novel—yet it deliberately fails to do justice to the psychological torments that fill its pages. With modernism, such abstract titles became open to sharply ironical use by writers like Joseph Conrad. His novel *Chance* (1914) shows how actions are determined by psychological necessity; *Victory* (1915) is about the salvation that may be found in defeat. When Conrad died, he left a novel tantalizingly incomplete called *Suspense*. He also wrote a wonderful novella called *Youth* (1902), about not being young any more (which became the title of Coetzee's next novel after *Disgrace*).

The title of J. M. Coetzee's *Disgrace* is not exactly ironical, but it is forbidding. It insists on an unconsoling theme. We are being told what the novel—for all its characters and locations and events—is *really* about. The title sensitizes a reader to a theme, even to a word. Phrases that could otherwise have been casual hook our attention. 'The whole thing is disgraceful from beginning to end,' David Lurie's ex-wife, Rosalind, says of his affair with his student. 'Disgraceful and vulgar too' (45). Because of the book's title, we notice her easy, indeed vulgar, use of 'disgraceful', an empty expression of exasperation. She means rather little by it. We know, after all, that she is a fellow 'sensualist' and no believer in any moral requirement to curb desire. She is simply saying that people should not be so foolish. Yet we notice too how 'disgrace' means so much more than she realizes. Her ex-husband is in the process of disgracing himself, dragging himself down. In the end, this disgrace will even permit him a kind of humiliated self-recognition.

A complaint is made against him for his sexual pursuit of his young student Melanie Isaacs, and an official investigation begins. Lurie is given the opportunity by his university to save his job by displaying a token penitence. Angered by the self-righteousness of those who sit in judgement on him and the dishonesty required of him, he refuses. He will not 'express contrition' (54) in some insincere public gesture of humility and shamefacedness. Yet he comes to experience and accept a deeper feeling of disgrace. He is made to feel old, futile, truly ashamed. The would-be 'servant of Eros' (52) is, after all, a mere sexual predator. He is driven to a strange 'ceremony' of self-abasement when he visits the family of the girl he has forced himself on; 'he gets to his knees and touches his forehead to the floor' (173). He tries 'to accept disgrace as my state of being' (172). He loses everything as a punishment for the affair; disgrace is his feeling that this is what he deserves.

In *Disgrace* those who feel disgraced are also those who have been punished or humiliated. Lurie's daughter Lucy is gang-raped, but it is she who tastes disgrace, taught the lesson of her weakness and made to suffer for the sins of her white tribe. As if she deserved it. Lurie imagines the rapists driving away in Lucy's car, contented. 'They must have had every reason to be pleased with their afternoon's work; they must have felt happy in their vocation' (159). He, the father, has been locked in the lavatory while it happens. He cannot save his daughter. 'Lucy's secret; his disgrace' (109). He is stripped of all that once gave him power and authority. When he first moves out into the arid countryside to live with Lucy, he works helping put down the unwanted dogs who plague the locality. He has become a 'dog-man'. (Not since *King Lear* have there been so many references in a literary work to the analogies between humans and dogs.) He observes that the condemned dogs 'flatten their ears' and 'droop their tails', 'as if they too feel the disgrace of dying' (143).

As if disgrace were the recognition of what is most terrible in life. Coetzee's title contests, in advance of the critics, any assumption that the novel is some kind of allegory of the state of South Africa. The singular abstraction suggests that the book wants to bring to life a universal condition. Surprisingly, rather like those didactic titles of the early nineteenth century, it suggests not just a theme but a lesson: disgrace is salutary, even necessary.

The other common type of title that presents itself as an authorial hint at a novel's implicit subject matter is the quotation title. This signals a relationship with another book, another author. The habit of using quotations for novel titles seems itself to have been Victorian in origin. One of the earliest examples is the best-seller *Not Wisely But Too Well* (1867) by Rhoda Broughton (the quotation, from *Othello*, applies to a heroine whose virtue triumphs over her amorous inclinations). The earliest famous example is probably Hardy's *Under the Greenwood Tree* (1872), an untypically cheerful story of Wessex life. The title refers the reader to a pastoral song in Shakespeare's *As You Like It* (ii. v), sung by an exiled courtier in the Forest of Arden.

> Under the greenwood tree
> Who loves to lie with me,
> And turn his merry note
> Unto the sweet bird's throat,
> Come hither, come hither, come hither!
> Here shall he see
> No enemy
> But winter and rough weather.

The immediate suggestion of the title is that the novel's bucolic delights are timeless; we have encountered them before. When he came to naming *Far from the Madding Crowd* (1874), however, Hardy used quotation ironically. The phrase is taken from Thomas Gray's 'Elegy Written in a Country Churchyard'. Those who recall the original context—and in Hardy's day the 'Elegy' was still one of the best known and best loved poems in the language—would have their appreciation of the novel slightly changed. In his poem, Gray speaks of rural life 'Far from the madding crowd's ignoble strife'. If you know this, Hardy's subtly amended use of the quotation is striking: the countryside he depicts is full of strife. The novel depicts the economic precariousness of rural life, as well as the destructive passions of several of its main characters. Its title is an anti-pastoral irony.

There is a difference between titles made from quotations that we are likely to recognize and those that most readers would have to look up. Aldous Huxley's *Brave New World* (1932) is memorable partly because Miranda's wondering exclamation in Shakespeare's *The Tempest* was already a famous quotation. Huxley's application is effectively ironical because the dystopia of his novel is indeed a 'wonderful' world, apparently without pain or discontent. Ernest Hemingway's *For Whom the Bell Tolls* (1940) recalls probably the best-known words that John Donne ever wrote: 'and therefore never send to know for whom the bell tolls; it tolls for thee'.[4] Here, we readily gather, is a novel about our common mortality. Graham Greene's *The Power and the Glory* (1940), like *Brave New World*, works by irony or 'antiphrasis'. Set in Mexico, its 'hero' is an alcoholic priest who practises his Catholicism at a time of religious persecution. Only because Greene's title is such a well-known phrase from the Lord's Prayer (in St Matthew's Gospel) can the author rely on his reader recognizing a religious thesis. On the one hand, the ignoble truth about ordinary, compromised human beings will not match the conventional swell of religious aspiration. On the other hand, in the most unlikely ways, Catholicism is indeed to be vindicated by Greene's story of suffering.

But what of the quotation that most readers will not recognize? The title of Michel Faber's novel of Victorian sexual mores *The Crimson Petal and the White* is strange and resonant enough to suggest that it must have some source, but is scarcely an oft-quoted phrase. Indeed, in interviews Faber has often been asked to explain it. The frequency of the request is itself evidence that the novelist has been using the title to quiz his readers. It is hardly self-explanatory, and is not actually used within the novel. Contrast this with, say, Alan Hollinghurst's *The Line of Beauty* (2004): the reader who does not already recognize Hogarth's phrase for the serpentine line that characterizes beautiful forms will be told about it in the course of the book. Hollinghurst even includes an explanation of how the phrase applies to his protagonist's winding pursuit of beauty, while his acquaintances follow the straight paths of ambition. Faber's title asks the reader to try to decode it. A moment with any good dictionary of quotations will identify the quotation, though it might take a little more reading to interpret it. The phrase is taken from a lyric by Tennyson that is itself mysterious. The lyric is found within his long narrative poem *The Princess* (1847). In this poem's frame narrative (see 'The Framing Device', below) a group of undergraduates entertain some ladies in the gardens of a country house with 'A tale for summer' (*The Princess*, Prologue, line 205). There is agreement that the tale will be punctuated by the ladies singing 'From time to time, some ballad or a song | To give us breathing space' (Prologue, lines 234–5). In the story, one of these songs is supposedly read aloud to herself by the beautiful Princess Ida, who is overheard by the love-struck narrator. (He is a prince, in love with Ida, who has renounced male company to devote herself to women's education.)

> Now sleeps the crimson petal, now the white;
> Nor waves the cypress in the palace walk;
> Nor winks the gold fin in the porphyry font:
> The fire-fly wakens, waken thou with me.
>
> (*The Princess*, VII. 161–4)

It is a yearning, strangely narcotic lyric, in the form of a *ghazal*, a Persian love poem. Its images, which are also the ornaments from some Eastern verse, seem to stand for inexpressible desires.

We are invited to think of the long poetic association between flowers (in this context, especially roses) and women. Faber's novel has two women at its centre: Agnes Rackham, the pure and religious wife; Sugar, the prostitute with ideas above her station. Agnes may be 'white', but she is also a hysteric, pursued by religious visions and terrified by menstruation. (This seems to have become our cliché about 'innocent' Victorian femininity: think of the sexually fearful Victorian wife in A. S. Byatt's *Possession* who drives her husband to infidelity.) Sugar may be 'crimson'—a scarlet woman, no less—but she longs for a good life. Agnes mistakes her, clad in white in the street outside her house, for a guardian angel. She enters the Rackham household in this role, as governess to their neglected daughter Sophie. Sugar is the mistress of Agnes's husband, Arthur, a perfume manufacturer who turns petals into an industrial commodity, both cultivating and destroying beauty. The novel details these cosmetic products, many named after flowers and petals. Faber's title is an idealizing poeticism, ironical given his novel's insistence on the physical sufferings of his female characters. This quotation title requires us to compare his novel's images of female desirability and frailty with all those pure or fallen women of Victorian literature.

Its very title lets us know that Faber's novel is both a Victorian novel and a corrective to the myths of femininity peddled by Victorian novelists. Faber appears happy to let his reader chase the quotation, as if tracking down a Victorian secret. It is like those other bits of nineteenth-century bric-a-brac (clothes, magazines, furnishings, wrappings, and advertisements) that, recovered from his research, he scatters through his novel. It is itself a genuine relic of Victorian culture. In working out its significance we are asked to see how a twenty-first-century novel reinterprets the versions of womanhood that we might recognize from nineteenth-century literature.

THE EPIGRAPH

The resonant quotation at the head of a novel can seem portentous. In *Paratexts*, his survey of extra-textual devices such as titles, prefaces, and notes, the literary theorist Gerard Genette calls the epigraph 'a password of intellectuality'. The author attaches himself to some great name; 'he chooses his peers and thus his place in the pantheon'.[5] The filiation may be credible if you are Thomas Hardy using a shard of Shakespeare at the head of *Tess of the d'Urbervilles* or James Joyce prefacing *A Portrait of the Artist as a Young Man* (1914–15) with a quote from Ovid. But don't lesser mortals risk absurdity? The potential for absurdity was recognized by the first English novelist to use a sonorous epigraph at the head of a novel. Henry Fielding in *Tom Jones* (1749) humorously exploits the potential for self-importance of the prefatory literary motto. His zestfully ignoble tale of Hanoverian lowlife carried on its title page a quotation from Horace's *Ars Poetica*: 'mores hominum multorum vidit'—'He saw the customs of many men'. This was Horace's translation into Latin of the first line of Homer's *Odyssey*, referring to the knowledge that Odysseus wins through his travels. The quotation is appropriate, for Tom Jones, Fielding's foundling cast adrift in a dangerous world, must learn his lessons on the high road of Georgian England. It is also gloriously inappropriate, mock-heroic in fact, for Tom's bed-hopping and brawling hardly match the mythical ordeals of Homer's epic hero.

Fielding provided neither an attribution nor a translation for his epigraph. The educated reader might be expected to recognize it. Fielding's method throughout his novel is to combine ancient learning with modern comedy, to use gentlemanly prose to describe 'low' behaviour. The incongruity of the epigraph epitomizes this method. When Laurence Sterne chose an epigraph for the first volume of *Tristram Shandy* (1759–67), he expected even more erudition of his reader. His novel had on its title page an epigram in Greek, without translation: 'Ταράσσει τοὺς Ἀνθρώπους οὐ τὰ Πράγματα, ἀλλὰ τὰ περὶ τῶν Πραγμάτων, Δόγματα'. It is taken from Epictetus, not an author whose writing every educated gentleman would be expected to know. (Hardly any women readers, of whom Sterne had many, would have known Greek.) It means 'Men are disturbed not by things, but by their opinions about things', fitting for a novel where characters are comically tormented by their own fixed ideas. The inaccessibility of the epigraph seems calculated. Sterne's novel is full of buried allusions and plagiarized fragments, hidden jokes for some future scholar. For all its conversational brio it is a novel larded with eccentric learning.

It is rare for a contemporary novelist not to translate an opening epigraph in a foreign language. Donna Tartt gives English versions of the suitable lines from Nietzsche and Plato that decorate the entrance to her novel *The Secret History*. The fragment of Sophocles' *Oedipus Rex* at the head of Philip Roth's modern story of retribution *The Human Stain* is only given in English translation. Tim Lott's 2002 novel *Rumours of a Hurricane* chronicles the effects of Thatcherism on a working-class family, but it has a Latin epigraph from an Elizabethan epigrammatist, John Owen: 'Tempora mutantur et nos mutamur in illis'. The epigraph is unattributed, but it is translated: 'Times change and we change with them'. It is a fitting motto for a tale about a time of change—about how the winners adapt and some cannot. But it also implies, especially by being given first in its original Latin, that this historical tale is a universal exemplum. Latin is the unchanging language. When, in contrast Alan Hollinghurst prefaces his novel *The Folding Star* (1994) with a verse epigraph in French, without any English gloss, he invites the reader to sense a private significance. The lines are attributed to Henri de Régnier, a poet of the late nineteenth and early twentieth centuries, whose work has been little translated into English. Perhaps the majority of Hollinghurst's readers will let this epigraph go its way, though even the many who do not exactly understand it will surely keep some lingering sense of its appropriateness (if only because it must stem from an author with a refined and literary cultural vocabulary). Only a scholarly reader, with access to an academic library, will be able to pursue it to its source. The melancholy verses may fit Hollinghurst's story of an Englishman's stay in a melancholy Flemish city, but only the author can know quite their resonance.

Yet even these verses have none of the absolute obscurity of Elizabeth Gaskell's untranslated German epigraph to her first novel, *Mary Barton* (1848). This story of poverty and class conflict in Manchester is prefaced by four lines of unattributed verse.

> Nimm nur, Fährmann, nimm die Miethe,
> Die ich gerne dreifach biete!
> Zweien, die mit nur überfuhren,
> Waren geistige Naturen.

Even the most erudite amongst her readers would be unlikely to know that the lines are by Ludwig Uhland, from his 'Auf der Überfahrt' ('In Passing Over') (1826). They might be translated as 'Take, ferryman, take the fare, which I gladly pay three times over! The two who crossed with me were ghostly beings.' The epigraph has no obvious connection to the events in the novel. Instead it appears to refer to Gaskell's two dead children: a stillborn daughter (her first child) and a son who had died three years before the novel was written.[6] The epigraph is pointed, for Gaskell had undertaken *Mary Barton* in order to distract herself after her son's death. (In the novel, which is full of death, John Barton's son has died of scarlet fever, the same disease that killed Gaskell's son.) Its essentially private meaning is represented by its untranslatedness, in a language that few Victorian novel readers would have known. Its inaccessibility is fitting.

As in Fielding's case, however, epigraphs perhaps work best when they are not entirely fitting, when incongruity is part of their meaning. This seems the case with Richard Yates's *Revolutionary Road*, a novel first published in 1961 but rediscovered, along with his short stories and some of his other novels, in the last few years. It opens with a quotation. Before his tale of suburban discontent begins, there, on a page of its own, is an unfamiliar fragment from a familiar writer. 'Alas! when passion is both meek and wild!' The author is identified as John Keats. It is a puzzle that presses on the reader to find its significance. The Keatsian 'Alas!', that poetic expression of regret, implies that the story that follows will end badly. The rest of the line suggests the disastrous potential of a combination of contradictory qualities (Keats has pointedly made a surprising contrast out of that lifeless cliché: 'meek and mild').

In *Revolutionary Road* the epigraph tells of the characters' resentful timidity. Frank and April Wheeler bridle at the conventions and restrictions of suburban life, yet they live this life because of their own compliance. As we read the novel, we can apply the epigraph. We are invited to notice how timidity and fierce inclination combine destructively in its leading characters. April Wheeler, with her thespian ambitions and her plans to move to Paris, is doomed to mortification. The opening scene, in which she stars in an embarrassingly bad amateur dramatic production, is painful because her hopes are so earnest. She nurses aspirations. Her fantasies about Parisian life are the more absurd for being supported by her belief that her husband is fluent in French (he knows the language hardly at all, but once drunkenly boasted about his proficiency). Frank Wheeler too feels meekly and wildly, his self-regarding sense of his lawless masculinity coexisting with his bland acceptance of his futile corporation job.

The point of Yates's epigraph is its apt unlikeliness: Keats speaking out in order to gloss a small-time drama of suburban life in 1950s America. Incongruity fits the story. The Wheelers like to speak as if they transcend the banal comfort of their existence: they read better books and think of higher things than their neighbours. They are mentally unfettered, they think. They chafe at the lives that they have meekly chosen. They share with their friends Shep and Milly Campbell conversations of excruciating complacency on 'the elusive but endlessly absorbing subject of Conformity, or The Suburbs, or Madison Avenue, or American Society Today' (59). Yates mercilessly details these exchanges as endlessly repeatable performances—conversations contrived only to reassure the participants. 'They would all agree, and the happy implication was that they alone, the four of them, were painfully alive in a drugged and dying culture' (60).

The epigraph implies that we are witnessing a new version of some old calamity. It draws attention to the finding of an old story in an unlikely new setting. The line is taken from Keats's poem 'Isabella; or, The Pot of Basil' (though Yates does not tell us this). A strange verse tale adapted from Boccaccio, it narrates the tragedy of two lovers, Isabella and Lorenzo. Neither rich nor noble, Lorenzo is murdered by Isabella's greedy brothers, who wish a better match for their family. Isabella recovers her beloved's head, which she keeps beside her in a pot, under a basil plant. (The combination of tragedy and absurdity no doubt appealed to Yates.) Finally, she pines to death. She and Lorenzo, reticent lovers, have been crushed by a cruel world. Frank and April's story also ends in a catastrophe: attempting to induce a miscarriage, April haemorrhages and dies. 'The Revolutionary Hill Estates had not been designed to accommodate a tragedy' (323). But tragedy there is.

THE PROLOGUE

A prologue is a unit of narrative that begins a novel but is detached from it. Usually it is baldly labelled 'Prologue', signalling that separation. A notable early example of the device is in Wilkie Collins's *The Moonstone* (1868). Collins's novel recounts the mysterious theft of a fabulous diamond from an English country house. It begins, however, in a different place and time. A prologue, set almost half a century earlier, tells us of the diamond's sacred origins in India. This narrative, '*Extracted from a family paper*', is dated 1799 and purports to be written by the cousin of the English adventurer John Herncastle. It tells how Herncastle murders the diamond's guardians as the British army storms the stronghold of Tippoo, sultan of Seringapatam, and steals the wonderful gem. The prologue allows us to know of the supposed curse upon all those who seek to possess the Moonstone. 'The dying Indian sank to his knees, pointed to the dagger in Herncastle's hand, and said, in his native language:—"The Moonstone will have its vengeance yet on you and yours!" He spoke those words, and fell dead on the floor' (4). Without requiring any actual crediting of the supernatural, the prologue will overshadow the subsequent narrative. Violence will surely return upon those who yearn to possess the diamond. The novel's denouement sees the thief murdered by mysterious agents from India and the diamond returned to its origins. The logic of the novel's beginning has been realized.

Prologues are not uncommon in novels of murder and mystery. Colin Dexter's Inspector Morse novels, Ian Rankin's Rebus novels, and Patricia Cornwell's thrillers about the criminal pathologist Kay Scarpetta, for instance, all use them. Prologues are also favoured by James Ellroy and Henning Mankell, who both use the convention with an intentional jolt, confronting the reader immediately with a passage of inexplicable violence. Ellroy's *LA Confidential* (1990) and Mankell's *One Step Behind* (1997), for instance, both begin with men being killed ruthlessly in entirely mystifying circumstances. In such novels of detection, we have to work back to the events of the prologue, only seeing their true significance by the novel's end. Comparable is the prologue that begins Donna Tartt's second novel, *The Little Friend* (2002). Set twelve years earlier than Chapter 1, it inflects all that follows. A child has been murdered. The child's family, we are told, will not talk about the events of that day, so the prologue is there to let us know what cannot find its way into dialogue. We are taken through the last minutes before his body is found, the unease growing to panic, a woman screaming, the terrible discovery. The reader must not escape the pain of it. We are made to imagine the apprehension and the agony that the characters knew.

The Little Friend too is some kind of novel of detection. When the main part of it gets under way, the protagonist, Harriet, sister of the murdered child, is determined to find the murderer. A baby at the time of the killing, she is now 12 years old. The prologue has set in motion an unease, a narrative imbalance, that must be resolved. Tartt also opens her first novel, *The Secret History*, with a prologue, and here too creates a gap of time, across which the novel then reaches. The prologue of *The Secret History* allows a time shift in the reverse direction, for it tells us of events that occur some time after the novel's official opening. Richard, the narrator, has done something that shapes every subsequent turn of his narration. Before we even know his name, we know his 'secret'. The prologue has told us that Bunny has been killed, that the narrator has been 'partially responsible' along with three others, that 'all those years' later he is still haunted by the recollection of the deed (1–2). 'This is the only story I will ever be able to tell.'

It is an odd business: the whole terrible point of the narrative seems to be given away in advance. But while this sacrifices uncertainty, it purchases a sense of fatality. We are made to know that the relationships between the six main characters, a self-selected group of classics students in a small New England college, will lead five of them to murder the other. 'It seems to me that psychology is only another word for what the ancients called fate,' declares their charismatic teacher, Julian (31). The prologue is a means by which Tartt turns psychology into fate. 'I'm afraid my students are never very interesting to me because I always know exactly what they are going to do,' observes Julian (32). He is wrong, both because they do in fact surprise him, and because, for the reader, knowing 'exactly what they are going to do' is just what gives a voltage to their undergraduate mind games. The students' tricks and rivalries will, we know, turn nasty, so we are ready to detect their nastiness. Tartt's prologue influences every episode that follows. We know that Bunny will be murdered by his friends, and we must understand why—what Bunny is like. The novel's greatest success is to let you see how it has to be. Slowly and carefully, justifying the foreknowledge that she has given the reader, Tartt makes it all inevitable, and makes Bunny a person you might almost want to kill.

THE FRAMING DEVICE

Some stories account for their existence. The framing device is the means of doing so, the fictional explanation of how a narrative has been discovered or recorded. As the metaphor implies, the frame (or explanation) surrounds the rest of the narrative. A framing device must therefore be used at the beginning of a novel (this distinguishes it from other kinds of metanarrative: see Chapter 6). The first great novelist using elaborate framing devices was Sir Walter Scott, whose novels invariably begin with lengthy explanations of how the story that follows has come to us. *The Heart of Midlothian* (1818), for instance, begins with a 'prolegomenon' by the pedantic Jedediah Cleishbotham, schoolmaster and parish clerk of the fictional Scottish village of Gandercleugh, who is publishing a story recorded by Peter Pattieson, his former assistant. In the opening chapter, 'Being Introductory', Pattieson tells how he assisted at a coach crash just outside the village. Two of the passengers were worldly Edinburgh lawyers, who stayed in the village inn that night and talked to him of Edinburgh's Tolbooth Prison, which is called the Heart of Midlothian. From them he learned the story that he now relates.

Scott's new work of fiction masquerades as an old tale, yet we cannot take this literally. The huge novel can hardly be what Pattieson actually heard the two lawyers say, however garrulous they might have been. But then framing devices are often relinquished once the story is under way. This is the case throughout Scott's novels. Scott, who liked to draw both on history and on traditional stories, used his framing devices—his stories about his stories—to treat his own narrative as recorded rather than invented. There are other uses for such devices. Henry James's *The Turn of the Screw* (1898), for instance, unsettles us partly through being introduced by an unnamed narrator, one of whose friends, Douglas, will read the story to a group of acquaintances. They evidently tell each other ghost stories, but here is a tale of possession to disturb them all. One of the group expresses his desire to hear Douglas's story. 'I can see Douglas there before the fire, to which he had got up to present his back, looking down at this converser with his hands in his pockets. "Nobody but me, till now, has ever heard. It's quite too horrible"' (145). The framing device allows for the introduction of the governess's narrative, read aloud by Douglas 'with a fine clearness that was like a rendering to the ear of the beauty of his author's hand' (151). It also presents a story that will change the mood of amused complacency at the pleasures of a 'gruesome' tale. Comparably, Joseph Conrad's *Heart of Darkness* (1902) is told us by an unnamed narrator who, one evening, in a boat moored in the Thames Estuary, listens with four others to Marlow's perplexing tale of his journey up the great African river to find Kurtz. As this narrator puts it, 'we knew we were fated, before the ebb began to run, to hear about one of Marlow's inconclusive experiences' (21). Our doubts about the significance of the events narrated are set in motion by the very form. The troubling and puzzling effects of the story are included within the work. Our narrator is but a listener, with no direct access to those 'inconclusive experiences'.

There are contemporary novelists too who like to begin by framing the story, pushing back its true beginning. In *The*

Human Stain, Philip Roth uses a framing narrative in order to approach with investigative curiosity a tale of passion. The novel does not just tell a story, it also scrutinizes that story. *The Human Stain* concerns a New England classics professor, Coleman Silk, who is hounded out of his job for alleged racism. (In fact he has made one innocent but misinterpreted remark.) His story is told by Nathan Zuckerman, who has, literally speaking, been employed as narrator. Silk has actually asked him to produce the true account of the witch-hunt that has ruined his career ('the day he burst in all but shouting, "Write my story, damn you!"'; 337). He has also told Nathan about the sequel: his secretive affair with Faunia Farley, a woman half his age who cleans at the college. Silk's story is contained within Nathan's account of how he came to find it out. Nathan recalls sitting on Coleman Silk's porch and listening to him pour out the strange facts of his new life. We have not just the picture of Silk's experiences, but also the frame that Nathan puts around them. The narrator, who tells us of 71-year-old Coleman's all-possessing, Viagra-enhanced sexual passion, is himself impotent after prostate cancer. The sexual delirium, heady and destructive, is seen from the outside. And it includes more than Coleman envisages. For Nathan says that it was when, after Coleman's death, he learned the secret of his racial origins that he 'began this book—the book he had asked me to write in the first place, but written not necessarily as he wanted it' (213).

Nathan is a character whom Roth often uses for such a purpose and who has aged with the author. He first featured in *My Life as a Man* (1974), and *The Human Stain* explicitly recollects his appearance in another Roth novel of the 1970s, *The Ghost Writer* (1979). Coleman Silk teaches at the same university that, we are told, once employed E. I. Lonoff, the great Jewish author whom Nathan Zuckerman visits in that earlier novel. Ever since, Nathan has been encountering characters on Roth's behalf. Roth's persistent use of the framing device suggests that he is but discovering stories that are out there. By thus framing his narratives, Roth also unsettles our sympathies. In *The Human Stain*, Nathan recollects 'that April day two years back when Iris Silk died and the insanity took hold of Coleman' (10). He is drawn into the story when Coleman, furious and persecuted, bangs on his door one afternoon. 'All restraint had collapsed within him' (11). His exorbitant feelings seem mad. He is a person to be explained, a man whose fate is a fable of American prejudices.

As in *Heart of Darkness* (though not *The Turn of the Screw*), the framing device is insisted on at the narrative's conclusion. Conrad's novella ends with Marlow falling silent and the unnamed narrator who began the story taking over again, now made to feel by what he has heard that the Thames itself seems 'to lead into the heart of an immense darkness' (124). The story now told, the narrator notices that it is dusk and overcast, but the darkness is as much an effect of the narration he has just heard as of the dying daylight. In *The Human Stain*, the final chapter also returns us to the narrator, to Nathan Zuckerman, writing his book and measuring the reverberations of Coleman Silk's life and death. Yet, quite as much as *Heart of Midlothian*, it has earlier required us to forget what we have been told about how the story has come to us. For within the frame of Nathan's record, the reader has been allowed to know more than Nathan could ever know. We have been taken into Coleman's unspoken thoughts and into his secret past: his childhood, his sexual awakening, his making of a new identity for himself.

We might think these the narrator's imaginative prerogative; Nathan does say 'As I reconstruct it . . .' before one description of an episode that he never witnessed (63). But then the novel includes the solitary actions and private reflections of characters other than Coleman without any such apology or explanation. We listen to Coleman's lawyer talking to his wife about Coleman's case. We enter the mind of Delphine Roux, Coleman's feminist nemesis in his faculty, as she daydreams in the library about the handsome man reading post-structuralist theory opposite her. In a slab of virtuoso interior monologue, we are even taken inside the maddened resentment of Les Farley, Faunia's psychopathic ex-husband. The novel extends itself to these other minds and other voices in order to chasten our sense of what we might know about others. Nathan tells of meeting Coleman and Faunia at an outdoor concert sometime after he left his job, seeing them talking intimately together, 'but about what, of course, I did not know' (208). The poisonous, anonymous letter that Coleman has received about his affair with Faunia (sent by Delphine Roux) had said

> Everyone knows you're
> sexually exploiting an
> abused, illiterate
> woman half your
> age.
>
> (38)

And Nathan's ignorance of what, perhaps trivial, talk passes at a certain moment between Coleman and Faunia recalls the wording of this letter in a salutary stumble of the narrative.

> Because we don't know, do we? *Everyone knows* . . . How what happens the way it does? What underlies the anarchy of the train of events, the uncertainties, the mishaps, the disunity, the shocking irregularities that define human affairs? *Nobody* knows, Professor Roux. (208–9)

Here the frame that Roth has made for himself is suddenly made prominent. Nathan Zuckerman is angrily *there.* Elsewhere it is sometimes a convenience to be forgotten. This is why it is important that Nathan is so clearly Roth's representative, a way in for the author's feelings about his material. The very flouting of the framing convention expresses the author's own passionate, lucid exercise of his imagination. The passion and lucidity are caught in the novel's most audacious use of its framing device. Near its end, Nathan encounters the homicidal

Les Farley, out fishing on the ice, no one around for miles. They have a charged, dangerous conversation and Nathan admits to being a writer, who writes 'about people like you' (356).

> 'Is that right?'
> 'Yes. People like you. Their problems.'
> 'What's the name of one of your books?'
> '*The Human Stain.*'
> 'Yeah? Can I get it?'
> 'It's not out yet. It's not finished yet.'
> 'I'll buy it.'
> 'I'll send you one . . .'

Often such self-referential tricks are merely self-regarding, but here the narrative risk of it exactly suits and imitates the risk that Nathan takes in the dialogue. If Les were to read the book he would want to kill its author. At the novel's conclusion the framing device is more than convenient: it is a dramatic necessity.

THE OPENING

When we talk about famous openings of novels we usually mean resonant first sentences rather than beautifully crafted first scenes or chapters. The memorable first sentence will epitomize in a small way the logic of the novel as a whole. Those famous openings of *Pride and Prejudice* (1813) or *Anna Karenina* (1873–7) are not merely clever statements in themselves, they are also perfect specimens of their different authors' narrative spirit and confidence. In some novels, the first sentence can enact the shock of entering a world governed by perverse rules. George Orwell's *Nineteen Eighty-Four* (1949) is exemplary. 'It was a bright cold day in April, and the clocks were striking thirteen.' The statement is made as if it were natural and already we are made to inhabit the logic of a dystopia. Something is very wrong but nobody inside the book notices.

Comparable is the opening sentence of Kafka's *The Trial* (1925), which can be translated into English as 'Someone must have been telling lies about Josef K., for without having done anything wrong he was arrested one fine morning.' This gives us the novel's synthesis of banal normality and paranoia, but in the original German the effect is the more unsettling. 'Jemand mußte Josef K. verleumdet haben, denn ohne daß er etwas Böses getan hätte, wurde er eines Morgens verhaftet.' The past tense of 'mußte' and the subjunctive of 'hätte' (expressing uncertainty) imply that this sentence is free indirect discourse (see Chapter 2): it follows the thoughts of the character. His innocence is his self-image, not the narrator's assurance.

In a comparable vein, the thriller writer Ruth Rendell also likes to open with a simple yet disturbed statement. 'The world began to fall apart at nine in the evening': *The Crocodile Bird* (1993). 'Violent death fascinates people': *The Bridesmaid* (1989). 'The clothes of the dead won't wear long': *The Brimstone Wedding* (1995). At once, you are to be unsettled. The arresting opening statement epitomizes her method. Typically, her novels take you into the strange reasoning of twisted characters. In *The Killing Doll* (1984) a teenager thinks that he has made a pact with the Devil. In *Going Wrong* (1990) a criminal mistakenly believes that a glamorous, upper-class woman is in love with him. Each novel invites us to inhabit some parallel world of obsession or deranged conviction. The narrator will record deluded thought processes, yet without the distance that would permit judgement.

So it is with Rendell's *Adam and Eve and Pinch Me*. Immediately, you are into it. 'Minty knew it was a ghost sitting in the chair because she was frightened.' 'Minty knew . . .', not 'thought' or 'imagined'. We simply follow her perceptions. It sounds like a statement of fact, yet contains a strange circularity. That 'because' explains nothing, while suggesting that there is some logic at work. This suggestion is at the heart of the novel and of much of Rendell's fiction. The logic is in the mind of a character whom we might call 'disturbed'—who, in an earlier age, would have been called 'mad'. As the opening chapter unfolds, we find out that she lives her life without anyone else, except the reader, noticing that she is ruled by such delusions. She keeps down a job, she socializes with her neighbours; and she sees ghosts and hears voices.

Even the name is off-balance. 'Minty'. It could be some term of endearment, an affectionate nickname maybe, but here it sounds simply peculiar. And it will be important in the plot. 'Minty' will be turned into a nickname, 'Polo', by the predatory conman who befriends her and then becomes her lover. This will later enable another of his victims to trace her. The conman calls himself 'Jock' and thinks he has the measure of Minty's vulnerability. 'You never were all that balanced, Polo,' she hears him say (11). Teasing is Jock's way with the women he tricks. The novel's title is the first line of one of his childish rhymes. 'Adam and Eve and Pinch Me | went down to the river to bathe. | Adam and Eve were drownded | Who was saved?' 'Pinch me,' says the gullible Minty—and so he does. 'Very gently on her upper arm' (25). But then she is weirder that he can guess and she will finally kill him. The nastiness of the rhyme becomes real. 'When you talk to God it's praying but when God talks to you it's schizophrenia' (21), jokes the owner of the dry cleaner's to Minty, not guessing why she does not laugh.

'More people are nuts, as you call it, than you'd think,' Minty's policeman neighbour tells his wife (245). Minty has what psychiatrists call an 'obsessive-compulsive disorder'. She is always cleaning herself and everything around her, and the narrative painstakingly follows all her purifying procedures. One leading character is a male anorexic, and we are taken in detail through all his special aversions. The narrative, as in that opening sentence, adopts the very patterns of fixation. Another central character, a rich, lordly, gay Tory MP, is, in comparison with these obsessives, a mere stereotype. You might think that from her experience in the House of Lords, Rendell would have had every opportunity to make him credible. Yet it is not him but Minty—in all her exacting peculiarity—who comes to life. We see how she becomes a murderer, not because she is evil or psychopathic, but because she is living in a world of her own. The novel interests us precisely by implying that, in different circumstances—if 'Jock' had not picked on her as a victim—she would have gone on living her peculiar life. Indeed, she has no notion that she is a killer. '"It's wicked to murder people," Minty said. "Look at the trouble it causes"' (249).

2
Narrating

How is a story told? There are two ways of thinking about this. One involves looking at a narrative from a distance to see its structure. We ask how it is arranged—in what sequence, with what divisions, and so on. This is the subject of Chapter 6. The second way of tackling the question is to ask, Who is speaking? From what viewpoint? In what voice? This is the subject of this chapter.

One basic distinction is between first-person narration and third-person narration. Novelists are themselves often conscious of this as a choice to be made when they sit down to a new work. The English novel begins with the first person. The first word of what is usually taken to be the earliest novel in English is 'I'. 'I was born in the Year 1632, in the City of *York*, of a good Family, tho' not of that Country, my Father being a Foreigner of *Bremen*, who settled first at *Hull*.' This is the opening of Daniel Defoe's *Robinson Crusoe*, published in 1719. *The Life and Strange Surprising Adventures of Robinson Crusoe* was, according to its original title page, '*Written by Himself*'. Robinson Crusoe was supposed the author as well as the hero. The novel includes a preface, purportedly penned by the editor of Crusoe's autobiography, but nowhere did Defoe's name appear on the first edition. All of Defoe's subsequent novels were, similarly, fictional memoirs. Each is given over to the individuality of its protagonist.

Some important novels that followed, like Samuel Richardson's *Pamela*, also took it for granted that, if the purpose of fiction was to explore the inner life of a credible character, a first-person narrative was the best means. *Pamela* is written in letters, but for much of her ordeal at the hand of her sexually predatory master, Mr. B., Richardson's heroine is unable to receive correspondence and her own letters become a kind of diary. The epistolary novel was to die out as a form at the beginning of the nineteenth century, but first-person narration would continue to hold attractions for certain novelists. It is no accident that the two novels in which Dickens most obviously uses memories from his own life, *David Copperfield* and *Great Expectations* (1860–1), are also the only two that are told throughout in the first person. Yet there have been great novelists whose very scope has seemed to forbid this way of narrating. George Eliot's range of sympathies and her generosity to her characters preclude the partiality, however interesting, of the first-person narrator. Henry James, another novelist whose analyses of motivation require, at least in all his novel-length fiction, a third-person narrator, even believed that the first-person method was inherently inferior. In his 1909 preface to the New York edition of *The Ambassadors* (1907), he declared that 'the first person, in the long piece, is a form foredoomed to looseness'.[1] The trouble is exactly that the first person can speak all too freely and directly to us, 'his possible readers, whom he has to reckon with . . . so loosely and vaguely after all, so little respectfully, on so scant a presumption of exposure to criticism'. Strether, the protagonist of *The Ambassadors*, is restrained and 'encaged' in his dealings with others in the novel, and we are to feel the force of the 'proprieties' that shape him. There would be something false about escaping into 'the terrible *fluidity* of self-revelation'.[2]

James is making an argument about a singular novel, but that last phrase is evidence enough of his disdain for the form in general. He expresses this elsewhere in his criticism and correspondence, notably in an extraordinary letter to H. G. Wells. In 1911 Wells had sent James a copy of his latest novel, *The New Machiavelli* (1911), which is narrated in the first person. In his letter of thanks James praised the novel in high terms ('rare & wonderful & admirable') before launching into an attack on 'that accurst autobiographic form which puts a premium on the loose, the improvised, the cheap & the easy'.[3] 'Save in the fantastic & the romantic (Copperfield, Jane Eyre, that charming thing of Stevenson's with the bad title—"Kidnapped"?) it has no authority, no persuasive or convincing force—its grasp of reality & truth isn't strong & disinterested.' The aesthetic value of fiction required the novelist's 'detachment', a shaping influence that could be felt at work in the narration.

James's judgement—or prejudice—implies a certain confidence in the novelist's capacity to observe human behaviour and infer human motives. That 'detachment' he so values might seem lordly to later novelists (though, as my discussion of the 'omniscient narrator' in this chapter indicates, omniscience is not necessarily the consequence of this detachment). David Lodge has reported his 'impression' that 'a majority of literary novels published in the last couple of decades have been written in the first person'.[4] He was clearly influenced in this by his experience as chairman of the judges of the Booker Prize in 1989, when five of the six shortlisted novels had first-person narrators. My own count of novels on the Booker Prize shortlists of the ten years between 1995 and 2004 shows that thirty-three out of fifty-nine are narrated wholly or partly in the first person. This includes some, like Mick Jackson's *The Underground Man* (1997) or Matthew Kneale's *English Passengers* (2000), that have more than one narrator, and others, like Ahdaf Soueif's *The Map of Love* (1999) and David Mitchell's *Cloud Atlas*, that mix first-person and third-person narratives. Even with these qualifications, we seem to have a large proportion of first-person narratives, larger surely than the proportion amongst novels in general. It might suggest that first-person narration has become a special feature of the 'literary novel' in English. Lodge's observation is made in order to suggest that contemporary novelists have lost faith in narratorial 'omniscience' or truthfulness, though the evidence might equally support a recent freedom for novelists to experiment with different kinds of narrator.

The 'autobiographic form' does sometimes require a kind of 'detachment', at least on the part of the reader. This is when we are required to infer what the narrator does not tell us or cannot perceive. The first three sections below discuss how we become aware of a narrator's limitations. The most common term for a narrator who is fallible is 'the unreliable narrator', a phrase coined in the 1960s by the American critic Wayne C. Booth.[5] Yet this is not always helpful. It may work for, say, Ford Madox Ford's *The Good Soldier* (1915), whose narrator, John Dowell, keeps evading telling us the truth about his own feelings. It does not apply to Christopher, the autistic narrator of Mark Haddon's *The Curious Incident of the Dog in the Night-Time.* His understanding certainly needs to be supplemented by the reader, but we are not invited to be sceptical about what he tells us. As he says several times, 'I always tell the truth.' His very truthfulness is a limitation on his understanding of the world. Other descriptions are needed of the contrived limitations of first-person narrators. Some novelists have made a virtue of first-person partiality by finding a viewpoint normally denied them (a male author inventing a female narrator, or vice versa) or splitting a novel between more than one narrator.

Yet, while many novelists wish to inscribe partiality in the very form of narration, the traditional omniscient narrator is not dead. Omniscience, we should say, is a way of describing potential knowledge rather than practical revelation. For novels with third-person narration will not, cannot, allow us equally into every character's thoughts. Most of the sections here treating such narration examine how attention is focused or divided between characters, how we get to know things from a certain point of view. Henry Fielding was the first English novelist elaborately to employ an omniscient narrator, able to view the motives of all his characters. Yet he spends a good deal of time in *Tom Jones* wondering why some of his characters act as they do. When a baby is deposited at the door of the good-hearted Squire Allworthy, Bridget Allworthy, his sour, uncharitable spinster sister, surprises us by intimating 'compassion for the helpless little creature' (bk. I, ch. iv, 38). The narrator lets us speculate. 'Perhaps the reader may account for this behaviour from her condescension to Mr Allworthy, when we have informed him, that the good man had ended his narrative with owning a resolution to take care of the child, and to breed him up as his own.' The 'perhaps' is entirely rhetorical; Fielding knows very well her motivation, which is that she herself is the mother of the foundling. However, we must not find this out until near the end of the novel, so both she and Fielding disguise the fact from the reader and from Squire Allworthy, making up for what she withheld from the infant with a tirade against 'the poor unknown mother', whom she calls 'an impudent slut, a wanton hussy, an audacious harlot, a wicked jade, a vile strumpet, with every other appellation with which the tongue of virtue never fails to lash those who bring a disgrace on the sex'. The consummate omniscient narrator will often leave the reader to work out why characters act as they do.

There remains a final matter of how to tell a story that again takes us back to the origins of the Novel. Samuel Richardson described his novels-in-letters as being 'written, as it were, to the *Moment*, while the Heart is agitated by Hopes and Fears, on Events undecided' (*Sir Charles Grandison*, 1753–4, preface, 6). Lovelace, the brilliant villain of his great novel *Clarissa* (1747–8), writes of his predilection for 'this lively *present-tense* manner', with events, and feelings, recorded almost as they are happening (Letter 256, 882). There was a presumption on the part of some early English novelists that the present tense best conveyed the fluctuating consciousness of a particular individual. Comparably, Laurence Sterne's *Tristram Shandy*, though it concerns past events, is memorable for a narrator who is always speaking, thinking, digressing in the present tense.

These two great novels are narrated in the first person; a modern invention is the third-person narrative in the present tense, considered below. Novels might choose to use more than one tense, moving between immediacy and reflection, and examples of this are also considered. The last section of this chapter is devoted to a technique—unknown to Fielding—by which a novel can marry the narrator's superior knowledge to the character's distinctive viewpoint: free indirect speech. This revolutionary yet mysterious development in the history of the Novel allowed novelists to escape the choice between, on the one hand, knowing everything, while seeing their characters from outside, and, on the other hand, letting us inhabit their characters' minds, while knowing events only as partially as they do.

FIRST-PERSON NARRATION

Donna Tartt's *The Secret History* has a narrator who has helped to commit a murder. He tells us this in the very prologue to the novel. The choice of a first-person narrator for a novel whose protagonist is guilty of a crime is rather traditional. From *Moll Flanders* to *Lolita* (1955), first-person narration has been the means of drawing a reader into some disturbing sympathy with a character's misdeeds. Confession has long been a form in which fiction is cast. Such a narrative engages us not simply by giving access to a character's thoughts (an 'omniscient' narrator can also provide this) but by opening a gap between the 'I' who tells the story and the 'I' who is the past self. Here, potentially, is the drama of a person trying to make sense of him- or herself. *The Secret History* begins by highlighting this. 'It is difficult to believe I could have walked through it—the cameras, the uniforms, the black crowds sprinkled over Mount Cataract like ants in a sugar bowl—without incurring a blink of suspicion' (1–2). Richard looks back on himself with a kind of incredulity. Narrator and leading character are supposedly the same 'person' but the narrative method separates them, if not as completely as Richard would like. 'I thought I had left that ravine forever on an April afternoon long ago, now I am not so sure.'

Tartt's narrator recalls himself and his actions with ruefulness, or surprise, or even disbelief. In such a narrative, occasional uses of the present tense remind us that the person narrating stands beyond the experiences recounted. Thus the importance of those apparently inert tags like 'I suppose that...' and 'Now I see that...'. When he remembers being embarrassed and taunted by Bunny in the days before he helped murder him, Richard sympathizes with his own mortification. 'I cannot find words to adequately express the torments I suffered when he chose to ply this art of his in public' (259). As here, the moments when the narration switches into the present tense are often those when something cannot be recaptured. Recalling the afternoon when he was first enchanted by his charismatic teacher Julian, Richard avoids replicating their dialogue. 'I wish I could remember more of what was said that day—actually, I do remember much of what *I* said, most of it too fatuous for me to recall with pleasure' (31).

Yet a novelist who chooses a first-person narrator has problems as well as resources. Does the author want us to pay constant attention to the narrator's present struggles to make sense of the past? Or will this get in the way of the plot? At one extreme is Defoe. In his novels, the narrator is always reflecting penitently on a foolish younger self. On every page there are two tenses: the past of the character's actions and the present of the narrator's self-criticism. 'Alas!' exclaims the narrator of *Moll Flanders* as she tells us of how her younger self was first seduced, made vulnerable by her own 'Vanity and Pride' (25). Dickens does this too in his two first-person novels, *David Copperfield* and *Great Expectations*. When Pip remembers the first meeting with Mr Jaggers, at which he and Joe Gargery are told of Pip's 'great expectations', he switches into the present tense after Joe refuses Jaggers's offer of money. 'O dear good Joe, whom I was so ready to leave and so unthankful to, I see you again, with your muscular blacksmith's arm before your eyes, and your broad chest heaving and your voice dying away' (vol. I, ch. xviii, 141). Yet this narrator also lets us share the delusions that he once had. Earlier in the same scene, after Jaggers's announcement that Pip 'will come into a handsome property', the narrator says this: 'My dream was out; my wild fancy was surpassed by sober reality; Miss Havisham was going to make my fortune on a grand scale' (138). The first-time reader is allowed to believe this until the moment when Pip is told by the convict Magwitch that he is in fact the mysterious benefactor. The older, sadder Pip who tells his story, keeps back facts that he knows in order to spring his surprises.

Some novelists have made creative use of the uncertainty about the distance between narrator and character. In Charlotte Brontë's *Jane Eyre*, against all the conventions of fiction in her day, the narrator switches entirely to the present for the most charged episodes of her story—as if she were, entranced, re-experiencing it rather than 'telling' it (see 'Tense Shift' below). However, it is not clear if Tartt has decided what she is doing with this type of narration. Sometimes she wants to show that her narrator looks back with amazement on his past self—that he is now horrified at what he was once drawn into. Yet sometimes she wants to credit her narrator's infatuation and make him still in love with the friends with whom he plotted the murder. In the first case he would be a 'reliable narrator', in the second an 'unreliable narrator'. Does she quite know which she has on her hands?

RECOLLECTION

Your memory is probably not as good as that of most narrators of novels told in the first person. Those who professionally deal with testimonies—detectives, say, or criminal lawyers—must find extraordinary the exactitude of recollection in such works of fiction. Robinson Crusoe, looking back some forty years later, can tell us that, when washed up on his desert island, he saw no sign of his shipmates 'except three of their Hats, one Cap, and two Shoes that were not Fellows' (46). Exactly so. Even less plausibly, Jane Eyre, supposedly writing years afterwards, recalls pages of precise and passionate dialogue with Mr Rochester. Doubt her record and the fiction crumbles. Brontë, like many others, relies on a convention that contradicts experience. We might remember a phrase or emphasis from a recent conversation, but we are unlikely to recall the exact words said to us, or by us, even minutes ago. Yet novels with first-person narrators invariably behave as if the narrator could replay a tape of dialogue made in his or her head.

Iris Griffen, the main narrator of Margaret Atwood's *The Blind Assassin*, reaches back decades to remember what was once said. She is in her eighties, and is telling the story of her and her sister Laura's entwined lives. Even the most recent event in her narrative, Laura's suicide, took place half a century earlier. Yet she gives us not just telling episodes, but also the dialogues that accompanied them. She recalls how, aged 9, she hid with Laura under the kitchen table, overhearing the cook and her friend discuss her mother's recent miscarriage.

> 'Did she have a lot of pain?' asked Mrs. Hillcoate, in a pitying, interested voice.
>
> 'I've seen worse,' said Reenie. 'Thank God for small mercies. It slipped out just like a kitten, but I have to say she bled buckets. We'll need to burn the mattress, I don't know how we'd ever get it clean.' (113)

And so on. The mixture of platitude and frankness is completely credible, and even as the conversation continues ('"Some women shouldn't marry," said Mrs. Hillcoate'), the fact of recollection becomes credible too. Reenie's precise words lodge, for

Iris remembers how she and Laura later sneaked upstairs to try to find 'the kitten'.

Yet Atwood's narrator does not have consistent recall. There are those novels like *Robinson Crusoe* or *Jane Eyre* that simply require us to suspend disbelief about the narrator's memory, but pointedly *The Blind Assassin* does not. Sometimes Iris herself doubts her recollections. When she tells us how Alex, the rebellious young man whom she and Laura shelter from the police, suddenly kissed her, she wonders if she did something to provoke him. 'Nothing I can recall, but is what I remember the same thing as what actually happened?' (266). Her own wedding is a blur. 'Speeches were made, of which I remember nothing. Did we dance? I believe so' (293). Often she cannot produce the telling detail, or remember exact words. 'Where am I?' she asks more than once as she turns from the present to resume her story. Almost every chapter of her narration makes visible the gap between the recent and the distant. She is writing to the moment, week by week, noting the changing weather, the slow turn of the seasons. 'I pay out my line, I pay out my line, this black thread I'm spinning across the page' (345). In the present, this narrator worries about what she has recollected. 'I look back over what I've written and I know it's wrong, not because of what I've set down, but because of what I've omitted' (484). Iris's doubts about her own account are part of that account. 'I've looked back over what I've set down so far, and it seems inadequate' (509). We are to believe in that inadequacy.

Above all, Atwood cleverly sets the passages of remembered dialogue against prevailing silence. Iris recalls a particular conversation with her father, but this is one of the few times that any words of his are remembered. She tells you exactly what her despicable husband, Richard, said when she found out that he had destroyed telegrams telling her of her father's death. Little else that he says is recorded (though there is much indirect reporting of the gist or the effect of something that he has said).

The commands of his baleful sister Winifred are summarized, but only the narrator's first ever, horrible conversation with her is transcribed. Recollection in Atwood's novel is eloquently uneven. What matters is exactly the difference between what is remembered and what is not. It is a kind of dramatic convention that earns our belief. The conversations that have been picked out from the past acquire a special energy because they are edged by silence or forgetting.

THE INADEQUATE NARRATOR

There is a special type of first-person narrative that requires the reader to supply what the narrator cannot understand. Much of what 'happens' in Mark Haddon's *The Curious Incident of the Dog in the Night-Time* is not grasped by Christopher, its narrator. The reader comprehends, as Christopher never will, the farcical drama of parental discord that he witnesses. Even when Christopher discovers that his mother is not dead, as his father has told him, but living in London with her lover, a former neighbour, he has no idea of his father's reasons (cowardice and protectiveness) for lying. Christopher, the book jacket tells you, has Asperger's syndrome, though this is never named in the novel. He has no understanding of others' emotions, though he doggedly records their symptoms. 'He looked at me for a long time and sucked air in through his nose,' he observes, when his father is, we infer, near despair (27). Yet requiring the reader to fill in these gaps allows for a tragicomic intuition of characters' feelings that a more adequate narrator could not invite.

The 'inadequate narrator' is not an established critical term. Yet the more usual 'unreliable narrator' seems inaccurate for a narrator who, however uncomprehending, is entirely trustworthy. One reason why he cannot negotiate his way through conversations is that he is 'inappropriately' (as the psychiatrists would say) truthful. Arrested after hitting a policeman, he is interviewed by a police inspector who is evidently keen to take the matter no further.

> He said, 'I have spoken to your father and he says that you didn't mean to hit the policeman.'
>
> I didn't say anything because this wasn't a question.
>
> He said, 'Did you mean to hit the policeman?'
>
> I said, 'Yes.' (22)

He registers the police officer's exasperation without actually being able to recognize it. 'The policeman closed his mouth and breathed out loudly through his nose' (23).

Narrative inadequacy is not so unusual in fiction. One of the greatest of all American novels, Mark Twain's *Huckleberry Finn* (1884), relies on its 13-year-old narrator's mingled canniness and innocence, as in this analysis of his father's behaviour. 'After supper pap took the jug, and said he had enough whisky there for two drunks and one delirium tremens. That was always his word. I judged he would be blind drunk in about an hour, and then I would steal the key, or saw myself out, one or 'tother' (ch. 6, 79). Think of Alice Walker's *The Color Purple* (1982), whose narrator is qualified by her inarticulacy. We infer what she suffers through her inability to express it. Then there is the model for the inadequate narrator, the eponymous heroine of Samuel Richardson's *Pamela*. A 15-year-old servant girl, she must be too innocent to comprehend the schemes of her predatory master, though we as readers must see them all too clearly. These narrators are innocent, like Christopher, but they are also limited by their language. One effect is a satirical indictment of those nominally sophisticated adults whom each narrator describes and tries to understand.

Christopher's peculiar ingenuousness is as much fictional device as medical condition. You do not have to check him against a psychiatric textbook to believe in him as a narrator. He leaves the reader to piece together the meanings and motives of the characters around him; he never explains or interprets.

'When I was little I didn't understand about other people having minds. . . . But I don't find this difficult now' (145). He has decided to turn life into a detective story, for 'if something is a puzzle there is always a way of solving it'. This inadequate narrator lets us glimpse the inadequacies of all the adults he encounters. The reader senses the torment and the forbearance of Christopher's father, never comprehended by his son. Christopher knows things about others only by their conventional signs. When his father shouts, this means anger. When there are tears 'coming out of his eyes' (27), he must be sad, though he wrongly and characteristically supposes that the cause must be the death of their neighbour's dog Wellington.

Christopher is also detached from his own torments. When things become too much, he curls into a ball and hides in a small space, or simply screams. When he reads the letters from his mother that his father has hidden from him, he has no description to offer of his feelings, just an account of a kind of seizure. 'I couldn't think of anything at all because my brain wasn't working properly.' This is no figure of speech. When the patterns of thought and habits of behaviour on which he depends collapse, there is nothing else. The irony is that his inadequacy as a guide to human psychology is balanced by a fastidious accuracy in matters of report. 'I am really good at remembering things, like the conversations I have written down in this book, and what people were wearing, and what they smelled like' (96). His exactitude shows up the evasions of the other characters. Imagining things is what makes Christopher frightened. 'And this is why everything I have written here is true' (25).

A MAN WRITING AS A WOMAN

Nick Hornby's decision to have a female narrator of his novel *How To Be Good* surprised its first reviewers. The success of his autobiographical *Fever Pitch* (1992) had proved this writer's ability to make supposedly male preoccupations widely accessible and generally amusing. His books were seen as close to his own life and experiences, his memoir hardly being distinguished in its genre from his subsequent novels. The title of the second of these, *About a Boy* (1998), even seemed to declare the author's preoccupation with maleness. Whether thought of as a searching anatomy of modern masculinity or just witty 'lad-lit', Hornby's writing was always, as the academics say, 'gendered'. So the narrative convention signalled in the first sentence of *How To Be Good* is an experiment upon the novelist's reputation as well as upon the reader's capacity to suspend disbelief. 'I am in a car park in Leeds when I tell my husband I don't want to be married to him any more' (1). We soon discover that the novel's territory is so familiar from Hornby's other books that you can hardly forget the author. We are back in Highbury, North London, with more of Hornby's self-perplexed, middle-class characters. Yet this narrator is evidently female: Katie, a 40-year-old GP with two children and an unhappy marriage. Apparently we are now to see things from a woman's point of view. Was the novelist abandoning his hard-earned knowledge of the modern male in some daring exercise of creative sympathy?

Oddly enough, the Novel in English began this way, with men writing as women. Daniel Defoe's *Moll Flanders* and *Roxana* (1724), are the supposed first-person accounts of female characters. Defoe chronicles the opportunities and risks of a commercial world, and women are its most prized or most despised commodities. More influentially, in *Pamela*, written in the voice of a servant girl, Richardson conflated the Novel genre with female experience. His novels record secret feelings, and suppose the language of feeling to be peculiarly feminine. Some of this might still apply. For those early pioneers, the Novel was the genre that examined private life and audaciously made heroic the private person. Hornby, turning his eye on modern marriage, finds it convenient to do so via a female narrator. It takes a woman to measure the costs of all that has to be sacrificed for a marriage. It takes a woman, in *How To Be Good*, to fail any longer to have the right feelings about her children, thinking her daughter a 'prig', 'lazy and uncaring and spoiled' (102), her son 'a horrible, whining boy' (125). Yet Hornby's switch of attention is not so complete. Long narrative passages, in Katie's 'voice', are in a familiar vein of gentle satire on male habits. Even after Katie's husband has become 'good'—the unlikely conversion that provides the novel's comedy—she recalls his previous varieties of masculine sourness and resentment. Cannily, Hornby uses his female narrator as an echo chamber for mid-life male dissatisfaction.

For Richardson, feminine narration involved a searching, often anguished inwardness. For Hornby, psychological depth is not really the ambition. In interior monologue, his narrator is still jokey, mock-flippant. In the privacy of her own head, she makes the same remarks that she does to her family and friends. 'Is it possible to want to divorce a man because he doesn't want to be rude about Ginger Spice? I rather fear it might be' (133). She thinks like she chats over the Chardonnay. Hornby has made his narrator female not for the exploration of character but because his book is about goodness. Defoe's women had to trade their 'virtue' to survive. Richardson's women defended their 'virtue' to the last (and 'Virtue Rewarded' is the subtitle of *Pamela*). In a rather old-fashioned way, Hornby's narrator seems to be female so that she can be some representative of goodness, however compromised, muddled, desperate. Once narrators had God to help them be good. Moll Flanders and Pamela examined their lives to see God's design for them, and to discover their sins and errors. Telling your story is a religious exercise. Being accountable to God makes you a reliable narrator. Katie (though she toys farcically with religion) has only her profession to reassure her. 'I'm not a bad person. I'm a doctor' (6), and 'I'm a good person, I'm a doctor' (75), are her internal, never-spoken refrains.

Hornby's narrative sex change is a literary convention that readers, unstartled, readily accepted, as they have often accepted it before. Other contemporary novelists have successfully attempted it. To name just a few prominent examples, J. M. Coetzee's *Age of Iron* (1990), Alan Warner's *Morvern Callar* (1995), and Kazuo Ishiguro's *Never Let Me Go* (2005) have male authors and female narrators. Donna Tartt's *The Secret History*, Rose Tremain's *Restoration* (1989), and Beryl Bainbridge's *Master Georgie* (1998) have female authors and male narrators. Hornby uses the gender metamorphosis to flesh out and affectionately mock what we might call liberalism. One good reason for his hold on his readers is that we can see that this is really self-mockery, amusingly disguised.

MULTIPLE NARRATORS

Why would a writer divide his or her novel between several different narrators? Orhan Pamuk's *My Name Is Red* is told in some twenty different voices. What is more, half of these are fabulous: the personified elements of the exquisite illuminations painted by several of the leading characters. The chapters spoken by these voices are decorative and digressive. The human voices belong to ten characters who tell us, in alternating chapters, their parts of what is a murder story. Or rather, there are nine characters: the narrator who calls himself 'the Murderer' is identical with one of the other named narrators. We have to find which one.

Multiple narrators serve the historical aspect of Pamuk's fiction. A sense of the past is to be pieced together from separate testimonies rather than grasped by some 'modern' narrator. Another successful example of the historical mystery, Iain Pears's *An Instance of the Fingerpost* (1998), comparably uses several narrators, though many fewer than Pamuk. For Pamuk, the mystery too fits the narrative technique; uncertainty about events is enacted in the very form. There is no all-knowing narrator to see the truth. A leading Victorian experimenter with multiple narrators was a mystery writer, Wilkie Collins. His novel *The Moonstone* comprises the testimonies of ten characters, used in an appropriately forensic manner. It is as if they were witnesses testifying at a trial. The solution to the crime, the theft of a priceless diamond, is to be pieced together from the different narratives. Pamuk can avoid the possibility of the incoherence that multiple narrators can bring by, like Collins, making them all serve one pressing plot. They narrate as if aware of each other, knowing where to take up the story or leave it. At the end of one chapter, the Murderer tells how he confessed his guilt to Enishte, the master of painters. The next chapter, narrated by Enishte, begins a moment later, as if seizing the narrative baton. 'A silence filled the room when he confessed he'd murdered Elegant Effendi' (199). This effect is frequent throughout: character A ends a chapter arriving at character B's house; character B begins his chapter by opening the door. The narrators are not to wander.

Multiple narrators came to the English novel quite early in its development, via the novel in letters. Samuel Richardson's *Clarissa* (1747–8) and Tobias Smollett's *The Expedition of Humphry Clinker* (1771) are leading eighteenth-century examples. Both are 'told' by a number of fictional correspondents. One ambition of the Novel has always been to show how the truth about human behaviour can depend on one's vantage point. *Clarissa* shows tragically and *Humphry Clinker* comically how the same events may be viewed differently by different characters. Pamuk also wants disparities between viewpoints. In the book's love story, the very disconnection of narratives is used to focus our sympathies. The lovers, Black and Shekure, cannot hear each other's passions and doubts. Their meetings are snatched, sometimes silent. They are brought together by the murder story that each narrates only partially, but the novel's very form has them warily manoeuvre around each other, eventual consummation elaborately delayed.

Pamuk's model for his discrete narratives is oral. His narrators are speaking, like the storyteller in the Istanbul coffee house to whom he keeps returning. Reading in translation probably blurs the effect, for any original distinctions between the voices of the different narrators have faded in the move from Turkish to English. To hold the narratives together Pamuk needs the reader, the person to whom his characters confess. This can seem to disrupt the very convention he is using. Characters keep turning to us for confirmation. When Shekure describes finding her father's body, she pauses to establish that she is talking to someone who has read the accounts given by other characters. 'Listen, I can tell by your tight-lipped and cold-blooded reaction that you've known for some time what's happened in this room' (216). 'Have I gained your trust as well?' one of the suspects typically asks the reader (462). 'You had until you asked me' might be the reader's answer.

SKAZ

In the first paragraph of Martin Amis's *Money* (1984), John Self is in the back of a taxi that bucks over a ridge in the road on its mad charge into Manhattan:

> to the sound of a rifle-shot the cab roof ducked down and smacked me on the core of my head. I really didn't need that, I tell you, with my head and face and back and heart hurting a lot all the time anyway, and still drunk and crazed and ghosted from the plane.
>
> 'Oh man.' I said. (1)

Welcome to New York and the narrator's distinctive style, shaped from habits of contemporary speech. From the idiomatic understatement ('I really didn't need that') to the colloquial marker of emphasis ('I tell you') to the insistent listing ('my head and face and back and heart . . .') to that blunt quantification ('a lot all the time') narration attaches itself to the spoken word. To read *Money* is to imagine listening. The narrator, after all, would never bother *writing* his story. John Self hates 'people with degrees, O-levels, eleven-pluses, Iowa Tests, shorthand diplomas. . .' and takes pride in being ill-read (58). Naturally his language is extravagantly non-literate. Yet there is brutal expressiveness too. His exaggerations are inventive as well as colloquial. 'Drunk and crazed and ghosted' takes us from the usual consequence of duty-free indulgence through the extreme effects of economy-class confinement to an idiosyncratic word for the enervated strangeness of the transatlantic traveller. And what about his 'heart' hurting like those other bits of his body? 'I have this heart condition and it hurts all the time anyway' (27). Is this *Weltschmerz* or fear of the grim reaper? Self's little lists often combine incongruous elements like this, as when he meets the evidently violent father of a young film actor. 'I was in no sort of nick for this encounter, I admit, full of fear and afternoon scotch and the homeward tug' (139). Something like melancholy emerges from the clichés that tip into confession.

Academic critics sometimes use the term 'skaz' to refer to a first-person narrative that seems to adopt the characteristics of speech. It was employed by Russian formalist critics in the early twentieth century to designate a type of folk tale (derived from *skazat*, 'to tell'). Originally it referred to an eyewitness account of some episode of rural life. It was, above all, a story that preserved some of the qualities of oral performance: the teller's embellishments or mistakes were part of the tale. Now it refers to novelistic prose that consistently exploits the habits of colloquial language, especially those usually excluded from proper written prose. Skaz traditionally included slang, proverbs, dialect, and significant errors of decorum or style. Self uses all these, as well as expressions that are normally censored before they reach any page. He uses 'bad language' freely in narration as well as speech: 'Broadway always contrives to be just that little bit shittier than the zones through which it bends'; 'I feel invaded, doped, fucked around.' He also resorts to the insults characteristic of demotic narration. He talks of 'fags' and 'throwbacks', of 'yobs' and 'bitches' (he is one of the former, his girlfriend one of the latter). Yet while Amis gives Self colloquial habits, his monologue is also artificial and brilliantly contrived. Like the narrators of Anthony Burgess's *A Clockwork Orange* (1962) and J. D. Salinger's *The Catcher in the Rye* (1951), he 'speaks' a language minted for the occasion. He has his bits of personal slang: his 'rug' for his hair; his 'sock' for his expensive yet squalid bachelor flat. His very torments generate colloquial wit. 'There's a definite swelling in my jaw now, on my upper west side. It's a fucking abscess or something, maybe a nerve deal or a gum gimmick' (4).

The first classic of skaz in English is probably Mark Twain's *Huckleberry Finn*, in which Huck's uneducated English magically shows up the foolish or hypocritical adults he encounters. Here he is on Miss Watson, 'a tolerable slim old maid, with goggles on' who tries to teach him about heaven and hell.

> Then she told me all about the bad place, and I said I wished I was there. She got mad, then, but I didn't mean no harm. All I wanted was to go somewheres; all I wanted was a change, I warnt particular. She said it was wicked to say what I said; said she wouldn't say it for the whole world; *she* was going to live so as to go to the good place. Well, I couldn't see no advantage in going where she was going, so I made up my mind I wouldn't try for it. (ch. 1, pp. 50–1)

For Twain, this was a peculiarly American escape from literary English, and American writers have used skaz more readily than British writers. John Self shuttles to New York and Los Angeles to chase money and flaunts the Americanese of his diction. 'Fear has really got the whammy on all of us down here. Oh it's true, man. Sister, don't kid yourself' (4). He brandishes phrases overheard from American television and cinema, as if they qualify him as a citizen of the modern world. He also, naturally, has contempt for Americans and the way they speak. He loathes what he lives off and you can hear it in his voice.

THE SELF-CONSCIOUS NOVEL

It is not uncommon for novels to have novelists as leading characters. Some, from Dickens's *David Copperfield* to Ian McEwan's *Atonement*, tell the 'back-narrative' of how a character has become a novelist. In these cases, learning to write fiction is inextricable from a larger narrative of self-discovery. Others, from Trollope's *The Way We Live Now* to Martin Amis's *The Information* (1995), satirize the business of manufacturing fiction and attempting to fit it to the public's tastes. Here the novelist observes mockingly, with an insider's jaundiced knowledge. In Carol Shields's *Unless*, however, the author's own case is more central. The novel sharply, inescapably, focuses a reader's attention on the ambitions and limits of Shields's own fiction. The narrator of *Unless*, Reta Winters, has come late to novel-writing after acting for years as translator for a famous woman of letters, Danielle Westerman. In her forties, Reta writes a slim novel with the gratingly whimsical title *My Thyme Is Up*. It is unexpectedly successful. Sales are good; reviews are complimentary, if condescending—'"Oddly appealing," the *New York Times Book Review* said' (80); she wins one of the lesser literary prizes. During the course of *Unless*, Reta is writing a sequel, often as a distraction from domestic calamity—her eldest daughter's inexplicable withdrawal from family, society, even life itself. As Reta thinks about her fiction, we are nudged into thinking about the reach of this novel, and indeed Shields's œuvre. Reta's work is praised by those who deplore 'the opaqueness of the contemporary novel' and commended for avoiding 'convolution and pretension' (81). One typical admirer talks of its 'sunniness', while inwardly Reta seethes.

Yet she concedes that her writing records the social and domestic life left out of 'the modernist tradition', which 'has set the individual, the conflicted self, up against the world' (121). She calls her chosen genre '"light" fiction' (206). In one of the several truculent, unposted letters that she writes to journalists and critics, she complains about references to women writers as 'the miniaturists of fiction'. She has been numbered as one of these, in contrast to male novelists with the social range of Don DeLillo or the erotic intensity of Philip Roth. Naming these contemporaries (Reta also notices Margaret Atwood winning the Booker Prize) mischievously makes Reta's self-awareness all the more clearly a version of Shields's. How sick she must be of such contrasts. (Though, ironically, the story of Roth's lauded *American Pastoral* (1997)—the narrative of a man whose daughter, in political indignation, becomes a self-deprived recluse—brings it very close to the territory of *Unless*.) In a satirical cameo, Reta's new editor tries to flatter and bully her into rewriting her new novel to make it more 'important'—to 'move it toward the universal' (282). She should escape her small woman's world.

Unless is a book about the proper concerns of fiction and it makes its subject out of the dissatisfaction of critics who want something grander than what Shields provides. Reta keeps quoting back at herself the unadmiring praise ('bard of the banal') of the reviewers. This tactic is older than might be thought. In the 1760s Sterne used it in *Tristram Shandy*, published during the earliest years of book reviews. Critical responses to one instalment of his novel would duly be mocked in the next. Should a reviewer 'gnash his teeth, and storm and rage at me, as some of you did last MAY', Sterne, in the guise of Tristram, would tolerantly recall that 'the weather was very hot' (vol. iii, ch. iv, 133). Hostile reviewers were pitiably overheated, in implicit contrast with cool and broad-minded readers. Behind *Unless* you can imagine a career's worth of patronizing reviews being noted. Where Reta is rueful, we sense the author's angrier self-vindication. Even the potential awkwardness of this self-consciousness itself becomes encoded in Shields's novel. Reta makes her own heroine, Alicia, into a writer and then worries about 'being in incestuous waters' (is that clumsy mixed metaphor hers, or Shields's?). She is 'a woman writer who is writing about a woman writer who is writing' (208). Which makes Carol Shields a woman writer who is writing about a woman writer who is writing about a woman writer ... Sometimes, as here, a reader can infer the author's impatience with the very devices of self-consciousness she has employed.

ADDRESSING THE READER

'Reader, I married him.' That bold first sentence of the last chapter of *Jane Eyre* seems to encapsulate the special intimacy with its reader that a novel can achieve. The novel developed as a genre that reached out to each individual reader, and held him or her in its embrace. In *Jane Eyre* and *Villette* (1853), Charlotte Brontë invented narrators who demanded intimacy with the reader and whose candour was downright. Here is Lucy Snowe, narrator and protagonist of *Villette*, telling us about the absence in the West Indies of Monsieur Emanuel, the man she seems to love. 'M. Emanuel was away three years. Reader, they were the three happiest years of my life. Do you scout the paradox? Listen. . . .' (ch. 42, 593). This is private communication. A novel, being what Henry Fielding called 'a private history', could draw you aside for confession and self-justification, directly addressing an imagined confidante. Brontë's way was unusual. Other novelists, like Fielding himself, talk rather formally to someone called 'the reader' (a convention rare after the mid-nineteenth century). 'Reader, I think proper, before we proceed any farther together, to acquaint thee, that I intend to digress, through this whole history, as often as I see occasion' (*Tom Jones*, bk. I, ch. ii, 33). A few, of whom Laurence Sterne was probably the first, slip into making 'you' a kind of character in the narrative, to be pleaded with, teased, flattered, or hectored.

And 'you' are certainly there in Martin Amis's *Money*. John Self's confidences make us complicit in all his bad, bad thoughts. Told that his old friend Alec Llewellyn is in prison, he shares the *schadenfreude* with the reader in full expectation of recognition: 'I felt a gulp of innocent, bright-eyed pleasure that my best and oldest pal was in such serious trouble. Mm, it's so *nice* when one of your peers goes down. You know the feeling? A real buzz, isn't it? Don't be ashamed, if you can possibly help it' (131). The reader is an antagonist as much as an intimate. Self imagines someone who is fastidious and educated, recoiling from his unrefined self-indulgence. 'And you hate me, don't you. Yes you do' (58). Yet this reader is a hypocrite. When Self has sex with sex symbol Butch Beausoleil, he is fulfilling, he is sure, everyone else's fantasy. 'You've thought about it, pal, take my word for it. You too, angel, if you're at all that way inclined' (275).

John Self addresses those who are as grubby as himself. 'You're in this too, brother, sister, among the weather, the ageing and the money' (316). The imagined reader is a descendant of the readers addressed by other novelists with a satirical bent, like Fielding, Sterne and, perhaps especially, Thackeray. In *Vanity Fair*, another dark comedy of the money world, the 'kind reader' is asked to accompany the narrator through a world where everything is to be bought and sold. 'This, dear friends and companions, is my amiable object—to walk with you through the Fair, to examine the shops and the shows there' (ch. xxix, 228). Thackeray addresses a reader who lives in Vanity Fair, the world of consumption and worldly ambition. Equally, Self talks to us as if we should know as well as him how money makes people do what you want. Musing on his discovery that pornographic models are not really as they appear in pornography, he asks, 'How did *I* get to check out one or two of the chicks in the pornographic magazines?' Suddenly this is our leering question. 'Well how do you think? Money—that's right' (236).

This narrator has different tones. He can joke with the reader about his obnoxious behaviour. He says that after a civilized dinner with the cultured Martina Twain he rammed his hand up her skirt and . . . 'Relax. I didn't really. In fact I behaved doggedly well all evening' (215). He bullies and boasts, but also looks for reassurance. Given a copy of *Animal Farm*, he turns to us and asks, 'Have you read it? Is it my kind of thing?' (203). In one of his many absurd new suits ('off-white with charcoal seaming') he feels uncertain. 'I'm not sure about it—I wish you were here, I wish you were here to tell me it looked okay' (195). After the kidding and boasting, he just has to tell the reader everything. 'I have a confession to make. I might as well come clean. I can't fool *you*' (211). Addressing the reader means truth-telling. Just as much as Charlotte Brontë's Jane Eyre, John Self tells the reader more than he can say to any of the other characters. The nineteenth-century heroine let us know her unspoken passions. The 1980s anti-hero tells us all the amoral, unspeakable truths of his heart and his libido.

So the device draws us in. In *Money* it combines two implications. First it suggests that the reader is also a citizen of the modern city: worldly, unsentimental, up to date—and qualified to get the satire. The reader knows the score, a connoisseur of human nature like Fielding's or Thackeray's reader—no fool. 'You' recognize what John Self describes: all the ways in which urban humanity pursues its appetites in the late twentieth century. And here is the other implication: that the reader too is variously voracious, faithless, self-disgusted. If he were not a despiser of literature, John Self might have turned to the reader with the line in which T. S. Eliot's *The Waste Land* echoes Baudelaire. 'You! hypocrite lecteur!—mon semblable,—mon frère!'[6]

THE OMNISCIENT NARRATOR

Logically speaking, all authors of novels are omniscient: their characters are their creations, so they can surely know whatever they want to know about them. But not all narrators are omniscient. Henry James, for instance, frequently speaks in his novels to indicate that he cannot know everything about his characters. Here are some extracts from James's report of a scene—a conversation—in *The Awkward Age* (1898–9).

> Mr Longdon, as he faltered, appeared to wonder, but emitted a sound of gentleness. 'Yes?' . . . Mr Longdon's momentary mystification was perhaps partly but the natural effect of constitutional prudence. . . .
>
> Mitchy, as if with more to say, watched him an instant . . . (bk. III, 11)

This is the characteristic syntax of narration in this novel: '. . . appeared . . . perhaps . . . as if'. The author can know everything, but the narrator declines to do so, presenting the scene to us as if he had already puzzled over it, without quite getting to the bottom of things. His partial knowledge, of course, is as artificial a convention as another narrator's complete knowledge. What matters is that the convention be used consistently.

Michel Faber's *The Crimson Petal and the White*, a novel set in Victorian London, goes back to Victorian habits of narration that Henry James was transforming. Like many of the most ambitious novelists of the nineteenth century, Faber allows himself an omniscient narrator. This narrator has access to the unstated feelings that lie behind the characters' words and actions. He can take us into the most hidden recesses of their minds. In one typical passage he shows us the members of the Rackham household as they lie in bed at night, possessed by their private passions. In consecutive paragraphs he describes William Rackham's dream of a commercial rival's destruction, his daughter Sophie's hunger for approval, and the fears about her apparent pregnancy of Sugar, the prostitute turned governess (738). This narrator can even tell us that William's dream is permeated by 'the extraordinary odour of burning soap', a smell that 'he'll forget the instant he wakes'. We are allowed to know more about his inner world than the character himself. This omniscience seems to offer the novelist the possibility of extensive sympathies. When, near the end of the novel, William is searching for Sugar and his missing daughter and barges into the house of the prostitute Caroline, we follow his fevered (and mistaken) thoughts. 'William detects the heady stench of a secret that can no longer be kept hidden.' But the narrator can suddenly step aside to say something about Caroline to William, a mere bit-part player in his drama. For she suddenly realizes that she recognizes William, the 'well-dressed stranger', as the brother of a man who was once kind to her. 'The memory of that sweet man fetches her a sly blow in the pit of her stomach, for she's had no warning, and memories can be cruel when they give you no warning' (829).

It is a sympathetic aside, reminiscent of the great Victorian practitioner of omniscient narration George Eliot. In *Middlemarch* she perfected her method of using narratorial omniscience to effect intriguing shifts of sympathy. The most audacious occurs after twenty-eight chapters of the novel, when she suddenly chooses to enter the mind of Casaubon, a character who has previously seemed cold, impervious, utterly unlikeable. 'Mr Casaubon had an intense consciousness within him, and was spiritually a-hungered like the rest of us' (bk. 3, ch. 29, 278). Now she will give us the grounds for sympathy with someone we have previously thought baleful. Indeed, she will even show us why he has not attracted sympathy before. 'His experience was of that pitiable kind which shrinks from pity, and fears most of all that it should be known' (279). He repulses the fellow feeling not only of other characters, but of the reader too. Eliot uses her omniscience to unsettle us from the comfort of easy allegiance or antipathy. Faber, like Eliot, wants narratorial omniscience in order to do justice to a whole society. It is also necessitated by his interest in a psychological underworld of Victorian life. In particular, omniscience accommodates a secret history of sexual mores. One of Faber's frequent words is 'secret', invariably used to refer to what he is in the process of revealing to the reader. Yet do we want to know, or would we prefer to imagine? Faber gives us the nicely delineated conversations between two evangelical do-gooders, Henry Rackham and Emmeline Fox, stiff with suppressed tenderness, eloquent with affection indirectly expressed. But then he will also tell us, in unflinching detail, of each character's 'secret' sexual fantasies about the other.

The novelist undoes the repressed. Faber's narrator flaunts a power of which post-Victorian novelists became suspicious. Writers like Henry James, Joseph Conrad, and Ford Madox Ford make their fiction out of uncertainty about their characters' motivations. For omniscience brings its own problems. If we have access to a character's thoughts at one time, why not at another? In *The Crimson Petal and the White*, it even generates obscurities of plotting. When William identifies the decomposed body dragged from the Thames as his wife, Agnes, does he believe what he is saying? Or does he just want the mystery of her disappearance to be ended? Why are we not informed? In the last part of Faber's novel, with Sugar living in William's house, we are told little of his thoughts. As she becomes more affectionate to his child, Sugar grows less tender towards her employer, and so do we. Much of the time the door of William Rackham's study is closed to us as well as her. Yet suddenly, solicitously, the narrator decides to tell us what is behind William's resistance to her advances. Apparent hostility is in fact his terror of sexual failure. The insight is a discomfiting moment of 'understanding'. What was convincingly unclear is all too sympathetically explained.

POINT OF VIEW

There are some great novels that seem to encounter no limitation upon their ability to know the minds of any of their characters. Tolstoy's *Anna Karenina* is an extraordinary example of how fiction might move at will from one character to another, catching the point of view of each. The strange yet logical extreme of Tolstoy's method is reached when he even feels able to tell us the thoughts of an animal. Levin is out hunting with his dog Laska and has seen a snipe. He encourages her to set the bird flying. 'Go, Laska, good dog, go!' (pt. 6, sect. 12, 624). But the dog, Tolstoy is happy to tell us, has her doubts. She has not yet spotted the prey. '"All right, if that's what he wants, but I can't answer for myself now," thought Laska, and rushed forward.' We are even to understand the distinct difference in viewpoints between a hunter and his dog. Most novelists do not try to exercise Tolstoy's freedom. While it might be easy to do so slackly or opportunistically, it is very hard to do so while retaining the reader's faith. The more characters known, the more viewpoints represented, the more difficult it becomes to maintain narrative coherence. In practice, novels with third-person narrators tend to represent events from the point of view of a limited number of characters—perhaps just one. It is as if fiction were duty-bound to be true to our experience of the world, in which the perspectives of most people we encounter are guessable, but not knowable.

When a novel does move freely from one character's point of view to another's, the effect can be strange. In Ann Patchett's *Bel Canto*, for instance, the narrative easily slips into the minds of many characters. In some South American city, guests at a diplomatic party are taken hostage by guerrillas. Soon the residence is surrounded and a siege begins which takes up most of the novel. As it develops, we are given access to the thoughts of four or five of the hostages. We are taken as far as their childhood memories or their never-spoken feelings about their spouses. We also, fleetingly, get the private reflections of some minor characters, whom we meet only once or twice (including some of the terrorists). The novel can do this because, in effect, almost nothing is happening. If a plot were being unfolded, Patchett's unpredictable shifting of point of view might well make us suspicious. We would always be wondering why we were being told how things looked to one character rather than another, wondering what was being concealed from us. But in the suspended animation of a siege, it is possible to drift from one consciousness to another without seeming to cheat.

We notice a narrative's point of view most of all when it changes. When delicately managed, the effect can be memorable. Take the moment in *Pride and Prejudice* where Austen suddenly, briefly, lets us see events from the viewpoint of Elizabeth Bennet's friend and confidante Charlotte Lucas. Shortly before she allows Elizabeth to discover that Charlotte has become betrothed to the absurd Mr Collins, Austen not only tells the reader about the engagement, but allows us to know what Charlotte thinks about his proposal and her own acceptance of it. 'Her reflections were in general satisfactory. Mr Collins to be sure was neither sensible nor agreeable; his society was irksome, and his attachment to her must be imaginary. But still he would be her husband' (vol. i, ch. xxii, 94). Here are Charlotte's comically, appallingly, lucid private thoughts. To avoid impecunious spinsterhood, she chooses to spend her life with someone whose very company she believes 'irksome' (this is her judgement, not the author's). By letting us into Charlotte's thoughts before she tells Elizabeth, to whom Mr Collins proposed a couple of days earlier, Austen changes our understanding of Elizabeth's response. She is taken aback. 'Engaged to Mr Collins! My dear Charlotte,—impossible!' (96). We are not surprised, and, knowing Charlotte's 'reflections', can find a shade of presumption in Elizabeth's amazement. From Charlotte's point of view, Mr Collins's offer is 'good luck'.

Many novels do this, slipping away briefly from one dominant point of view. What is more unusual is to begin a novel from the viewpoint of one character, and then change it. In *The Constant Gardener*, John le Carré plays just this odd trick with our sympathies. His novel begins with Sandy Woodrow, the Head of Chancery at Britain's High Commission in Nairobi, receiving the news that the wife of a fellow British diplomat has been murdered. We see Woodrow, meeting events in his English way, 'jaw rigid, chest out' (9), but we are also shown his thoughts. We are told about his secret, unconsummated infatuation with Tessa, the murdered woman. For the first six chapters we take it that this shambling, intelligent Africa hand, with his private heartaches, is our hero, the focus of the narrator's attention. He is a likely enough protagonist for a le Carré novel: superficially awkward, though really clever and calculating; unhappily married; a public-school guardian of a lost British imperium.

Then we are suddenly shifted. Justin, Tessa's middle-aged husband, has been to stay with the Woodrows after his wife's murder, and when he leaves Kenya after her funeral, the reader leaves with him. It is an ordinary moment but a narrative jolt when Woodrow and Justin part. 'And the next minute Justin was walking down the steps to the red car.' We expect this to be Woodrow watching him leave, but the following paragraph gives us dialogue between Justin and his driver, Mustafa (confidential dialogue, in which Justin asks Mustafa to pass a secret message to a friend). Previously, the narrative insisted on seeing Justin from the outside. We viewed his reaction to his wife's death only through Woodrow's eyes. Even at Tessa's funeral we were still inside Woodrow's head.

A certain kind of shift in point of view is one of le Carré's characteristic techniques, and he particularly likes to open a novel through the perceptions of a character who is not to be his protagonist. He does it often, never more cleverly than in his best-known novel, *Tinker, Tailor, Soldier, Spy* (1974). For the most part, its narrative is focused through the thoughts of the secret agent George Smiley. Yet most of its opening chapter is given to the observations of Roach, a lonely boy at the boarding school where ex-spy Jim Prideaux has taken refuge. Roach will never understand Prideaux's history or know anything of the elaborate plot that is to unfold, yet it is he who notices how his secret past is returning into his schoolmaster's life. Approaching the story in this way conveys the distance of le Carré's spies from everyone they meet, the lonely inaccessibility of the secret world into which the novel takes us.

There are hazards in the method. In *The Constant Gardener*, le Carré is tempted to switch his narrative focus onto characters besides Woodrow and Justin. The previously enigmatic Ghita, Tessa's friend, becomes less enigmatic late in the novel when we are suddenly allowed into her thoughts as she pursues the truth about the murder. Tim Donoghue, the resident British spy in Nairobi, is a faux-naive actor until the moment, hundreds of pages in, when le Carré wants us to know what he is thinking 'inside his operational skull'. But why should the focus suddenly be shifted to them? For le Carré's spies and diplomats, dialogue is always performance. Every leading character operates behind some innocuous exterior, and you can understand the novelist's inclination suddenly to take us beyond this. His method emphasizes the gap between the way they speak and the way they think. Woodrow's speech is all clipped old-school cliché and archaic idiom. Yet he calculates like a sophisticated Foreign Office operative. Provoked by this difference between appearance and inner calculation, some of the novel's shifts of points of view seem merely convenient for the plot. The major change of focus of the novel's opening, however, is carefully judged. It dramatizes the revelation of a troubled, enquiring, bloody-minded protagonist 'behind' the bland, cooperative exterior of Justin Quayle, Foreign Office man. The 'Constant Gardener' of the title becomes a character of unguessed passions.

TENSE

What makes the opening sentence of J. M. Coetzee's novel *Disgrace* so unusual, so perturbing? 'For a man of his age, fifty-two, divorced, he has, to his mind, solved the problem of sex rather well' (1). Is it its chilly humour? The central character, David Lurie, will disgrace himself by pursuing his sexual appetite, but the first sentence gives him a temporary sense of complacency. He thinks he has found a neat 'solution' to a primal problem. He has a weekly arrangement with a taciturn but sympathetic prostitute, and so the itch of the flesh is under control. Yet what is most arresting about this opening is its manner, not its matter. The odd, risky thing is the tense: the present perfect ('he has . . . solved'). The whole book is in this or the present tense. None of it is in the past tense. It is not unusual for novels with first-person narrators to do this, as if replicating the immediacy of experience. Coetzee has done it before in *Waiting for the Barbarians* (1980) and *The Master of Petersburg* (1994). Margaret Atwood likes to do it, in imitation of the confidential tone of her narrators (*Surfacing* (1972), *Cat's Eye* (1989)). Jay McInerney and Brett Easton Ellis do it for more exhibitionist reasons, displaying the up-to-the-momentness of a modish style.

Third-person, present-tense narration is, however, much rarer. You have it in John Updike's Rabbit novels, where it gets us into, but not inside, the mind of the protagonist, Rabbit Angstrom. Updike's anti-hero is put in the present tense because he is a man caught in a round of habits, and a man who never seems to know what is going to hit him. Updike uses a present tense designed to make Rabbit some American Everyman, his fate ever a surprise to him. Why does Coetzee use it? Because it gives to the narrative voice a numbed, helpless quality. Lurie is intelligent and self-analytical, yet somehow powerless to shape his life. His emotions bleached by disillusion, he succumbs to sexual impulse. The normal past tense of narrative—'he *had*, to his mind, solved the problem of sex'—would have implied some vantage point beyond the events of the story. Usually we look back in the company of a narrator from the other side of an ending. The pattern of a story has been decided, even if we do not yet grasp it. The present tense, however, makes everything provisional. It edges us closer to the situation of the character while refusing us any actual identification with him.

Disgrace in fact contains its own rumination on tenses. Lurie is a professor, once of modern languages, a subject that has now, to his disgust, been retitled 'communications'. An affair with a student, Melanie Isaacs, leads to his resignation. As he contemplates his new life with his daughter in an arid South African outback, he recalls how he once spent his days 'explaining to the bored youth of the country the distinction between *drink* and *drink up*, *burned* and *burnt*. The perfective, signifying an action carried through to its conclusion' (71). The distinctions are repeated when he penitently visits Melanie Isaacs's father and tries to explain what drove him to the affair with his daughter.

> 'Yet in the olden days people worshipped fire. They thought twice before letting a flame die, a flame-god. It was that kind of flame your daughter kindled in me. Not hot enough to burn me up, but real: real fire.'
>
> Burned—burnt—burnt up. (166)

'Burnt up' because Lurie, who has lived for the present, has had something finished in him. The grammatical nicety recalls him to his now unrooted state and we are given a clue to his destiny. His 'disgrace' will have to become 'perfective'; all his pride and complacency will have to be eradicated. In the present tense, the story makes it seem that he has no idea of the conclusion to which he is heading. So the tense also matters to our sense of the novel as a tale of South Africa. In this new nation, violence is unleashed in new ways, and Lurie and his daughter become victims. The rules have changed and he cannot know where he is going, where any of them are going. All kinship and all security are frail. Everything is temporary, except the rhythm of mere animal life. The novel finally leaves us and its protagonist in the present tense, without any assurance that we have reached a point from where we can see the story's shape, in a provisional world.

TENSE SHIFT

Most novels are narrated in the past tense, some in the present tense, but a few, like *The Constant Gardener*, oscillate between the two. In le Carré's novel, the effects of the shifts from past to present tense and back again are counter-intuitive. The past tense is for action, the present tense is for memory. For fifty pages or so the novel is narrated in the past tense, from the point of view of the British diplomat Sandy Woodrow. We follow him to the Nairobi house of a murdered British woman, Tessa Quayle, in the company of her shocked husband. Ostensibly Woodrow is to help Quayle recover personal documents. In fact, he wants to find and destroy a drunken love letter that he once wrote to Tessa. In the Quayles' house, the past floods back. 'He reached the middle of the room and stopped, arrested by the power of memory' (56). We hardly need to be told about this 'power', for the narrative now switches to the present tense, re-performing Woodrow's last meeting with the woman who is now dead. '"I thought the best thing I could do was call by," he begins sternly.' He is in the same room at a different time, and Tessa is smiling at his poor excuse for his visit. 'Woodrow can't see the smile because she is backlit. But he can hear it in her voice' (57). It seems to be happening now.

This is the first of many occasions when the present tense is used to show that something is taking place in a character's head, brought to immediacy by the force of memory. For most of the novel, the memories are Quayle's, retrieving the personality of his wife but also bringing back the events that will enable him to work out why she has been killed. He is first taken from past to present tense as he leaves Nairobi airport after her murder and sees a poster advertising the miraculous drugs of the sinister ThreeBees company.

> The poster held him.
>
> Exactly as it had held Tessa.

> Staring rigidly up at it, Justin is listening to her joyous protestations at his right side. (148)

He is remembering the couple's first arrival in Kenya, when they saw the very same poster. He is also sensing a clue to Tessa's fate. From then on, such tense shifts structure the narrative. When a paragraph begins 'It is evening . . .', you know that you are being taken into Quayle's memories.

This making the past present, as if re-enacting it, is a device discovered by some nineteenth-century novelists. Charlotte Brontë's *Jane Eyre*, a work often audaciously disobedient of narrative proprieties, uses it to memorable effect. When Brontë's narrator recalls episodes of special significance she suddenly shifts into the present tense, tasting delight or pain afresh. So when she recalls the evening on which Rochester proposed to her, she begins in a conventional past historic: 'I walked a while on the pavement; but a subtle, well-known scent—that of a cigar—stole from some window' (vol. ii, ch. 8, 278). Then, as the summer smells from the garden rise again, the tense changes, to the heady passage that Thackeray knew by heart (see Introduction). 'Sweet-brier and southernwood, jasmine, pink, and rose have long been yielding their evening sacrifice of incense: this new scent is neither of shrub nor flower: it is—I know it well—it is Mr. Rochester's cigar. I look round and listen' (279). With Brontë, it is usually a few sentences or paragraphs before the controlling voice of past-tense narration takes over again.

Le Carré too tries using the present tense to register what we might call perturbation. Poring over the documents that his wife has left behind, Quayle finds death threats made against her. 'As Justin struggles to recover his balance, his eye falls on a hand-addressed envelope' (272). It is Woodrow's compromising letter. Such a perturbed present tense can seem overemphatic. 'Justin the deceived husband is struck motionless by the moonlight as he stares rigidly at the sea's silvered horizon . . .' (274).

Shifting tense works better for le Carré when it distinguishes between the unfolding of events (in the past tense) and the scrutiny of memories (in the present tense). Here psychological realism—Quayle's bereavement leads him into all that remembering—is at one with plot; the solution to the mystery is discovered only by reanimating the past.

FREE INDIRECT STYLE

Take this opening (it is a complete paragraph) of William Trevor's short story 'Against the Odds' from his collection *The Hill Bachelors*:

> Mrs Kincaid decided to lie low. There had been a bit of bother, nothing much but enough to cause her to change her address. From time to time she was obliged to do so. (180)

The cliché in that first sentence should signal what is going on. Mrs Kincaid is someone who needs to conceal herself. The idioms and euphemisms ('a bit of bother') used to explain her subterfuges are themselves evasive, and echo, in their refusal to be specific ('nothing much'), her own evasive thoughts. As we read further we will slowly discover what the narrative is talking around here: the outwardly respectable, 60-year-old Belfast lady is a conwoman; any 'bother' must arise from one of her deceitful schemes. She has to move on to escape retribution.

This is free indirect style (sometimes also called 'free indirect discourse'): the narrative adopts the sentiments of the character. It is a technique that was pioneered by Jane Austen—odd as it might be to think of Austen as a technical innovator. David Lodge has pointed out that it can be found 'briefly and fragmentarily' in the slightly earlier fiction of Fanny Burney and Maria Edgeworth, novelists whom Austen read with keen interest.[7] Yet they did not really discover its potential for combining both distanced observation of a character and a sense of how he or she sees the world. The technique, arguably her most important gift to later novelists, is used most brilliantly in *Emma*. When Emma returns to the room in which she has arranged for Harriet Smith and Mr Elton to be alone, in the hope of a marriage proposal, the novel says, 'The lovers were standing together at one of the windows. It had a most favourable aspect' (vol. i, ch. x, 72). In fact, the two are not 'lovers' at all; Mr Elton is actually angling for Emma herself. The 'aspect', the appearance of things, is being interpreted erroneously. But the narrative insists on adopting Emma's illusions, allowing us both to laugh at and to share her perspective.

The technique has become so common that we hardly notice it. Trevor uses it with considerable subtlety, often to let us glimpse what is not directly expressed. The effect is peculiar and subtle in 'Against the Odds' because we find that Mrs Kincaid never speaks in confidence to anyone. The free indirect style reflects her never-spoken thoughts. Even in her silent talking to herself, she avoids the truth. The story goes on to let us witness with pity her manipulation of her next gull, a lonely widower called Blakely whom she will effectively fleece. But it keeps us within her thoughts. When she first encounters Blakely in a café, it replicates her observations. 'He'd be a bachelor or a widower, else he wouldn't be taking his dinner in a café every day. You could tell at once the foot he dug with, as decent a Protestant foot as her own, never a doubt about that' (188).

That first sentence sounds just like speech. The English reader can hear its Ulster accent. But it follows the character's entirely silent calculation (unmarried, he will be a suitable victim). The next sentence, with its weird idiom ('Which foot does he dig with?') reveals her prejudice in a moment of comically inappropriate kinship. Because he is a fellow 'decent' Protestant, she will find it all the easier to trick him out of his money.

Free indirect style gets us immediately close to Trevor's characters while keeping their deepest thoughts or fears unspoken. It is a means of concealment as much as disclosure. In the collection's title story an elderly widow on a lonely farm wonders what will become of her after her husband's death. What will her five children, all of whom have grown up and left, decide to do? 'It was up to them; she couldn't ask. It wouldn't be seemly to ask, it wouldn't feel right' (224). In most third-person narratives the very appearance of those colloquial contractions—'couldn't', 'wouldn't'—would signal the narrative's replication of the character's thoughts. Here the character thinks about what cannot be said ('she couldn't ask') but also avoids contemplating the possibilities herself. If she has hopes or fears, they are suppressed. And that peculiar, carefully chosen word 'seemly' lets the reader into her mind while forbidding curiosity. 'It wouldn't be seemly' is something she says, we imagine, that brooks no further argument.

This use of free indirect style to show how things are left unthought as well as unsaid is common in Trevor's stories, and especially appropriate in 'The Hill Bachelors'. The widow's youngest son, Paulie, finds himself drawn back to the hill farm, compelled to give up his hopes of escape and of marriage to take up his dead father's work. Or what will his mother do? Nothing has been said about the inevitability of this; his mother has not even let herself think about it. But her silence has done its work. It is ironical that free indirect style is sometimes called 'free indirect speech' when so often, in Trevor's short stories, or in *Emma*, it allows unspoken assumptions to enter the narrative.

3
People

NOTHING is stranger or more important in our reading of novels than the sense that we are encountering real people in them. Academic critics tend to steer away from the business of characterization, even though it is invariably the ordinary measure of a novelist's achievement. It is as if succumbing to the illusion that a 'character' in a book is a person implies losing your critical faculties. Long ago, in a famous essay called 'How Many Children Had Lady Macbeth?', the critic L. C. Knights made it clear that the discerning reader should resist this weakness. How can we maintain 'the necessary aloofness from a work of art', he asked irritably, if we 'treat a character as a human being?'[1] Literary theory, while speaking in different terms, has preserved this aloofness. Sometimes its determination to avoid all talk of characterization is inadvertently comical. Here is Mieke Bal, a renowned narrative theorist, solemnly perplexed in her 1985 book *Narratology* when faced by the troubling illusion of a human presence in texts. 'That no one has yet succeeded in constructing a complete and coherent theory of character is probably precisely because of this human aspect. The character is not a human being, but it resembles one.'[2] Just so.

How is this resemblance achieved? The first section of this chapter discusses a special and especially satisfying case: the representation of a person that seems so unscripted by the author that it cannot be an illusion. Here is a character who can even surprise his or her inventor. Such a character must be not just complex but contradictory. Not every person depicted in a novel is like this, but here is one, George Eliot's Dorothea Brooke. In the opening chapter of *Middlemarch*, Eliot tells us of Dorothea's religious enthusiasm, but also of some of her other interests, including riding.

> Most men thought her bewitching when she was on horseback. She loved the fresh air and the various aspects of the country, and when her eyes and cheeks glowed with mingled pleasure she looked very little like a devotee. Riding was an indulgence which she allowed herself in spite of conscientious qualms; she felt that she enjoyed it in a pagan, sensuous way, and always looked forward to renouncing it. (bk. 1, ch. 1, 10)

How much of self-mockery and how much of self-deception is there in this? The development of the narrative, and especially Dorothea's foolish acceptance of Casaubon's marriage proposal, would suggest a good deal of the latter. Here, charmingly, Dorothea hardly knows herself, or her own contradictoriness, and we glimpse what seems truly the complexity of her character.

Middlemarch is one of those novels whose heroines get things wrong; Jane Austen's *Emma* and Henry James's *The Portrait of a Lady* are two other brilliant examples. These books would not work if they did not also conjure a powerful sympathy with their central characters, just as in that passage above we can smile sympathetically at Dorothea's self-serving delusion. The matter of sympathy with a character is dealt with in both of the first two sections of this chapter. 'No novel is anything, for purposes either of comedy or tragedy, unless the reader can sympathise with the characters whose names he finds upon the page,' declared Anthony Trollope.[3] If we believe this, we put a premium on motivation, the subject of the second of the sections below. I begin this section with another illustration from *Middlemarch*, for George Eliot's fiction lives by its ability to convey the complexities of human motivations. (One sure sign of this is her ability to allow us to understand her characters' failures to understand each other.) Yet not every novelist tries to be like George Eliot. In the section entitled 'Motivation', we see that complexity in the rendering of motivation is an aim of only a certain kind of fiction. Sometimes, as in the Muriel Spark novel that I discuss, a denial of sympathy might also be a purpose of a novelist.

A novel does not necessarily take us into the deepest recesses of a character's mind. Even Austen or Eliot or James look in from the outside. '"Character", one might say, is what other people have, "consciousness" is ourselves.'[4] Character is one person known by another. A first-person narration has singular opportunities precisely because its narrator cannot have access to the thoughts of the novel's other characters. Reading a first-person narrative, the critical issue is not what we think of the characters, but whether we believe what the narrator thinks about them. The apparent failure of a novel to imagine the depths of its characters might, with a first-person novel, be a kind of achievement. Dr Primrose, the innocuously obtuse narrator of Oliver Goldsmith's *The Vicar of Wakefield* (1766), or Nick Carraway, the half-comprehending narrator of F. Scott Fitzgerald's *The Great Gatsby* (1925), do not understand the characters about whom they care most. They fail, we might say, to flesh them out. But then we are invited to infer what the narrators do not see. Such narrators can always be surprised by the characters they describe, and such surprise can be an index of their authenticity.

Even a third-person narrative that seems to go deep into the thoughts of some of its characters will probably have minor characters whom we know very little, or know only on the surface. *Middlemarch* may keep stretching our understanding to include one person after another, but at its edges are the cardboard cut-outs of provincial types that it needs for its plausibly crowded scene of Midlands life. Some of the most memorable or amusing characters in fiction are designedly not like real people, in all their complexity. From the beginning, a *character* has been a type. Such a character has often been called 'Theophrastian', after the ancient Greek author Theophrastus, who composed a collection called *Characters*. These were various 'kinds of men': the flatterer, the garrulous man, the buffoon, the pretentious man, and so on. Following the publication of a Latin translation of this work at the end of the sixteenth century, the genre became popular in England, and a series of writers, including John Donne, produced their own collections of characters. Over 300 different editions of such collections were published in England during the seventeenth century.

Novelists like Fielding, Smollett, Dickens, and Thackeray employ Theophrastian characters, their presence likeliest when the fiction is satirical and often signalled by their names (see Chapter 9, 'Names'). It is not therefore necessarily a criticism of a novel to say that one of its characters is a 'type', for a character may be designed to be representative. There are types for which novels are peculiarly responsible. Typicality does not rule out distinctiveness. Wilkie Collins's Count Fosco from *The Woman in White*, discussed below, has typical characteristics of 'the villain' and yet is utterly idiosyncratic. Characterization means distinctiveness. In Eliot or James this might imply the unique combination of inclinations and circumstances that form an individual. In Dickens, however, it might mean a habit of speech or an odd twist of the body. He sometimes candidly takes one quality to be representative of a person. Miss Pross, Lucie Manette's loyal, fiery companion in *A Tale of Two Cities* (1859), is unceremonious and sharply to the point, a woman 'whose character (dissociated from stature) was shortness' (bk. 2, ch. 6, 99). There she is, in dialogue always exhibiting her 'shortness'. In Miss Pross's case, being 'short' means being truthful, undeceived, true. With Miss Pross, we might say, there is no beating about the bush. 'Shortness' is her virtue and her strength. In one of the novel's climactic scenes, she gives short shrift to the villainess, Madame Defarge, and defeats her in both a physical and a verbal duel. Dickens makes her real by catching one thing about her, as we might do in recollecting a particular person we know.

Finally, there is a different way in which 'real people' have long inhabited fiction. These real people are historical personages or public figures or, as in Andrew O'Hagan's *Personality*, discussed below, celebrities. In recent years there has even evolved a genre of what might be called 'biographical fiction'. Some examples of this, like Colm Tóibín's novel about Henry James, *The Master* (2004), imagine an inner world beyond the normal reach of biography. Examples might include John Banville's two accomplished novels about Renaissance astronomers: *Doctor Copernicus* (1976) and *Kepler* (1981). Others have imitated the reach of conventional biography. Gore Vidal's *Lincoln* (1984) exhaustively piles up administrative detail and presses dates on us as if determined to have us accept its basis in fact (testily asserted in the novel's afterword). Yet another species of biographical fiction makes the fanciful reconstruction of a dead person's life just one of its narrative strands. Examples include Malcolm Bradbury's *To the Hermitage* (2000), which is about Diderot, and Michael Cunningham's *The Hours* (discussed elsewhere in this book), about Virginia Woolf. Both have parallel narratives in modern times, in which the writings of their famous authors are revivified in the lives of appreciative readers. As fiction usurps the province of biography, however, it risks condemning itself to a kind of triviality. The more it stacks up its evidence, its sources, its academic credentials, the more it confesses to a secondary status—something perhaps more entertaining than the truth, but something less than the truth too.

More compelling has often seemed the autobiographical invention of character. The last section of this chapter deals with a personage who is not unique to late twentieth- and twenty-first-century fiction, but has become a powerful presence in the fiction of some of its best writers: the alter ego. Here I discuss how a novelist makes a character of him- or herself. The exercise might, of course, be a self-indulgent substitute for invention. In the fiction of Philip Roth, discussed in this section, it lends a peculiar passion and urgency to the narration.

CHARACTERIZATION

It is easy to presume that successful characterization involves taking the reader to the heart, the inner core, of an imagined person. Once, however, 'character' meant something different, something as much to do with the outer appearance of a person as with the inner being. 'I have begun to acquire a composed genteel character very different from the rattling, uncultivated one which for some time past I have been fond of,' wrote James Boswell in his Journal for 1762.[5] Your 'character' was what you presented to the world. Boswell reported a coffee house acquaintance thus: 'Mr. Nicholls I found to be sensible and elegantly learned; with an agreeable moderation of sentiment intermixed, his character was finely completed.' The last observation is made entirely in admiration. This ideal of presentational achievement is a long way from our common association of 'character' with selfhood. The sense of 'character' as the world's judgement upon you was once explicitly active in novels. 'Colonel Brandon's character . . . as an excellent man, is well established,' says Elinor, the heroine of Jane Austen's *Sense and Sensibility* (1811, vol. iii, ch. ix, 295). 'Character' here means reputation as well as individuality. (It is a meaning of the word preserved in our notion of the 'character reference'.) The truth of a person is often established in Austen's fiction by measuring the one idea of character against the other. Edward Ferrars says to Elinor, 'Colonel Brandon seems a man of great worth and respectability. I have always heard him spoken of as such' (vol. iii, ch. iv, 253). Elinor, who has come to know Colonel Brandon well, confirms that he is just as he is said to be. '"Indeed," replied Elinor, "I believe that you will find him, on farther acquaintance, all that you have heard him to be."' Character is defined by this fit between reputation and individuality. It is social as much as psychological.

Some contemporary novels are also interested in 'character' as a social phenomenon. One of the successes of Monica Ali's *Brick Lane* is a triumph of characterization that can be understood in just these terms. Chanu, the protagonist's husband, is not the novel's central character but finally emerges as its most believable person. He begins as someone the reader is invited to resent. His marriage to Nazneen has been arranged. She does not know him before she becomes his wife. He has been foisted on her and us. We are given plenty of reasons to be irked by him. He is self-important; 'rolls of fat' hang low from his stomach (23); he lectures his children; he makes his wife cut his corns. Yet slowly he becomes human. His incongruous quotations from Open University philosophy modules, his pronouncements on the 'village' habits of his fellow Bangladeshis, his sociological explanations of British culture: these become sympathetic without ceasing to be absurd. His intellectual generalizations and ill-founded ambitions are irrepressible. Those older expectations of 'character' are some guide to Ali's method with Chanu. For she does not require sympathy by giving us access to his thoughts or fears. We are notionally seeing his private self—his behaviour within the family home, even in the marital bed—but we keep meeting him through only his outward habits and his would-be wise pronouncements. He partly lives in 'his own private world of theory and refutation, striving and puzzlement'. His sense of being educated is his defence against disappointment. 'It is lucky for you that you married an educated man. That was a stroke of luck' (45). A mini-cab driver on a Tower Hamlets council estate, he talks himself into optimism. 'Of course, when I have my Open University degree then nobody can question my credentials' (38). He has a cupboard full of certificates gained from various courses and examinations. He is going to get promotion. He is going to return to Bangladesh to make a fortune from a soap business.

Any novelist can simply tell us what a character thinks. Ali has decided to do so with only one of her characters, Nazneen. To the very end of the book we stay inside her head. We know for sure only her feelings about her marriage, only her sense of how she and her husband avoid each other's thoughts. This commits the novelist to a difficult trick of characterization with her husband: bringing Chanu alive from the outside. We must slowly sense him through the idiosyncrasies of his presentation of himself. There is a wonderful comic episode capturing this, where Chanu takes Nazneen and their two daughters on a tour of tourist London, ending at Buckingham Palace and a picnic in St James's Park. In ridiculous mid-calf shorts and baseball cap he enthuses about the history of building and monuments (history being another of his areas of self-declared expertise). He reduces his family to hysterical laughter. 'He swelled with pride at how marvellously he had managed the day. "It is a lot of fun"' (294). He does not get the joke, yet his declaration banishes embarrassment or ill will.

Ali never lets Chanu directly reveal his inner self. Indeed, the plot of *Brick Lane* turns on our uncertainty about his feelings. Near the end, are we to guess from his behaviour that he knows that his wife is unfaithful? Desperate to end her relationship with Karim, but somehow unable to do so, Nazneen wills him to know. 'Let my husband find out, Nazneen prayed' (384). Even she is not allowed to be sure that he has guessed at her affair: 'how many times had she willed him to know? He would not yield to her and yet he must know' (410). The novelist respects the character enough to allow him to keep things to himself.

MOTIVATION

One of the traditional tasks of novelists has been to seem true to their characters' motivations, and with subtlety of analysis usually comes sympathy. To know all is to forgive all. George Eliot's *Middlemarch* is probably the greatest English novel to be written upon such a principle, imagining every character to have his or her human reasons and fears. There is a famous self-interruption in *Middlemarch*, where George Eliot asks us to recognize this, chidingly turning on us, in the midst of an expository sentence, to regret the limitations of our readerly sympathies. It is in book 3 of the novel, with Dorothea, now Mrs Casaubon, returned from her honeymoon to the home of her desiccated husband.

> One morning, some weeks after her arrival at Lowick, Dorothea—but why always Dorothea? Was her point of view the only possible one with regard to this marriage? I protest against all our interest, all our effort at understanding being given to the young skins that look blooming in spite of trouble; for these too will get faded, and will know the older and more eating griefs which we are helping to neglect. (ch. 29, 278)

It is an audacious break from our attention to Dorothea. The picture of her ill-advised marriage becomes convincing exactly because of our painfully belated understanding of Casaubon's feelings. We have become so used to finding him ridiculous or repellent that the sudden access to his pride and fear seems to epitomize Eliot's ambition for her fiction (see Chapter 2, 'The Omniscient Narrator').

Everyone has their unspoken needs and their reasons. For much of its history, the Novel has been dedicated to discovering ever more discriminating ways of conveying the complexities of human motivation. In the late nineteenth and early twentieth centuries, fiction seemed to have reached the ultimate extent of such exploration in the novels of Henry James and Marcel Proust, writers for whom actual events became totally subordinate to psychological exactitude. Though these novelists may never have been widely read, they have deeply influenced later writers and readers. Subtlety of motivation is presumed to be a virtue of fiction. Yet there are novelists who, especially for satirical purposes, take a more diagrammatic approach to human psychology. A good example is Muriel Spark, a novelist peculiarly attentive—but hardly sympathetic—to the varieties of human vanity. She watches as her characters prey upon each other's weaknesses (no wonder that blackmail features in many of her novels). Yet she works by denying that there are depths to those characters' motivations. More than thirty years ago Christopher Ricks complained that 'she doesn't much like having to do with characters where she cannot altogether know what makes them tick'.[6] 'Mrs. Spark finds all her characters speedily exhaustible, whether she loves them or not.' Her admirers would hardly deny the charge, they would just deny that it is a charge. She merely observes the moves in what her fictional Lord Lucan, in *Aiding and Abetting*, thinks of as 'the gambling-den of life'. She shows you enough to let you see their selfishness or lack of scruple. Then she coolly goes no further.

Aiding and Abetting is a novel that has its origins in an infamous murder, and has as its lure an infamous murderer and fugitive: Lord Lucan. We know from detective fiction that murder stories are about motives. However, bringing Lucan alive here means creating a killer monstrous because of his sheer superficiality. 'He was stupid and boring,' declares Joe, who used to know him (101). 'Lucan himself had been a perfect bore,' decides Hildegard, the charlatan psychiatrist, 'a cut-to-measure gentleman with a pack of memories very, very like that of many another man of his class and education' (144). The murder was his one burst of originality. No wonder he is so difficult to find, for anyone with 'a smattering of information' about his past could assume his personality well enough to fool his own acquaintances.

Alfred Twickenham, one of Lucan's aiders and abetters, asks himself, 'Why did I cover up his whereabouts? Why? And so many of us did it' (70). In Spark's telling of the story, Lucan's escape was made possible by a conspiracy of snobs, none of them having a drop of admiration or sympathy for the fleeing aristocrat. 'What possessed Daddy to help him escape?' asks Twickenham's daughter Lacey (74). This being a Spark novel, she herself embarks on a search for Lucan not because she wants to strip bare the intrigue of which her father was a part, but because she fancies writing a book about him. 'People who want to write books', the narrator observes, bluntly, 'do so because they feel it to be the easiest thing they can do' (75).

Spark denies us any moral centre. Her main character, and investigator of Lucan's psyche, is Hildegard, a fraud who, while a professional analyst of motivation, is as monstrously amoral as Lucan himself. She values elegance and intelligence; her life is dedicated to remaining 'untroubled'. 'There is certainly a remoteness, a lack of ordinary compassion in her dealings with characters,' wrote Frank Kermode, much earlier in Spark's career.[7] This quality is still there, a matter of technique as much as temperament. Joe and Lacey, on the road together in pursuit of Lucan, begin a 'love affair', but Spark mordantly concentrates on trivia. She tells us nothing of the affair, but much about how Joe manages to get the hotel's credit card machine to work, and how as a consequence the couple feel blessed. 'His card then worked. They felt good to be on their way. They felt very good, anyway, at the grand beginning of a love affair, free and full of enterprise, without any mess of impediments' (106–7). The distance that Spark keeps from her characters leads you to suspect that every relationship is somehow manipulative or predatory. At the heart of the novel, Lucan and his useful double, Walker, are locked in mutual need and hatred. Lucan decides that 'it was Walker's destiny to die' (153), but then 'Lucky Lucan believed in destiny' (152). Destiny made him an earl, and his wife was 'destined to die': it is a code of irresponsibility. Spark's characters analyse the motives and consequences of human actions, but only in order to avoid any painful reflection. The novelist is true to their willed superficiality.

THE ANTI-HERO

It sometimes seems that the anti-hero is more at home in novels than the hero. One of the earliest novels to refer to its protagonist as its 'hero' is Fielding's *Joseph Andrews*, which is already making a joke out of the notion that he could be thought of as a heroic personage. 'Mr. *Joseph Andrews*, the Hero of our ensuing History, was esteemed to be the only Son of Gaffar and Gammer *Andrews*, and Brother to the illustrious *Pamela*, whose Virtue is at present so famous' (17). 'The illustrious Pamela' is the heroine of Samuel Richardson best-selling *Pamela*, and 'illustrious' is highly sardonic. Yet, like his rival, Fielding makes his protagonist a character—a domestic servant—who could never have been the hero of any other genre. This sense that a novel might draw us to a person not normally thought of as heroic is found in fiction into the nineteenth century. Thus the opening sentence of Jane Austen's *Northanger Abbey*: 'No one who had ever seen Catherine Morland in her infancy, would have supposed her born to be an heroine' (vol. i, ch. i, 1). If the hero of epic narrative is originally a man greater than ordinary men, than we might think of the novel, the genre of ordinary life, as inherently anti-heroic.

Most of the recent novels discussed in this book have a protagonist, a main character, a person whose fortunes we follow. Yet in most cases they are notably unheroic. Is Martin Amis's John Self or J. M. Coetzee's David Lurie a 'hero'? Is Nick Hornby's Katie or Ian McEwan's Briony a 'heroine'? Surely not. But then we are used to protagonists characterized by their failures or weaknesses. One use of the term 'anti-hero' has been to describe extreme cases of unheroic qualities. It has been applied to blundering, sometimes foolish protagonists: Schweik in *The Good Soldier Schweik* (1920–3), say, or Yossarian in *Catch-22* (1961), or Moses Herzog in Saul Bellow's *Herzog* (1964). The term is, however, disputed. These anti-heroes are good men baffled by the world. They are the distant descendants of Joseph Andrews and Catherine Morland, both of them innocents abroad. Yet the 'anti-hero' can also be something very different: a protagonist who draws us into sympathy despite doing things that should appal us. One such is Patricia Highsmith's Tom Ripley.

Simone, the wife of Jonathan Trevanny, the ordinary man whom Tom Ripley makes into a murderer in Patricia Highsmith's third Ripley novel, *Ripley's Game*, has no doubt what to call her husband's seducer: 'this monster' (218). Materialistic, unscrupulous, and manipulative, Ripley certainly qualifies as a bad man. He lives in high style off theft and forgery. In the course of *Ripley's Game*, he kills five men, one by garrotting, the other four by various kinds of bludgeoning. He performs the killings without hesitation or guilt. He also corrupts the previously innocent Jonathan, recruiting him as a Mafia hitman. Yet Jonathan himself, the very person whose life Ripley ruins, reacts to his wife's horror by thinking, 'Tom was not really such a monster.' As Ripley knows, 'people, once they got to know him . . . liked him' (147). The reader too.

The anti-hero takes possession of a narrative without any effective opposition. Villains, in contrast, are set against representatives of good. In the great majority of cases, a villain, however fascinating, exists to be defeated. But there is no one to defeat Ripley. No one, except the reader, really finds him out. The reader is therefore with him. In all Highsmith's Ripley novels, we hear Ripley thinking from the very beginning. Characteristically, the first thought that he has in *Ripley's Game* is self-critical: he regrets speaking to a criminal associate 'in a stuffy, pontificating way' (5). Ripley is all for candour and against pretension. He has values that seem almost ethical. Unasked, he turns up to assist Jonathan with his second murder for reasons that sound, if you can forget the context, almost principled. 'Tom had felt that Jonathan might botch this job, and having got Trevanny into this, Tom thought it behooved him to try to help him out' (111). 'It behooved him': the odd wording catches Ripley's own peculiar sense of obligation. It is not moral, but it is characteristic. Ripley sometimes likes people and sometimes he will help them. He enjoys companionship.

This is related to his manipulativeness, for he is psychologically acute. In *Ripley's Game* he uses his knowledge of Jonathan's terminal illness to exploit him. Persuading Jonathan that his condition is worse than it is, he convinces him that he has nothing to lose by trying to earn nefariously some badly needed money that he can leave to his wife and child. Like most anti-heroes, he has discernment rather than principles. Nabokov's Humbert Humbert in *Lolita* (published in 1955, coincidentally the same year as the first Ripley novel) is an outstanding example. Nabokov's paedophile narrator is a man of wit and fine sensitivities, alert to the delights of language. Like Ripley, he knows about art and beauty and good food. In imitation, later novelists with amoral, homicidal narrators have made their anti-heroes bons vivants and men of culture. Patrick Bateman in Brett Easton Ellis's *American Psycho* (1991) and Tarquin Winot, protagonist of John Lanchester's *The Debt to Pleasure* (1996), for example, are both self-styled arbiters of taste as well as murderers. Lanchester's narrator describes to a woman whom he is about to kill the analogies between 'the two most important cultural figures in the modern world, the artist and the murderer' (225). Ripley too is at once aesthete and killer. He appreciates art enough to arrange the forgery of works of a minor modern master: Derwatt. Even as his scheme for arranging the killing of a professional criminal is being developed, he is spending his days 'painting a full-length portrait of Heloise [his wife] horizontal on the yellow satin sofa' (27). He lives in an impeccably furnished chateau (Belle Ombre) where he tends the garden and paints. He reads Schiller and Molière—not in translation—and appreciates classical music (an important accidental meeting in *Ripley's Game* occurs because Ripley attends a performance of quartets by Schubert and Mozart). When a Mafia hood first intrudes on his elegant home life, he is seated at the harpsichord, 'playing the base of a Goldberg variation, trying to get the fingering in his head and in his hand' (161). Above all, he is 'civilized' (one of his own favourite terms of approbation).

He is also gifted with a sense of propriety. He disapproves of gambling and prostitution. He is earnestly concerned that Jonathan be paid in full for carrying out his killings. He suggests, 'in jest', to his criminal friend Reeves that a fake medical report indicating that Jonathan is close to death might help secure his cooperation, but then realizes that 'Reeves was the type to have tried it—a dirty, humourless trick' (88). For a moment we are inside the logic of Ripley's mind, feeling distaste for a scheme he has himself mooted. An odd monster, then. Partly, the anti-hero offers us the frisson of taboo-breaking. *Ripley's Game* is about how a 'basically decent' man (Ripley's own, entirely sincere, description of Jonathan) can be persuaded into murder (132). Yet Highsmith also has a curiously moral purpose. She has invented a character who lacks only a conscience. He has the other faculties, including those that might make us like a person. By creating such an engaging anti-type, she shows what an amoral life might be like.

THE VILLAIN

The villain is the property of certain kinds of fiction. Most novelists will want to credit every character with complications of motive. To have a pure 'baddy', as the childish slang indicates, is to risk the merest caricature. Novelists whom we value for psychological subtlety—George Eliot, say, or Henry James—do not have villains. Few novels feature any character as convincingly cold-hearted as Eliot's Henleigh Grandcourt in *Daniel Deronda* (1876) or James's Gilbert Osmond in *The Portrait of a Lady*, yet neither character can properly be called a villain. Both are too subtle and are too subtly represented; both act cruelly out of what are shown as complicated forms of selfishness. The true villain is driven not only by simple greed or lust for power, but also by a kind of glee at his own badness. There is therefore another kind of risk in depicting villainy. Give the representative of evil the intellect and perceptiveness that make him a worthy antagonist and he might well become all too intriguing. Literature offers many a role model, from Shakespeare's Iago or Edmund to the epitome of fascinating malignity Milton's Satan. This type of villainous contriver enters the European novel in the guise of Lovelace, the brilliant villain of Samuel Richardson's *Clarissa*. He lives on in fiction in the brooding Latin autocrats of any number of Gothic novels, the model being Count Montoni in Ann Radcliffe's *The Mysteries of Udolpho* (1794). Such figures command the attention of other characters as much as of the reader. 'This Signor Montoni had an air of conscious superiority, animated by spirit, and strengthened by talents, to which every person seemed involuntarily to yield' (*The Mysteries of Udolpho*, vol. i, ch. xii, 122).

It is no accident that the great Victorian novelists who specialized in villains were those closest to popular fiction. Wilkie Collins has several, including the wonderfully evil Count Fosco in *The Woman in White*. 'He looks like a man who could tame anything' is the first thing that the clever and resourceful Marian Halcombe tells us about him (Second Epoch, sect. II, 219). 'He is a most remarkable likeness, on a grand scale, of the great Napoleon' (221). He is a memorable character, but also, as Marian says, a figure entirely singled out 'from the rank and file of humanity'. Villains are not to be quite human. Dickens has many: Fagin, Carker in *Dombey and Son* (1846–8), Ralph Nickleby. Dickens likes to distort them, allowing them intelligence, even wit, but twisting them into menacing shapes. Conan Doyle was to give us the baneful Moriarty, prototype of the evil genius. One of the most influential modern purveyors of villains, Ian Fleming, borrows traits from all these, but his evil plotters are also triumphs of reductiveness. It is as if he were returning to the origins of the character, in the incarnations of unalloyed evil to be found in medieval mystery plays and Tudor 'moralities'. In James Bond novels, the villain's hold over the popular imagination is being rediscovered.

From Russia With Love established a convention followed since by many thrillers and by many films (including most of those featuring James Bond). Bond must, like any good knight, defeat in single combat the scarcely human champion of the enemy. In this novel, it is 'Red' Grant, former IRA intimidator, deserter from the British army, coiled psychopath, and Chief Executioner of SMERSH. But more exactingly, Bond must defeat the schemers that this evil warrior serves. He must win a fight, but he must also survive the machinations of someone with a malign imagination: the villain, the plotter who sends the assassin on his mission. No Bond novel could live without its villain. *From Russia With Love* has two, and is perhaps caught in two minds between them. The SMERSH planner is Kronsteen, whom we first encounter a few moves from victory in the final of the Moscow Chess Championship. 'To him all people were chess pieces,' and, like all satisfying villains, he is an expert analyst of human beings (ch. 7, 61). His vocation is 'to foretell their reactions'. He hatches the plot to disgrace as well as to kill Bond. He is abetted by the grotesque Rosa Klebb. Whoever looks at this 'toad-like' personification of malignity feels a shudder of sexual disgust. She is so venomous that, even as she is defeated on the last page, she poisons Bond with a blade in her shoe. (Fleming had toyed with the idea of killing Bond at the end of this novel.)

The villain is above all a plotter, and therefore we are obliged to him (or in rare cases her) for many of the pleasures of the story. The villain has made the plot for us. The villain therefore has to be intellectually gifted. Thus the first piece of information about Moriarty that Holmes gives Watson in 'The Final Problem' (1893): 'He is a man of good birth and excellent education, endowed by nature with a phenomenal mathematical faculty. At the age of twenty-one he wrote a treatise upon the binomial theorem, which has had a European vogue. On the strength of it he won the mathematical chair at one of our smaller universities'.[8] Fleming's Kronsteen is in a line of descent from this twisted prodigy, whom Holmes calls 'a genius, a philosopher, an abstract thinker'. Sometimes villainy is more like intellectual energy fretting to express itself, each new Bond novel being that self-expression. Dr No is a brilliant, mad scientist. Blofeld, who plays a large part in several Bond novels, is a qualified economist and historian, as well as an engineer and an expert in 'radionics'. He is also, like Kronsteen, a finely sensitive student of human nature. In *Thunderball* (1961), where he presides at the SPECTRE high table like the master of a satanic Oxbridge college, we see him gazing all-knowingly at his subordinates. His eyes 'stripped the guilty or the false and made him feel transparent' (ch. 5, 61). Piercing eyes are a prerequisite for the villain in a novel. He can catch 'the grains of truth, suspended in the void of deceit or attempted obscurity'. He is fat like Count Fosco, with 'a vast belly that he concealed behind roomy trousers and well-cut double-breasted suits' (62), and is, like him, compared to Napoleon (we might recall that Holmes calls Moriarty 'the Napoleon of crime'). Fleming happily adds to the recipe analogies with Genghis Khan and Alexander the Great (56).

From Montoni to Fosco, foreignness is often an aspect of the true villain. Fleming's villains are frequently 'foreign'. Here he imitates Buchan's Richard Hannay novels, whose arch-villains are the Germans von Stumm and von Schwabing and the Spanish-Irish Dominick Medina. Fleming lines up the 'half Chinese and half German' Dr No, Ernst Stavro Blofeld 'born in Gdynia of a Polish father and a Greek mother' (56), and Auric Goldfinger, at whose provenance Bond can only guess: 'Not a Slav. Perhaps a German—no, a Balt!' (*Goldfinger*, 1959, ch. 3, 29). These genetically strange, everywhere foreign, beings are outside all normal laws, yet gifted with special powers. They have to be defeated, yet, before this happens, they must dazzle us a little with their clear-eyed analyses of the world.

REAL PEOPLE

Novelists are commonly suspected of basing their fictional characters on real people. Sometimes the singularity of a character is such that even the uninformed reader will suspect that there must be have been a real prototype (Muriel Spark, we sense before we are told, must have got Miss Jean Brodie from life). Historical novels also embody 'real people', but in the great majority of cases these characterizations compete with historical accounts (or other novels), not with our own knowledge. Only a certain kind of novel includes 'real people' who, by some kind of celebrity, are already known to us—whose voices we have heard. This is a fictional possibility largely because of radio and, especially, television. When Giles Foden's *The Last King of Scotland* (1998) gives us Idi Amin, brought to life in his buoyant, comical, boastful speech, he exploits the fact that the dictator's absurd and frightening pronouncements were frequently broadcast. The reader who is old enough will hear familiar cadences.

Another modern example is Andrew O'Hagan's *Personality*, which features real people in two ways. Firstly, his story of the singing star and anorexic Maria Tambini is based on the life of Lena Zavaroni, who became famous when she won the TV talent show *Opportunity Knocks* at the age of 13 and was for several years hugely popular on stage and television. A prefatory Note to the Reader concedes, elliptically, that the novel 'bears a relation to the lives of several dead performers', but does not name the original of its protagonist. An acknowledgements section at the close lists O'Hagan's main sources, which include the local newspaper for the Scottish island of Bute (where Zavaroni was born and brought up), but includes nothing to do with Zavaroni. While every review of O'Hagan's novel mentioned Tambini's real-life counterpart, not one of the many extracts from reviews that festoon the paperback edition actually names her. You are to know without ever being told. Other contemporary novelists (Joyce Carol Oates making a fictional protagonist out of Marilyn Monroe in *Blonde* (2000), Don DeLillo taking us into the mind of Lee Harvey Oswald in *Libra* (1988), for instance) have felt no such reticence. In the case of *Personality*, it seems to leave the novelist maximum room for invention while inviting readers to believe in the character's destiny. It is of a piece with O'Hagan's calculated refusal to know quite what is going on in his protagonist's head. We know about her, but we do not know her. And fiction must veer from biography; facts are changed. Maria's father is an unnamed American sailor, once stationed in Scotland, who had a brief affair with her mother, Rosa. In reality, Lena Zavaroni was brought up by both her parents and was close enough to her father for the two of them to perform together in later years.

O'Hagan's making of a fiction that everywhere suggests, but never specifies, its relation to a real person's life is not unique. Another example is John Banville's *The Untouchable* (1997), which is 'about' Anthony Blunt, the knighted art historian and curator of the Queen's pictures, who publicly admitted in 1979 that he had been a Soviet spy for decades. Banville gives him a new name, Victor Maskell, and similarly rechristens others with whom Blunt was associated—notably his fellow Cambridge spies Burgess and Maclean. Under the fiction is a true history, the sources for which are named in Banville's Acknowledgements. The fictional disguises are transparent, yet they are elaborately maintained. Banville's novel is more strictly a *roman-à-clef*: a novel in which actual persons are presented under fictional names. In *Personality*, celebrities appear as themselves. In *The Untouchable*, the supporting cast includes several whom we can enjoy recognizing. Guy Burgess becomes Boy Bannister, promiscuous homosexual and flamboyant drinker, revelling in the privileges of a social world that he holds in contempt. Querrell is surely Graham Greene, the Roman Catholic connoisseur of betrayal with his 'fishy look' and tight suits, who spends his time at parties 'leaning with his back against the wall, diabolical trickles of smoke issuing from the corners of his mouth, watching and listening' (34–5). 'He was genuinely curious about people—the sure mark of the second-rate novelist.' Greene actually played no part in Blunt's story, so the cameo is opportunistically venomous, an example of how biography is altered even as the reader is invited to identify real people in the fiction.

A sense of revealing what has been secret, of broaching the forbidden, commonly attaches to the *roman-à-clef.* So it is fitting for a novelist who wants to imagine the inner world of a spy. Banville doubles the effect of delicious indiscretion by writing in the person of Victor Maskell, who is recording his secret history for posterity. O'Hagan, in contrast, gives us 'real people', who are familiar, in some unreal way, from television. 'Show-business personalities enter the narrative under their own names,' as the Note to the Reader puts it. Maria meets Bernie Winters, Eric and Ernie, Lucille Ball, even Ronald Reagan. Some of these 'personalities' (a word that acquires a sardonic tone in the course of the novel) speak in the novel. There is Les Dawson in Maria's television dressing room, with a stream of bad puns and old-trouper gags to which many a reader will be able to put his voice. Here, as later when Dean Martin or Johnny Carson talk to her, the point is that the celebrity speaks just as we—and Maria—would expect. Maria duly reacts to Les Dawson's jokes as if she is 'lost in mirth' (131). 'Personality' is indefatigably acted out. 'Personality' was the title of one of Zavaroni's hits, duly given to Maria to sing in the novel.

Cause you've got—
Personality
Walk—
Personality
Talk—

Personality
Smile—
Personality
Charm—
Personality
Love—
Cause you got a great big heart. (171)

Personality is just that performance that the public recognizes.

There are odd precedents in the history of the novel for cameo appearances by 'showbusiness' characters. The actor David Garrick regularly appeared in eighteenth-century novels. Tobias Smollett gave speaking parts in his fiction to favoured actors and writers. The effect was to include novel readers within a circle of the cultured and knowing. Television has given some of O'Hagan's characters an aura of familiarity that makes their appearance in *Personality* disconcerting. The most prominent of them is Hughie Green, who has two chapters of dramatic monologue that artfully recall the gruesome phrase-making of his TV appearances. 'Showbusiness. Before you call it an illness you want to think what it does for people . . . Showbusiness is glory in the afternoon and sunshine after dark' (113). He is 'always speaking in headlines' says Maria, half in admiration. He keeps returning in the novel, eloquently platitudinous and self-serving, with a distinctive syntax of sincerity: 'Believe me . . . Don't get me wrong . . . There. I've said it now.' The novel artfully builds on the double bluff of his catchphrase: 'And I mean that most sincerely, folks!' (Being so self-aware about your display of sincerity is supposed to underline it.) In this novel's neatest feat of characterization, its version of Hughie Green is made grotesquely believable by virtue of his own performance of 'personality'.

THE ALTER EGO

Perhaps most novelists (including bad ones) make their protagonists like themselves. Drawing attention to the fact is risky. Dickens did it with *David Copperfield*, letting his readers know in a preface that the novel was his 'favourite child' and implicitly confirming that David (who indeed becomes a novelist) was entangled with himself. No reader of Joyce's *A Portrait of the Artist as a Young Man*, particularly given its title, would need a biographer to suppose that Stephen Dedalus is a fictional extension of Joyce. The real danger for a novelist of having an alter ego in your novel is that he or she is likely to be bland, blank, uncharacterized. A character is unlikely to take on an independent, surprising life if only a vehicle for the author's views. A good example would be Nicholas Jenkins in Anthony Powell's twelve-novel sequence *A Dance to the Music of Time* (1951–75). He may be the necessary figure around whom a large number of characters, observed over almost half a century, cohere. But in order to allow us to view what Powell wants us to see, he can be permitted no insight or opinion that is not the author's own. He is another protagonist of a novel who himself becomes a novelist.

It is telling that Nick more or less shares his creator's date of birth, so that he meets particular historical events at the same stages of his life as Powell must have done. Powell was born in 1905; *A Question of Upbringing* (1951), the first volume in the sequence, is set in 1921, with Nick a senior pupil at Eton. You can see why Powell would need a reliable ambassador to carry his narrative across twelve volumes, composed over such a span of time. But why else would a novelist need an alter ego? For much of his career Philip Roth has had one: a character who is known to be the author's double. He insistently features in Roth's novels, usually, though not always, as a narrator. He is called Nathan Zuckerman. He is a successful novelist, he lives in New England, he is Jewish. He first appeared in *My Life as a*

Man in 1974. A section of Roth's oeuvre since then is sometimes labelled 'Zuckerman novels'. He returns in *The Human Stain*, which even includes an allusion to an earlier appearance in *The Ghost Writer*. In an internal monologue, Nathan looks back sardonically on himself as an aspiring author, hungrily fastening on to the great writer Lonoff (5). Yet, more than forty years on, changed by age and the intervening American decades, he is still the ruthless observer whom we met in that first Zuckerman novel. Nathan is a narrator who can be unsympathetic even when he is right, and whose urge to fulfil himself as a writer is less than noble. Roth's alter ego is not there to be admired. In *The Human Stain* Coleman Silk half regrets getting sentimentally involved with this novelist, who loves catastrophe above all things. What has Coleman been doing, telling him things? 'Sharpening the writer's sense of reality. Feeding that great opportunistic maw, a novelist's mind' (170).

Roth knows that his reader will identify him with Nathan. In *Zuckerman Unbound* (1981), he actually warned against this reading habit. Author of a hugely successful novel, Zuckerman is shown being harried by admirers. Thirsty for autobiography, they believe him to be his own protagonist, Carnovsky (knowing readers will think of how Roth was identified with the protagonist of *Portnoy's Complaint*). 'They had mistaken impersonation for confession and were calling out to a character who lived in a book' (140). This novel's parade of foolish readers is scornful and hilarious. Much of it, like Roth's other Zuckerman novels, gets its voltage from the possibility that it might be what the author has himself known, that it might indeed be filched from Philip Roth's own life. Zuckerman's inner voice runs through a list of self-accusations that could be Roth's. 'Cold-hearted betrayer of your most intimate confessions, cutthroat caricaturist of your own living parents, graphic reporter of encounters with women to whom you have been deeply bound by trust, by sex, by love' (170).

The Human Stain exhibits some of the creative uses and

some of the dangers of this identification. In particular it allows a kind of passionate anger into Roth's fiction. Zuckerman makes his story out of 'my disgust . . . my shock' at what is said about Coleman Silk, at the lies of some and the self-righteous fantasies of others. Roth's alter ego is absolutely reliable in his commentary—we cannot doubt that his anger against political correctness and sexual puritanism is also Roth's—but he can vent the feelings that self-respecting authors keep out of their novels. Zuckerman's impotence allows this. He tries to get Faunia's father to hear the truth about his daughter's affair with Silk, but to no avail. He tells Silk's sons that Les Farley, Faunia's psychotic ex-husband, is responsible for their father's death, but they are not interested. He rages, but, unlike an author, he cannot have things his way. The fury animates the prose. Yet there are also problems when the alter ego seems to be Roth speaking directly. The opening pages of *The Human Stain* feature an eloquently sarcastic outburst inspired by the harrying of President Clinton for his sexual misdemeanours. Nathan Zuckerman inveighs against 'America's oldest communal passion, historically perhaps its most treacherous and subversive pleasure: the ecstasy of sanctimony' (2). The rhetoric is enjoyable, but there is an awkward possibility that the author is lecturing us.

It is more convincing when the pressure of authorial concern forces from the alter ego some passion exactly appropriate to his story. This happens in the novel's brilliantly written finale, when Nathan Zuckerman is drawn into a strange, frightening meeting with Coleman's probable killer, Les Farley (see Chapter 1, pp. 35–6). He finds him in winter, fishing through the ice on a remote lake. The two men have a strange conversation, charged with Farley's potential for violence (both men keep being drawn to the glittering auger, the 'strong, serious boring tool used to make the hole in the ice'; 346). Nathan feels threatened: does Farley know how much he knows? But he cannot resist the dangerous exchange in this lonely place. The novelist's curiosity becomes narratively absorbing as Nathan cannot help nudging their conversation into the dangerous areas near what must, we know, be Farley's murderous passions. 'This is what happens when you write books. There's not just something that drives you to find out everything—something begins putting everything in your path. There is suddenly no such thing as a back road that doesn't lead headlong into your obsession' (344). It fits the narrative moment; it might also be the motto for Roth's use of his alter ego to lead him into dangerous places.

4
Genre

'GENRE' is a word for types of writing; it is also therefore a word for habits of reading. Though novelists might like to cheat expectations, they need readers to have expectations that can be cheated. Genre alerts us to the readerly expectations learned from similar books. Imaginative literature relies on readers' knowledge of the generic conventions that it challenges or gratifies, even if this knowledge is often hardly conscious. Genre does not mean the imposition of rules, but the presence of conventions that may be altered or flouted. Without our awareness of genre, the alteration or flouting would be meaningless. 'Rightly understood, it is so far from being a mere curb on expression that it makes the expressiveness of literary works possible.'[1] A genre is not just a category for literary critics, it is also a resource for the writer. 'Far from inhibiting the author, genres are a positive support. They offer room, as one might say, for him to write in . . . a proportioned mental space.'[2]

It is an interesting question as to whether 'the Novel' itself is a genre. Early pioneers of the Novel like Defoe and Richardson did not even use the word 'novel' for what they were writing. Fielding's *Tom Jones* calls itself, with mock-solemnity, 'this Heroic, Historical, Prosaic Poem' (bk. IV, ch. i, 132). However, thanks to these writers and those who came after them, novels were, by the mid-eighteenth century, established with a strong *raison d'être*, if not quite a set of rules. They were justified by their adherence to the standard of 'probability' (the reason why Swift's *Gulliver's Travels*, with its midgets and giants and talking horses, was not grouped with the fiction of

Richardson and Fielding). Nor had the various sub-genres of fiction, like the historical novel or the Gothic novel, developed. For a while, 'the Novel' was a coherent genre. Soon it began developing such varieties, however, that the generic label came to do little more than distinguish novels from, say, memoirs or works of history. By the latter part of the twentieth century, when 'the Novel' could seemingly include any fictional prose narrative, including types as wholly improbable as what we usually call 'magical realism' (see below, pp. 117–19), the genre had become so capacious as to be almost indistinct. Yet the Novel's very comprehensiveness has invited a proliferation of sub-genres. Many of them have been popular, with the odd consequence that 'genre fiction' has become a condescending label. It covers supposedly unliterary types of novel: science fiction, romance, detective fiction, horror, and so on. Literary novelists (Julian Barnes, Iain Banks) often dabble in genre fiction—for the sales, but perhaps also for the satisfaction of following the 'rules' of each species.

While the force of the Novel as a genre is weak, the power of genre within novels is still apparent. It was notably exploited and tested by one of the most popular 'literary' novels of recent years, David Mitchell's *Cloud Atlas*. Its selection in 2005 as the Richard and Judy Book Club Book of the Year says something about the contemporary reader's willingness to accept what would once have been thought experimental narrative technique. For Mitchell's novel arranges narratives not just set in different times, but also written in different genres. No sooner has a reader become used to the peculiar stylistic habits of one kind of narrator, and the expectations fostered by one kind of story, than there is a shift to a narrative world with new rules. The linking of distinct narratives set in different times is not unprecedented. Michael Cunningham's *The Hours*, for instance, had three parallel lines of narrative set in, respectively, the 1920s, the 1940s, and the 1990s. The gaps between the narratives in Iain Pears's historical mystery *The Dream of Scipio*

(2002) were more dizzying, spanning the fifth, fourteenth, and twentieth centuries. Formal generic shifts, however, are more unusual. Mitchell drew his inspiration from Italo Calvino's *If on a Winter's Night a Traveller* (1979), which contains a dozen snatches from different narrative genres. Mitchell set his six narratives in different times (two of them in the future), and wrote them as if they were extracted from six completely different kinds of novel.

With these six narratives nested one inside another (the author calls it a 'Russian doll structure'), there are ten jumps between genres. The novel's success is that, no sooner are you plunged into a new genre, than you find yourself taken up by it, carried along. Mitchell could have written a whole novel in any of his genres. This is also his problem. For a genre provides more than conventions for a writer; it also gives a framework for a reader's expectations. Once inside one genre you forget what it is like to be inside a different one. You may notice with gratitude the 'links' to other stories that the novelist has provided, but the imaginative worlds of those other stories are, of necessity, forgotten once you have left them. *Cloud Atlas* certainly shows that contemporary readers are to switch between the conventions of different sub-genres of the Novel. Yet it also makes us aware of how forceful those conventions can be.

Sometimes the conventions are explicitly announced. When sub-genres of fiction developed in the eighteenth and nineteenth centuries, some were entirely self-conscious. The title pages of many late eighteenth-century novels included the subtitle 'A Sentimental Novel' ('sentimental' being a term of approbation at this time). The declaration promised readers that they would be getting scenes of pathos and virtuous distress, enabling them, like these novels' heroes and heroines, to exercise all their better feelings. From the 1790s, novels that toyed with the supernatural often had the subtitle 'A Romance' on their title pages (see below, pp. 112–15). These novels were highly self-conscious about their genre. So, as a rule, were those that could be classified as distinctive types of the nineteenth century. Newgate Novels and Silver Fork Novels and Sensation Novels were not genres announced on title pages. They were, however, labels used by contemporary critics and categories of which readers were sharply aware. These three genres may appear to be literary fossils, yet Newgate Novels were the ancestors of crime fiction and Sensation Novels have become 'thrillers' (see below). Apparently dead genres can indeed return, as the section in this chapter entitled 'The Novel of Circulation' suggests.

The genres treated below are only samples from a greater range of possibilities. The most significant type of novel not given its own section here is historical fiction, which is discussed instead in Chapter 7, 'Research'. One of the new genres of the twentieth century has been a special version of the historical novel: the historical mystery (discussed in this chapter). Perhaps this is therefore a sub-sub-genre. Another kind of novel, for example Peter Ackroyd's *Hawksmoor* (1985), A. S. Byatt's *Possession*, or David Mitchell's *Cloud Atlas*, is partially historical. (These three novels all involve the discovery of old documents, to which we are given direct access.) This should alert us to a final truth about genre. Types of fiction do not constitute some set of pigeonholes into one of which every novel must fit. Sometimes only parts of a novel belong to a special type of writing. The phases of satire in Zadie Smith's *White Teeth* discussed below are intermittent. Without dividing a novel up between mutually exclusive genres like David Mitchell, a novelist can still, within a single novel, excite changing expectations in the reader.

THE THRILLER

In many bookshops and public libraries you will find a large, discrete section of novels labelled 'Crime and Thrillers'. This pairing of categories is true to two lines of writing that Ruth Rendell follows. Invariably there are crimes in all her novels, but only some of them follow the pattern of detection suggested by the heading 'Crime'. Rendell has returned intermittently to her fictional detective Inspector Wexford, who appeared in her first novel *From Doon with Death* in 1964. A notably decent, reasonable man, he plies his trade in the provincial town of Kingsmarkham. Whatever he uncovers, whatever nastiness he might unearth in middle England, the narrative is finally given over to sense and morality. In contrast, her 'thrillers' (including those that she publishes under the name Barbara Vine) promise no triumph of order. The police might well arrive at some stage, but only belatedly and uncomprehendingly.

Historically the detective novel has a different lineage from the thriller. The detective story is often said to have been invented by Edgar Allen Poe, with his stories of Inspector Dupin. He features in 'The Murders in the Rue Morgue' (1841), the first narrative constructed in order to display the ingenuity of a professional detective. Poe influenced French fiction and made possible the first great English detective novel: Wilkie Collins's *The Moonstone*. We might note, however, that Dickens's earlier *Bleak House* (1852–3) included a mystery that is eventually solved by a detective, Inspector Bucket. Indeed, it was Dickens who first used the word 'detective' in a literary context: he entitled an 1850 article about the activities of London detectives 'Three "Detective" Anecdotes'.[3] At the end of the nineteenth century detective fiction found new popularity with the most influential of all such narratives: Arthur Conan Doyle's Sherlock Holmes stories. In the 1930s the mass-produced murder mystery became known, first of all in America, as the 'whodunnit'.

The first thriller, however, is arguably William Godwin's *Caleb Williams* (1794; entitled *Things As They Are* when it was first published). Written in the first person, it is the story of a man who discovers the secret of a crime, but whose discovery leads him into torment. Years after it appeared, Godwin was to give an account of its composition that was itself to influence later novelists. He plotted the novel backwards, beginning with his conception of his hero, Caleb, being a fugitive 'in perpetual apprehension of being overwhelmed with the worst calamities, and the pursuer, by his ingenuity and resources, keeping his victim in a state of the most fearful alarm'.[4] Having escaped from prison, Caleb is pursued by his former employer, Falkland, and his inexorable agent, Gines. In a plot followed by many a 'psychological thriller' since, Caleb finds that, however clever his disguise or hiding place, Gines keeps discovering him. There will have to be a final confrontation between Caleb and his tormentor. Godwin described how he planned this before working out why Caleb was being pursued. 'I was next called upon to conceive a dramatic and impressive situation, adequate to account for the impulse that the pursuer should feel, incessantly to alarm and harass his victim.' Now Godwin envisioned 'a secret murder, to the investigation of which the innocent victim should be impelled by an unconquerable spirit of curiosity'. The murderer would thus be given a motive to persecute Caleb. Finally, Godwin turned to the first part of his novel, establishing Falkland, the villain to be, as a man once worthy to be admired by his victim. The 'overpowering interest' of his story, Godwin believed, would depend on 'his appearing to have been originally endowed with a mighty store of amiable dispositions and virtues'. The interest would be psychological.

Rendell writes what are often called 'psychological thrillers', specializing as they do in the murderous rationality of disturbed individuals. Her distinctive achievement is to make inescapable the logic by which banal obsessions become deadly. Because we know what genre she inhabits, we are guessing from the first at the terrible consequences of her characters' peculiarities. In *Adam and Eve and Pinch Me*, her central character, Minty, becomes convinced that stabbing the spectres that seem to haunt her is the only way of banishing them. We know that someone is going to be hurt. Minty has been fleeced by 'Jock', a practised conman who latches on to women with money. When he wishes to disappear, he fakes letters advising his former paramours of his death in the 1999 Paddington train crash. His other lovers, fooled out of their money, their eyes now opened, know that this must be another trick. Minty, however, presumes that the letter is real and that Jock is indeed dead. So when she catches sight of him she naturally believes that she is seeing his ghost. If we know this kind of thriller, we should also know that Jock, the cheery deceiver, blithely wandering London in search of his next victim, chose the wrong woman in Minty. She is going to do something nasty with the butcher's knife that she wears strapped to her body to defend her against ghosts. Knowledge of the genre fills us with apprehension—a special power in the hands of a skilled writer. We wonder less what will happen than how it will be brought about.

Rendell did not invent this type of book, where ordinary weirdness leads to fatal violence. *Adam and Eve and Pinch Me* in fact pays a little homage to Patricia Highsmith, Rendell's most notable predecessor in the genre. Rendell sends several of her characters to watch the film of *The Talented Mr Ripley*, though naturally they do not notice that they too live in a world where murder is a few logical steps away. The reader sees it all, but none of the characters does. In fact, there is no one in the novel to comprehend everything, like the sleuth at the denouement of a whodunnit. When the police enter Rendell's novel it is as gullible visitors from a different world. We are told, rather too explicitly, that Minty's obsession with cleanliness makes her seem 'conspicuously innocent' to the detectives who arrive at her door (368). 'The police are nearly as likely to be favourably impressed by cleanliness, neatness and respectability as anyone else.' Ironically, the symptoms of Minty's very obsessiveness reassure the two visiting policemen. She smells of soap and lavender shampoo. Being, as we know, insanely deluded, she also seems guileless to them. This thriller reverses the logic of detective fiction. Only the reader understands the causal links between events, including two murders, whose connectedness remains hidden from both detectives and journalists. The murders of two otherwise unrelated individuals have both been committed by Minty, deluded into believing that she was ridding herself of 'ghosts'. Rendell flourishes at us the fact that only the reader of the novel can possibly see the connection. She tells us that newspapers call the murderer 'the "mindless" or "aimless" killer'. We, however, have been let in to the killer's mind, her aims. Little do they know; much do we.

ROMANCE

The declaration on the title page and the cover of A. S. Byatt's *Possession* suggests that this is a peculiar kind of novel, operating by special rules. *Possession: A Romance* its full title announces, as if indicating its difference from the usual run of novels. Already we might suspect that 'Romance' must imply more than our habitual, narrowed meaning: a love story. *Possession*, so sharp about academic literary criticism and its follies, frequently asks its reader to notice the peculiar properties of different genres. What does its subtitle lead us to expect? Byatt supplies an excerpt from Nathaniel Hawthorne's preface to *The House of the Seven Gables* (1851) as a guide. 'When a writer calls his work a Romance . . . he wishes to claim a certain latitude', a latitude not allowed to the novelist. 'Romance' does not heed 'the probable and ordinary course of man's experience', says Hawthorne, but presents 'the truth of the human heart' in circumstances 'of the writer's own choosing or creation'. 'Romance' has always implied remoteness from the events of everyday life, the territory of knights and damsels rather than men and women. From medieval stories of chivalry to the antique verse tales of Keats, Coleridge, and Scott, and on to the Victorian Arthurianism of Tennyson, Romance included what Congreve defined as 'miraculous contingencies and impossible performances', calculated to 'elevate and surprise the reader into a giddy delight', though leaving him 'flat upon the ground whenever he gives off'.[5] It has often been contrasted with the Novel. 'Truth distinguishes our Writings from those idle Romances which are filled with Monsters,' Fielding announces in his very earthbound novel *Tom Jones* (bk. IV, ch. i, 131). In its early years, the English novel, dedicated to all that was 'probable', often set itself against 'Romance'.

The work that seems to many the first novel-like narrative of European literature, Cervantes' *Don Quixote* (1605–15), is a sustained send-up of romances. Its crack-brained hero sallies forth expecting to find the adventures of Romance and collides ludicrously with the real world. 'Romance' has had a special presence in the English novel, as a frequent word for all that might be unlikely, unreal, miraculous. Romance has often been all that was inimical to the self-respecting novelist. So why does Byatt embrace it? She has her Victorian poet Randolph Ash use 'Romance' to mean both a fantasy about love and a literary tradition. After his first moment of 'madness' with Christabel LaMotte (we infer that, though he is a married man, he has, on impulse, kissed her during their secret meeting in Greenwich Park), Ash writes a letter that we could call passionate and 'romantic' (192–4). Yet he reassures her, 'We are rational nineteenth-century beings, we might leave the *coup de foudre* to the weavers of Romances' (193). There is no irresistible love at first sight in the real world, he assures himself, though he will find otherwise.

Possession wants to repossess Romance, as did some Victorian poets and artists. Ash and LaMotte both fabricate poetic romances based on legends. LaMotte tells her Breton cousin, a would-be writer, that 'Romance is a proper form for women . . . Romance is a land where women can be free to express their true natures' (373). She is not thinking of mere love stories but of 'Spenser's *Faerie Queene* or Ariosto, where the soul is free of the restraints of history and fact'. In a somewhat tendentious demonstration of literary origins, Byatt takes her characters and her readers to the storm-scoured coast of Brittany, where

LaMotte takes refuge after her affair with Ash and where she gives birth to their child. The author has chosen Brittany as the place of origin of primitive Romance narratives. Breton lays helped transmit Arthurian tales. LaMotte's poetry from this period of her life, artfully fabricated by Byatt, makes symbolic use of Breton legends, though the 'true story' of a clandestine passion that lies behind it will remain hidden from even the most ingenious of literary interpreters.

Possession's self-description has appeared before on the title pages of novels. Many early examples of what we now call 'Gothic novels' called themselves 'romances'. The first two best-sellers to secure the notoriety of Gothic, Ann Radcliffe's *The Mysteries of Udolpho* and Matthew Lewis's *The Monk* (1796), both carried the subtitle 'A Romance'. (Only the earliest of Gothic novels, Horace Walpole's *The Castle of Otranto* (1765), actually labelled itself 'Gothic'; it described itself, at the head of its first chapter, as 'A Gothic Story'.) A novel declaring itself 'A Romance' in the 1790s was setting out, at the end of a century in which novelists had asked to be judged by standards of 'probability', to rediscover the fantastic. This is what Byatt wants to do too, importing fairy tales and Gothic legends through the poems and stories that she has her characters invent. Simultaneously she turns the researches of her modern-day academics, and the quest of the reader after the truth of 'what happened', into a romance, bringing dead lovers back to life.

'Romance' is a much debated and frequently redefined word in literary history. In Jane Austen's *Northanger Abbey*, 'romance' is the name for Catherine Morland's delusions, fostered by her devotion to Ann Radcliffe's novels, and especially to *The Mysteries of Udolpho*. It is the word that Austen uses when Catherine realizes that life is not like a Gothic narrative. 'The visions of romance were over. Catherine was completely awakened' (vol. ii, ch. x, 159). She has opened her eyes to daylight, and to the folly of her novel-based fantasies. Colonel Tilney, in whose house she is staying, is not a black-hearted murderer of his wife (though he is a rude and mercenary man). The romance of plot-making has blinded her to reality. Yet literature can show how we grow into, as well as grow out of, a sense of the fantastic. In Austen's last novel, *Persuasion*, 'romance' is reclaimed by its heroine Anne Elliot. Having once refused the proposal of a man she loved, she knows, eight years later, the value of romantic longings. 'She had been forced into prudence in her youth, she learned romance as she grew older—the natural sequel of an unnatural beginning' (vol. i, ch. iv, 29). The popularity of *Possession* suggests that readers too relish the learning of romance.

SATIRE

Satire does not always live easily within novels. The mockery of vice and folly can thwart the very extension of sympathy to characters that is often the aim of novelists. Zadie Smith's *White Teeth* has satirical aspirations and some passages of unalloyed satire. These contribute to the sense that it is a novel whose picture of multicultural England has escaped obligations of political correctness. Its marginal characters are often satirically imagined types, their absurdity representative rather than distinctive. They are such as Archie's boss, Mr Hero, the racist who says, 'I'd spit on that Enoch Powell . . . but then he does have a point, doesn't he?' (72). Or the comprehensive school headmaster, who responds to pupil misbehaviour by 'not wanting anyone to feel boxed in' and worrying that any pupil 'felt the need to lie' (299). They are the stuff of satire, which asks us to see not how everyone is individual (the usual novelistic presumption) but how everyone with a certain occupation or rank is the same.

The novel also has satirical set-pieces. Daringly, Smith tries a cameo of ill-educated, moderately foul-mouthed Asian youths 'slouching towards Bradford' in their Nike gear to protest against Salman Rushdie's *Satanic Verses* (232). They talk happily of their outrage at a book of which they know nothing. '"My uncle says he can't even spell," said a furious Hifan, the most honestly religious of the lot. "And he dares to talk about Allah!"' (233). Smith likes to make space for gloriously absurd discussions. Especially good is the gathering of the animal liberationist group FATE (Fighting Animal Torture and Exploitation). Its members debate the best form of direct action at the public meeting where the scientist Marcus Chalfen will unveil his genetically programmed mouse. 'But surely the mouse in this case is a symbol, i.e. this guy's got a lot more of them in his lab—so we have to deal with the bigger picture' (484). His comrade demurs; 'to me that's absolutely the opposite of what FATE is about. If this were a man trapped in a little glass box for six years, he wouldn't be a symbol, you know?' The parody is pitch-perfect. 'The gathered members of FATE murmured their assent.' The comic earnestness of proceedings is emphasized because seen through the eyes of Joshua Chalfen, whose attachment to the group is motivated entirely by his hopeless, unstated lust for its ringleader, the delicious Joely.

Satire is also dominant in the depiction of the Chalfen family, the left-wing, middle-class clan who welcome the wide-eyed Irie and the abusive, exploitative Millat into their midst. 'Joshua was a star Maths pupil, Benjamin wanted to be a geneticist just like his father, Jack's passion was psychiatry, and Oscar could checkmate his father's king in fifteen moves' (313). Joyce and Marcus Chalfen speak with appalling openness about sex, openly boast of their children's intelligence, and encourage them to befriend 'brown strangers' (326). 'Their only after-school activity (they despised sport) was the individual therapy five times a week at the hands of an old-fashioned Freudian called Marjorie who did Joyce and Marcus (separately) on weekends' (313). The depiction pleasingly caricatures a certain smug yet affable middle-class Englishness, with its intellectually condescending, imperviously tolerant, rationalism. In themselves, the Chalfen chapters are droll. Yet their inclusion risks contravening the novelist's own contract. Her method with her main characters has been anti-satirical: to extend to each prevailing folly, if not exactly exoneration, at least the grace of a novelist's sympathy. The two characters who are Jehovah's Witnesses, their hopes absurdly fixed on some predicted date for the end of the world (with the selection of only a tiny minority for redemption), are treated with subtle amusement. Why not those self-satisfied bourgeois Darwinians too? In the disposal of her satirical portraits, Zadie Smith might be accused of the political correctness that she otherwise scorns.

MAGICAL REALISM

'Magical realism' was a term used by almost all the reviewers of Jonathan Safran Foer's *Everything Is Illuminated* to describe one strand of its narrative. A would-be novelist called Jonathan Safran Foer narrates episodes, between the 1790s and the 1940s, from the lives of his ancestors and their fellow denizens of their Ukrainian *shtetl*, Trachimbrod. Divided between two Jewish congregations, the Upright Synagogue and the Slouching Synagogue, it is a community of eccentrics visited by peculiar accidents, many tragicomic. Its characters and traditions have to be reimagined because they are erased by the Germans who invade the Soviet Union. In the tales of Trachimbrod, most readers would recognize narrative patterns that mimic the fantastic logic of folk tales. The story of Trachimbrod begins one day in 1791 when a wagon overturns while crossing a river. The driver is drowned, but amongst the curious flotsam that rises to the surface—'string and feathers . . . candles and soaked matches, prawns, pawns, and silk tassels that curtsied like jellyfish'—is a baby girl, 'still mucus-glazed, still pink as the inside of a plum' (13). There is to be no natural explanation for her bobbing up into the novel. Trachim, the wagon's owner, gives his name to the village, but his body is never found. By lot, the village's 'disgraced usurer', Yankel, is chosen as her father (22).

She is to be the narrator's great-great-great-great-great-grandmother.

Magical realism often features wonderful events depicted with pictorial exactitude. Think of the characters harmlessly falling out of a plane at the beginning of Salman Rushdie's *Satanic Verses* (1988). In fact the term 'magical realism' was first applied to paintings rather than novels. It was given currency by the German art critic Franz Roh in his 1925 book *Nach-expressionismus, magischer Realismus*. 'Magical realism' was, he argued, the special quality of a new kind of post-Expressionist painting involving fantastic or dreamlike imagery. Later, in the 1940s, the term resurfaced to describe the work of certain modern American painters, including Edward Hopper. Only belatedly did it become attached to fiction, and frequently it is fiction whose 'magical' elements have a strong pictorial aspect. The key novel in making this kind of writing into a recognized sub-genre was Gabriel García Márquez's *One Hundred Years of Solitude* (1967; trans. 1970). Márquez showed that it could be a way of fictionalizing complex and traumatic historical themes. So it is in Safran Foer's novel. The author's namesake writes an imagined history of his antecedents ending in the eradication of their *shtetl* by the invading Germans in 1942. In his narrative method you can feel the influence of precursors like Günter Grass's *The Tin Drum* (1959; trans. 1962) and Rushdie's *Midnight's Children*. These too are novels that provide a fantastic genealogy for their central character, telling the stories of improbable couplings and semi-miraculous births.

Such narrative falls into patterns that defy probability. Safran, the grandfather of the author's alter ego, becomes the sedulous sexual therapist of the community, coupling dutifully with the village's old maids and its virgins. There are fifty-two of the latter whom he 'visits', making love to them 'in each of the positions that he had studied from a dirty deck of cards' (195). The *shtetl*'s history is kept alive in its 'Book of Antecedents', a collection of surreal anecdotes about the oddest episodes and most eccentric characters of the previous two centuries. Like the time that everyone had a different-coloured dye put on their hands to see who was stealing the baker's rolls, with the unforeseen result that the community's hidden contacts (on the skin of another man's wife, on the pages of a forbidden book) suddenly became visible. 'The shtetl was painted with the doings of its citizens' (200).

This kind of narrative makes fiction aspire to the condition of myth. Some of the novelists most closely associated with magical realism (Márquez, Rushdie, Isabel Allende, Francisco Goldman) do indeed invoke the saints or gods with which their authors grew up. Secular novelists reclaim religious narrative to enrich their own novels. Safran Foer has the spirit of an ancestor 'speak' near the end of his novels to tell us how his narrator's grandfather survived the Germans' eradication of his community. Yet he seems sensitive to the possibility that it might all become whimsical, and therefore draws attention to his artifice. The very story we are reading is being sent in parts to Alex, his malapropism-addicted Ukrainian translator, who comments, sometimes in exasperation, about its development. It is all just a fiction. But does this not sound like a writer who distrusts his chosen genre?

THE NOVEL OF CIRCULATION

How do you write about a society? In particular, how do you write about American society, so huge and so uncircumscribed? Don DeLillo's *Underworld* is self-consciously a map of the American late twentieth century and, with its montage of narratives and its time shifts, often designated a 'postmodern' novel. Yet to hold together its different characters and their stories, it relies on an old-fashioned, even quaint, fictional trick. Running through this complex novel is the story of an object: a baseball. We first see the ball, in the novel's bravura opening section, being hit into the crowd for the winning home run in a famous game between the New York Dodgers and the New York Giants on 3 October 1951. *Underworld* gives us a history of this ball, a secular relic for those who wish to possess it. The novel's own historical investigator is Marvin Lundy, a collector of baseball memorabilia, a man dedicated to the preservation of national memory. He has set out to find the ball, but also to work out 'the lineage', as he calls it. Only the reader knows, from early in the novel, what happened to it in the seconds, then minutes, after it flew into the crowd. We see Cotter Martin, a poor black teenager who has gatecrashed the game, managing, by luck and quickness and finally ruthless strength, to get the ball for which many others are reaching. We also know where it has ended up. One of the novel's central characters, Nick Shay (a fan of the Dodgers, who lost to that last-minute home run), has bought it, for $34,500. Why would he want it so badly? As he explains to a puzzled English TV producer, 'It's about the mystery of bad luck, the mystery of loss' (97). The novel finds out the ball's history in between Cotter Martin and Nick Shay.

The idea of getting a society into a novel by following an object (or sometimes an animal) is an old one. The device was popular in the eighteenth century, especially after Francis Coventry's novel *The History of Pompey the Little* (1751). This anatomy of Georgian absurdities takes its title from the name of the lapdog whose fortunes Coventry describes. A novel whose episodes are connected by the progress of this animal is inherently satirical, as Coventry facetiously indicates in his novel's first chapter: 'the Politicians of the Age, and Men of Gravity may be apt to censure me for misspending my Time in writing the Adventures of a Lap-dog, when there are so many *modern Heroes*, whose illustrious Actions call loudly for the Pen of an Historian' (ch. i, 1). Each owner is a representative character (an aristocratic lady, a fop, a Methodist, and so on). Critics sometimes call such a narrative a 'novel of circulation'. One of the best-selling novels of the eighteenth century was another such: Charles Johnstone's *Chrysal; or, The Adventures of a*

Guinea (1760–5), which follows a gold coin through the hands of the great, the vicious, and the foolish. The title page advertised it as a novel 'Wherein are exhibited Views of several striking Scenes, With Curious and interesting Anecdotes of the Most Noted Persons in every Rank of Life, whose Hands it passed through In America, England, Holland, Germany, and Portugal'. Part of the appeal of Johnstone's narrative was the implication that the characters encountered were based on identifiable public figures. In the following decades, similar novels became popular. Amongst others, there were the stories of a cat, a watch, a pincushion, and a coach. In the nineteenth century they were rarer, though Douglas Jerrold, one of the founders of *Punch* magazine, did publish *The Story of a Feather* in 1843. It follows the passage of an ostrich feather, from hand to hand, through the different classes of Victorian society.

In DeLillo's hands, the genre becomes a way of spanning history. His 'Shot Heard Round the World' was struck on the baseball field on the day that the Soviet Union first tested an atom bomb. The aftershock of this event ripples through the novel. Seeing what happens to the baseball is a way of taking us through American life during the Cold War and its aftermath. In *Underworld* we discover that the true history of this true American relic will lead to further connections, whose web is invisible to the characters. So, for instance, the man to whom Cotter's father sells the baseball (for $34.25) gives it to his son Chuckie Wainwright. Chuckie flies on a B-52 in Vietnam that later gets made into conceptual art by Klara Sax, Nick's former lover. Another of the ball's temporary owners is shot by the Texas Highway Killer, whose terrifying, mysterious exploits recur through the novel. Following 'the long arching journey of the baseball' reveals other, unexpected links between characters (318). All are pulled in to the unsettling and underground connectedness of American life. 'Because everything connects in the end, or only seems to, or seems to only because it does' (465). Has there ever been a novel with more talk of mysterious 'connections'? J. Edgar Hoover and the effects of nuclear testing and the assassination of Kennedy and the waste disposal industry and the cold war. Yet DeLillo has to turn to an old and curiously artificial genre to hold it all together.

THE *CONTE*

French has many more terms than English to categorize the varieties of fiction. Some of these—the *roman-à-clef*, the *roman-fleuve*—have seemed so invaluable that English has purloined them. In order to characterize much of the fiction of Muriel Spark, including her novel *Aiding and Abetting*, we might reach for another French term, which was commonly used of fiction until the mid-nineteenth century: the *conte*. The *conte* is fantastic, witty, often satirical. It is a tale whose moral or philosophical content might be pronounced, but which has little interest in the psychological depth or circumstantial detail that most novels provide. For this reason, a *conte* is usually short. It might be profound, but it is not weighty. Early examples would be Voltaire's *Candide* (1759) and Johnson's *Rasselas* (1759). Later examples might include Oscar Wilde's *The Picture of Dorian Gray* (1890) or Walter Pater's *Marius the Epicurean* (1885). All of these tales have something in common with *Aiding and Abetting*: the fiction stems not from a number of realistically conceived characters but from a notion, a premiss, an intellectual experiment.

'Let us suppose . . .', begins the *conte*. That putting of an idea often has a mischievous ring. The writer is letting loose an experiment rather than trying to fill a believable fictional world. So the *conte* tends to be satirical, as *Aiding and Abetting* certainly is, and perhaps a little 'wicked', a word used not infrequently of Spark's fiction. *Aiding and Abetting* mocks the empty mutual assurances of therapists and patients, the amoral condescension of Lord Lucan's imagined community of aiders and abetters (all of them obdurate snobs), and above all the failure of everyone concerned, however resourceful, to react to anything in the right way. Looking like a condensed novel, it is in fact an extended parable.

Readers have always noticed, and critics sometimes complained, that Spark's novels are spare and schematic, fable-like rather than realistic. They seem unconcerned to conceal the narrative's plan under a wealth of convincing detail. Though psychologically acute, they do not attempt to flesh out their characters. *Aiding and Abetting* is characteristic in these respects. A book cannot expect us to suspend all disbelief when it introduces Lord Lucan, a paid double who goes by the name of Walker, but swears that he too is Lucan, and their psychiatrist, a charlatan who once swindled pious Catholics out of their savings by styling herself Blessed Beate Pappenheim The Stigmatic of Munich. The shortness of almost all Spark's books (*Aiding and Abetting* can comfortably be read in two or three hours) is part of their form: here is fiction stripped down, as if to a diagram of human behaviour. But what happens also removes it from the expectations of novel readers. There are extremes of coincidence, for instance. When Lacey, daughter of one of Lucan's former cronies, begins searching for him, she and her accomplice, Joe, keep nearly bumping into him. 'I could have sworn that the man along there, three people in front, resembled Lucan. But of course . . .' (159). They think they have seen him on a plane, in a car, at a racecourse, even exiting a Scottish monastery disguised as one of the brothers. In each case, we discover that they are right. Far from Lucan being nowhere, he becomes ubiquitous, a reflection of his pursuers' fascination with the apparent banality of his evil deeds.

There is also an undisguised metaphysical element, to which the *conte* is traditionally hospitable. Lucan introduces himself to the psychiatrist Dr Hildegard Wolf (as Beate Pappenheim has renamed herself) by saying, 'Twenty-five years ago I sold my soul to the Devil' (1). His opening line alerts us to the fact that we are reading a morality tale, whose characters have no real moral feelings. They might like to talk as if they do, but they do not. As the narrator says about Hildegard and her boyfriend, 'If you can comprehend a morality devoid of ethics or civil law, this was really the guiding principle of both people' (40). These two lead a life of propriety and aesthetic scruple. In their elegant Paris flat they voice a nice enough morality of sentiments and expressions, but never feel any pressing sense of the right or wrong thing to do. When we are invited to see 'the good Dr. Wolf' scrutinizing the infamous fugitive who is her patient, that 'good' speaks of her supposed (but in fact bogus) role as a professional therapist (11). It is the opposite of morally 'good'. In that most penetrating *conte*, *Candide*, Voltaire gifted his leading characters with an absurd faith in a providential order of things, which he then tested to extremes. For similarly mischievous purposes of fable-making, Spark has detached her characters from moral feelings, and then stepped back to observe.

THE HISTORICAL MYSTERY

Orhan Pamuk's *My Name Is Red* is in some ways a difficult novel. It is structurally demanding, being divided up between ten narrators, with interspersed parables offered by several imaginary voices (Death, A Horse, Satan). It is also culturally challenging. Set in Istanbul at the end of the sixteenth century, it is much concerned with the clash between Eastern and Western—Islamic and Christian—ideas about art. The Anglophone reader is required to imagine the formal delights of the illuminations painted by the miniaturists who are Pamuk's main characters. To them, the aesthetic and religious values informing these pictures are second nature. This is a novel of ideas about how East and West might meet. It is also an example of what has become a popular genre: the historical mystery. Pamuk likes to build his novels around mysteries, making detective stories of intellectual enquiries: *The Black Book* (1990; trans. 1994) is about a man whose wife has disappeared; in *Snow* (2002; trans.

2004) a journalist investigates a spate of suicides in a remote Turkish town. The main character of *My Name Is Red*, Black, attempts to solve the murders of a court painter and their master, who is also his own uncle. However formally elaborate or philosophically ambitious, the book is—to use that originally dismissive label—a whodunnit.

The combination of historical setting and murder mystery will remind many of Umberto Eco's 1984 best-seller *The Name of the Rose*. Eco's medieval crime puzzler led us through the byways of antique learning and made the solution of the whodunnit depend on a knowledge of medieval literary theory. Comparably, to solve the murders in Pamuk's novel we must find out something about theories of art in the Ottoman court. We are nudged into suspecting that an artist has been murdered because he has offended against an established, theologically approved code of artistic representation. (Thus the novel seems to offer itself as an allegory of fundamentalist intolerance.) The generic aspect of *My Name Is Red* shapes the reader's responses and speculations in this respect. Pamuk surely had Eco's book specifically in mind, for he appears mischievously to invite us to use our knowledge of the dénouement of *The Name of the Rose*. We are given every opportunity to believe that Pamuk's murderer will be a zealot for religious orthodoxy, as was the case in Eco's novel. This, it turns out, is a red herring.

The Name of the Rose was a more elaborate version of an established genre pioneered by Ellis Peters (real name Edith Pargeter), creator of the medieval detective Brother Cadfael. Academics like Eco have been drawn to the genre. One of Peters's commercially successful imitators is Candace Robb, a scholar of medieval literature before fiction became a full-time occupation. She has written a series featuring the one-eyed sleuth Owen Archer, set in and around fourteenth-century York. Rosemary Rowe, author of Roman whodunnits, is the pen-name of Rosemary Aitken, an English Language academic.

The Celtic scholar Peter Beresford Ellis is the prolific author of historical murder yarns under the name Peter Tremayne. The best-known are set in seventh-century Ireland and feature a female detective, Sister Fidelina. There are even historical detective stories for children, notably the series of Roman Mysteries written by Caroline Lawrence. Each of these includes a lexicon of useful Latin words, for the genre delights in popularizing erudition. The literary professor Margaret Ann Doody, author of a series of whodunnits set in ancient Athens featuring Aristotle as detective, makes her tales turn on knowledge of ancient mores. The Oxford art historian Iain Pears has produced erudite mystery novels, culminating in the best-selling historical whodunnit *An Instance of the Fingerpost*. In the course of its narrative its reader is instructed in the intellectual ferment of seventeenth-century Oxford.

One might think that with *My Name Is Red* Pamuk has attached a novel of ideas to this popular genre simply for good commercial reasons. Yet his choice of genre is also appropriate. To solve the mystery we follow an enquiry into the nature of Islamic art, and how it began to be influenced by Western, particularly Venetian, painting. Usually in historical mysteries the reader looking for clues is invited to be a kind of archaeologist. In Pamuk's novel you become, more strangely, an archaeologist of beliefs. In his melancholy transformation of the genre, the 'solution' is troubling rather than satisfying. The murderer has killed because of the irreconcilability of two aesthetic codes, Eastern and Western. Unlike the killer in Eco's novel, Pamuk's murderer has killed to protect heterodoxy—in his case to safeguard a workshop of miniaturists dabbling in 'Frankish artistry' (481). For Muslims to undertake lifelike portraits as the 'Christian idolaters' do is a kind of heresy, and the killer's victim is about to disclose this to a leading religious zealot. He dies for a question of theology that has, in the past, belonged only in obscure corners of history. Pamuk has imbued the quaintness of his chosen genre with a surprising gravity.

5
Voices

In one respect, speech in fiction used to be closer to speech in drama that it now is. There is plentiful evidence of novels being read aloud to family and friends in the eighteenth and nineteenth centuries; Jane Austen's letters, for instance, are full of references to this habit. So still in the early decades of the twentieth century. To take one example, Evelyn Waugh's *Brideshead Revisited* (1945) describes how it was the custom in Sebastian Flyte's family to ask his mother, Lady Marchmain, to read aloud 'on evenings of family tension' (ch. 5, 128). Waugh's narrator, Charles Ryder, tells us how she did so on the evening when Sebastian's chronic drunkenness became embarrassingly apparent. 'She had a beautiful voice and great humour of expression. That night she read part of *The Wisdom of Father Brown*.' Good writers might expect readers accomplished at performing their fiction. Waugh's *A Handful of Dust* (1934) ends with a nightmare version of this: poor Tony Last, trapped in the Amazonian jungle, having to read and reread the novels of Dickens to the sinister Mr Todd. 'He had always rather enjoyed reading aloud and in the first year of his marriage had shared several books in this way with Brenda' (ch. vi, 214). Now he will have to enjoy the exercise for ever. As Mr Todd observes, 'It is delightful to start again. Each time I think I find more to enjoy and admire.'

It would be interesting to know when this habit of reading novels aloud died out—perhaps with the widespread ownership of radios? Novelists once needed to consider their novels as scripts for amateur performers, and to give help to a reader aloud. This may be one reason why *idiolects*—forms of speech distinctive of an individual—used to feature far more in novels. We can of course picture Dickens's Uriah Heep in *David Copperfield*, but anyone reading aloud can immediately make him present.

> 'I am well aware that I am the umblest person going,' said Uriah Heep, modestly; 'let the other be where he may. My mother is likewise a very umble person. We live in a numble abode, Master Copperfield, but have much to be thankful for. My father's former calling was umble. He was a sexton.'
>
> 'What is he now?' I asked.
>
> 'He is a partaker of glory at present, Master Copperfield,' said Uriah Heep. 'But we have much to be thankful for. How much have I to be thankful for in living with Mr Wickfield!' (ch. 16, 191)

Could any person really repeat the mispronounced word 'humble' so often? Or use that euphemism for 'dead' alongside the absurdly qualifying 'at present'? Or so repeat their thankfulness? Yet these are irresistible cues for the performing voice. The brilliance of it is that sense that the habits of speech, the repetitions of 'umble', must somehow be sarcastic—and, of course, Heep is in fact bitter and ambitious and predatory. When he declares himself 'thankful' for living with Mr Wickfield he turns to servility his scheme to entrap Wickfield and obtain his daughter Agnes for his wife.

Dickens stylizes, but so does every novelist purporting to catch how people naturally speak (see 'Dialect', below). Only in rare cases does any novel make any thorough attempt to represent non-standard pronunciation, and even successful uses of non-standard vocabulary are likely to be highly selective and sparing. In life, a regional form of speech that is unfamiliar to us will often be difficult to understand; in novels, hardly ever. A novelist's reasonings now are likely to be similar to those of Thomas Hardy, defending the dialogue in *The Return of the*

Native (1878), which a reviewer had accused of artificiality. A novelist should be allowed, said Hardy, to convey 'the spirit of intelligent peasant talk' by retaining 'the idiom, compass and characteristic expressions', but not attempting to reproduce 'mispronunciations': 'if a writer attempts to exhibit on paper the precise accents of a rustic speaker he disturbs the proper balance of a true representation by unduly insisting upon the grotesque element.'[1] Hardy himself typically gives the impression of dialect through idioms and patterns of syntax, without attempting phonetic reproduction. He complicates this by having characters who can vary between dialect and standard English. One such is Tess Durbeyfield, 'who had passed the Sixth Standard in the National school' and 'spoke two languages; the dialect at home, more or less; ordinary English abroad and to persons of quality' (*Tess of the d'Urbervilles*, ch. iii, 27).

The artificiality of the means by which speech is made to seem natural is evident in novelistic dialogue, the subject of the second section of this chapter. No student of actual conversation—an imaginary sociolinguist with a tape recorder, let us say—would recognize the conversations in novels as 'realistic'. Even novelists who like to render the brute patterns of colloquial language will tactfully avoid the repetitions and redundancies, the endless qualifications and unfinished sentences, that characterize 'real speech'. Fiction smoothes speech. It also often translates it. The sections below entitled 'Languages' and 'Translation' deal, respectively, with novels in which characters are supposed to be speaking different languages, and novels that take place almost entirely in a language other than English. We are asked to believe in—to hear—the novel's voices, while knowing that the words on the page are not actually those that were spoken.

Fiction of recent decades has discovered some new fictional resources of speech. The phone conversation in novels is at least eighty years old, but is now a conventional element of fiction, with its own unwritten rules and its ever new variations. Meanwhile, some of the parts of speech that were once excluded from fiction have been put to creative use. In this chapter I give special attention to clichés and to swearing. Here too we might believe that a novelist is transposing into fiction the reflexes of actual speech. Yet here too we find elaborate stylization. Colloquialism is an impression that a writer must carefully create rather than a true record of what he or she often hears.

DIALECT

Gilbert, one of the narrators of Andrea Levy's *Small Island*, recalls how, as a Jamaican RAF recruit in wartime England, he heard children call out after him, 'It speaks, Mummy, it speaks' (165). The speech of a black man is the most surprising thing about him. In Levy's novel characters are preoccupied with how they and others speak. It seems to be one of the consequences of living on a 'small island'. In a Yorkshire village an elderly couple approach one of the West Indian RAF men and the woman asks, 'Would you mind saying something? Only my husband here says it's not English you're speaking' (138). 'Can you understand what I'm saying?' the English landlady Queenie absurdly keeps asking Hortense, who has newly arrived from Jamaica, as if different skin colour must imply linguistic incomprehension (231). 'You'll soon get used to our language.' All Hortense's articulacy will not shake Queenie's conviction that she needs a translator. In fact the West Indian characters, inculcated with antique respect for the Queen's English, pride themselves on their linguistic correctness. Arriving in wartime England, Gilbert's fellow Jamaican Lenval wants to know 'how so many white people come to speak so bad—low class and coarse as cane cutters' (140). Gilbert recalls how his mother's whispered commands to her eight children before attending the predominantly white Anglican church are all to do with polite speech. 'No cuss words, no blasphemy, no patois' (130). As a child Hortense is taught 'proper' English at school and solemnly tells her grandmother, Miss Jewel, who has brought her up, that she should improve on her rural Jamaican dialect. '"Miss Jewel," I told her, "you should learn to speak properly as the King of England does. Not in this rough country way"' (43).

Levy carefully differentiates speech habits. The Jamaican friends and relatives of Hortense and Gilbert tend to speak a more strongly marked dialect. Here is Gilbert's cousin Elwood, trying to persuade him not to return to England after the war. 'You stop run round to those fool-fool English—we gon' lick them. Nothin' gon' stop us now' (198). And here is Miss Jewel speaking in that 'rough country way': 'You nah need a likkle spell, me sprigadee. De Lawd haffe tek care a yuh' (62). Non-standard spellings mark this out as Jamaican dialect, though essentially distinguished from standard English only by pronunciation. You suspect that the real dialect of a poor Jamaican 'country woman' in the 1930s would have been more foreign than this. It is transparent compared to Emily Brontë's rendering of Yorkshire dialect in the speech of the servant Joseph in *Wuthering Heights* (1847). Here are his first words in the book, in an exchange with Mr Lockwood: '"What are ye for?" he shouted. "T'maister's dahn i' t' fowld. Goa rahnd by th'end ut' laith, if you went tuh spake tull him"' (ch. 2, p. 7). Though her sister Charlotte thought Joseph's speech 'exactly renders the Yorkshire dialect', she felt it necessary, when editing the novel after Emily's death, to bring it closer to standard English. 'I am sure Southerns must find it unintelligible.'[2]

Before the nineteenth century, novelists had little interest in dialect speakers, except to mark them off as comically foolish. It was Sir Walter Scott who began to give dialect—in his case Scottish dialect—to characters who might be intelligent or even noble. Here is the first character to speak in his novel *Old Mortality* (1816), set in the late seventeenth century. She is the mother of the ploughman in a 'wild district' of Lanarkshire, explaining why her son is not present for the landholder's muster of his men, a gathering regarded with great suspicion by local Calvinists: '"whether it were the colic, or a qualm of conscience, she couldna tak upon her to decide, but sure it was, Cuddie had been in sair straits a'night, and she couldna say he was muckle better this morning. The finger of Heaven," she said, "was in it, and her bairn should gang on nae sic errands"' (75). There is comedy in this, but not absurdity. In this novel, as in others by Scott, educated characters speak with only occasional marks of Scottishness ('Ay' for 'yes', for instance), while other characters have dialect speech patterns that would have challenged many genteel English readers. Scott made dialect an interest of novelists; for some Victorian writers the interest became almost scientific. Elizabeth Gaskell's use of Manchester dialect was spurred by the researches of her husband, William Gaskell. She attached his *Two Lectures on the Lancashire Dialect* to the fifth edition of her first novel, *Mary Barton*, in 1854—evidence of the attention to truth of her representations of speech in that novel. Gaskell gave her characters a carefully moderated form of Manchester dialect. Here is John Barton talking about his wife's sister, Esther: 'Ay, she was a farrantly lass; more's the pity now . . . You see them Buckinghamshire people as comes to work here has quite a different look with them to us Manchester folk . . . I never seed two such pretty women for sisters; never. Not but what beauty is a sad snare' (ch. 1, 6). Gaskell allows some grammatical deviations from middle-class English ('them people', 'I never seed') and one dialect word, 'farrantly', which she annotates with her own footnote ('comely, pleasant-looking'). This is the pattern throughout the novel, with dialect vocabulary used very sparingly.

Gaskell makes no attempt to catch the non-standard pronunciation of words. Most novelists interested in the patterns of dialect have not striven for authenticity like Emily Brontë, but have followed Gaskell's lead. Levy does this in the narratives of Hortense and Gilbert, which take on the characters' habits of speech. They are distinguished by small touches, like the use of *I* instead of *me*: 'it was left for I to tell him'. At moments of pressure, Hortense slips into a past tense without standard *-ed* endings: 'He smiled so sweetly I nearly pass out' (47). She also adopts a non-standard elaborateness of phrasing and diction: 'Would you perchance have a basin that I might get a use of?' she asks Queenie (228). (She and Gilbert both use *perchance*, having learned polite speech through Wordsworth and Shakespeare.) Distinctive speech habits are not necessarily distinctively informal.

Levy subtly gives touches to her characters' Jamaican English. Sometimes the speech and narrative of Queenie, her main non-Jamaican character, seems harder to believe. A butcher's daughter from Nottinghamshire who has spent her adult life in West London, the elocution lessons that she has had in her teens further confuse the sound of her voice. Her demotic omission of pronouns ('Turns out she'd been walking along the pavement'; 'Told me it wasn't her husband') and dated slang ('Blinking heck') make her use of words like 'motley', 'bemoaning', and 'errant' seem odd. Where would these have come from? Could an imaginable way of speaking include these elements? It is possible in life, but not quite convincing in a novel.

DIALOGUE

Fictional conversation is a literary skill rather than a hearing of voices. This is the point of an exchange in Muriel Spark's 2004 novel *The Finishing School*. Spark observes the jealousy felt by Rowland, a teacher of creative writing and failed novelist, towards Chris, his talented pupil. Chris has shown Rowland two chapters of his projected novel. 'On his second reading: "But this is quite good," Rowland had whispered, as if speechless with amazement' (9). The understatement is comically revealing; in his heart, Rowland expects anything written by his students to be contemptible. And what is it that most surprises him?

'The dialogue,' he said, 'how did you know about dialogue?'
'Oh, I've always read a lot.'
'Oh, you read a lot, I see.'

Dialogue, we infer, is the hardest thing for a beginner. The exchange practises what it teaches, capturing first Rowland's unguarded horror, and then the frightened blankness of his comprehension ('I see'). It also suggests, via Chris's mock-casual explanation, a tenet of Sparkean dialogue: it is an art, a matter of study. Reading, not listening, has taught Chris how to do dialogue.

We can see the artifice of novelistic dialogue most clearly where the talk is apparently least elaborate. In Graham Swift's *Last Orders*, the dialogue seems unstudied, as if overheard by the reader. Yet it has been arranged with great care. Though Swift's characters find words difficult and seem credibly inarticulate, there is never an 'um' or an 'er'. Their sentences do not lose their way or dwindle to nonsense. There is a kind of decorum even in the use of cliché. And hardly anyone ever swears. All of Swift's speakers are working-class and from South London; none is 'educated'. Yet though their dialogue is differentiated from middle-class English by small touches—the ubiquitous 'aint' for 'isn't', a sprinkling of double negatives like 'they didn't have no honeymoon' (29)—it is its clipped brevity that is distinctive. This might seem socially specific—these are not people who talk in a fancy way—but the dialogue is contrived for psychological effect rather than sociolinguistic accuracy.

Conversation has been stripped down to bare essentials: stoical, rudimentary, charged with things that cannot be said. Outside the hospital where Jack Dodds has died, his friend Ray sits with his widow, Amy. She holds a letter in which Jack has asked for his ashes to be scattered off Margate pier.

I say, 'You sure you wouldn't want to come?'
She shakes her head. 'Got my reasons, haven't I, Ray?'

> She looks at me.
>
> 'I suppose Jack had too,' I say, tapping the letter in her hand. I let my hand move up to give her arm a little squeeze.
>
> 'The seaside, eh Ray?' She looks again at the river. 'Yes, he had his reasons.' Then she clams up. (16)

Clamming up is a part of dialogue throughout the novel. Eventually we will find out about the 'reasons' referred to in this typically inexplicit exchange—complicated memories and resentments from a long marriage. We will discover the limitations that have been placed on what can be spoken, and discover that such limitations are always the point of dialogue in this novel.

Swift even makes his several narrators unforthcoming about just how words are spoken. The spareness of dialogue is an effect not only of terseness and condensed vocabulary, but also of the reticent 'reporting clauses', as linguists call them: 'He says . . .', 'I say . . .', 'He says . . .'. This is the typical rhythm of dialogue in Swift's novel.

> He says, 'You hear much from your Susie these days?'
>
> I say, 'Odd letter.'
>
> He says, 'You reckon she'd come, if you was—I mean, d'you think she'd show up?'
>
> Vic says, 'What a question.'
>
> Lenny says, 'It's a fair one.'
>
> I say, 'I aint thought about it.' But I have.
>
> Lenny says, 'It's a fair question.' (47)

Ray wonders whether his daughter would come to his funeral. Lenny, the 'stirrer', touches his loneliest fears. But not a single word directly represents any emotion to us.

Some novelists are keener to specify how words are spoken. D. H. Lawrence is a good example. In a couple of randomly selected but characteristic pages of dialogue from chapter vi of *Women in Love* (1920) one finds the words of the characters being 'protested', 'cried' (a frequent Lawrence usage), 'exclaimed', 'retorted', 'whispered', 'asseverated', 'stated', 'asked', 'persisted', 'commanded', 'jeered', 'replied rather superbly', 'said in contempt', 'said warningly' and 'squealed' (70–1). Lawrence tries to make each tone audible, as if turning up the volume of the talk. He pushes to extremes a traditional technique. In the nineteenth century it was taken for granted that a novelist should supply descriptions of how dialogue is spoken. A play might simply present the characters' lines, leaving all decisions about their delivery to actors and directors. Dialogue in a novel was not expected to be 'dramatic' in this way. Sir Walter Scott believed that dialogue must be 'mixed with the narration'. The novelist 'must not only tell what the characters actually said . . . but must also describe the tone, the look, the gesture, with which their speech was accompanied,—telling, in short, all which, in the drama, it becomes the province of the actor to express'.[3]

Last Orders refuses such specification, invariably declining even to provide the significant gestures that accompany speech. The most you usually get is 'I look at him', 'he looks at me', 'she looks away'. Even the spacing is telling. In early novels, like those of Henry Fielding, there was no convention of moving to a new paragraph for a new speaker. Dialogue was arranged in dense blocks, with each paragraph containing several voices, divided only by the opening and closing of inverted commas. The effect is, indeed, sometimes cacophonous. In Swift's novel, the very space at the end of lines carries implication. Here is Jack Dodds, dying in his hospital bed, mysteriously asking his hostile foster-son for money.

> He says, 'I want you to lend me some cash.'
> I say, 'Cash?'
> He says, 'Cash.'
> I say, 'You need cash?' (35)

We will find out that there is a whole family history behind this exchange but, as ever, nothing of what we need to know is in the words themselves. In such ordinary-sounding yet highly stylized dialogue, everything is in the gaps.

LANGUAGES

One of fiction's privileges is to make intelligible what in life would not be so. In her novel *Bel Canto*, Ann Patchett invents a cast of characters who all speak different languages, and for the most part cannot understand each other. Guests at a diplomatic party, now taken hostage by insurgents, they divide into small groups, each of which shares a tongue. Yet, as the narrative unwinds, they have to find ways of communicating with those to whom they cannot directly speak. So the strange thing is that, although all the printed dialogue is in English, English is hardly ever being spoken. We spend the whole novel inside the besieged residence. If we were really there, we would hear a babble of tongues. The most commonly spoken is Spanish (for we are somewhere in Latin America), but many of the guerrillas speak their own native language, while leading characters amongst the hostages are conversing in Japanese, German, French, Russian, or English. Some reviewers muttered that the novelist had merely found a means of bringing together various national stereotypes. Yet Patchett has done this so as to highlight the difficulties of making them comprehensible to each other. In reality one might have expected the diplomats to be better at languages: wouldn't the French and the Germans be fluent in English? But Patchett is determined to keep them to their own tongues. The Japanese comfort each other with the mere soft sound of their Japanese. The French ambassador and his wife, who had expected a better posting, joke together about 'ce pays maudit', translated for us, but no one else, as 'this godforsaken country' (36).

Sometimes a novelist will feel the need to register that he or she is 'translating'. The French characters in Dickens's *A Tale of Two Cities* may speak in English, but it is marked with traces of 'foreignness'. They use 'thee' and 'thou' and frame locutions that designedly sound un-English. The novel's first supposedly French sentence is 'Say, then, my Gaspard, what do you do there?' (ch. 5, 34). It is rather like the way that Germans in British war films used to speak to each other in English but with pseudo-German accents. Probably the first British novelist to experiment with 'translated' dialogue was Sir Walter Scott, who did it awkwardly. In *Ivanhoe* (1819), divided between Norman rulers and Anglo-Saxon 'inferior classes', there is a Monty Python quality about the heightened English of the French-speaking noblemen and the demotic Anglo-Saxon of the bumpkins. As an example of the former, here is Reginald Front-de-Bœuf, talking to a friar whom he suspects of sympathizing with the lower orders. 'Thou seest, Sir Friar, yon herd of Saxon swine, who have dared to environ this castle of Torquilstone. Tell them whatever thou hast a mind of the weakness of this fortalice, or aught else that can detain them before it for twenty-four hours. Meantime bear thou this scroll. But soft—canst read, Sir Priest?' (ch. 27, 221). This is most peculiar speech, by nineteenth-century standards as well as ours, but it is supposed somehow to suggest Norman French. The speech of 'the inferior classes' is quite as odd. '"The curse of St Withold upon these infernal porkers!" said the swineherd' (ch. 1, 13). But these are not his actual words, for Scott has just told us that to give this speech 'in the original'—Anglo-Saxon—would 'convey but little information to the modern reader, for whose benefit we beg to offer the following translation'.

In Scott's hands, the business of translation is sometimes inadvertently comic. So it often is in novels that wish to retain some sense of the foreignness of speech. The characters in George Eliot's *Romola* (1862–3) live in fifteenth-century Florence, but converse in the English of educated Victorians. Yet Eliot keeps wanting to remind us that this is a fiction: she has her characters sing in Italian and peppers their dialogue with exclamations like '*Va!*', '*Diavolo!*', and '*Che miraculo!*'—these marked off in italics from the 'translated' speech around them. In *The Moonstone*, Wilkie Collins has one of his main narrators, Gabriel Betteredge, casually tell us that he has changed the words of a character he quotes who is the wife of a local fisherman. 'I translate Mrs Yolland out of the Yorkshire language into the English language' (First Period, ch. xv, 125). Even the novel's wily detective, 'the all-accomplished Cuff', has trouble understanding her, so 'you will draw your own conclusions as to what *your* state of mind would be if I reported her in her native tongue.'

Patchett's novel avoids absurdity by offering the formal awkwardness of such translation as a virtue of her fiction. Her novel delights in the slowing-down of conversation, the simplest comments sometimes having to go through several languages. Gen, the character who is a professional translator, becomes the manager of exchanges that are always having to pause and dawdle. 'These were not men who were accustomed to waiting or speaking precisely' (114). But now they must. And the translator becomes the busy crystallizer of their sentiments. 'Every person in the room had a thought that was in need of translation' (172). Gestures and affections carry characters beyond their languages. Roxanne Coss, the diva whose performance was to have been the highlight of the party, sings the aria from Dvořák's *Rusalka* with matchless expressiveness, and only the translator realizes that 'this woman did not know a word of Czechoslovakian' (164). He himself falls in love while giving a language lesson to one of the would-be terrorists. 'They spoke of vowels and consonants. They spoke of diphthongs and possessives' (202). Reaching between languages becomes a special intimacy, for it is a way in which a person loses his certainties and assumptions. 'She wanted more of everything. More vocabulary, more verbs . . . She wanted gerunds and infinitives and participles' (209). What could be sexier?

TRANSLATION

Fiction may turn the speech of its characters into the language of its readers, but in the examples in the previous section at least the narrator was speaking in English. There are other novels, however, where we are to imagine the narration itself taking place in another language. Monica Ali's *Brick Lane* is one such, coming to us as if it were all a work of translation. We have to imagine that most of its characters are talking in Bengali, even though dialogue is presented to us in clear, standard English. The narrative consistently shares the perceptions of a protagonist, Nazneen, present in every scene, who initially knows no English at all. At the age of 19, she has been brought from her village in Bangladesh to East London for an arranged marriage. Everything is observed or heard by her, yet she only begins to learn English several years—and a couple of hundred pages—into the story. We are told her thoughts, yet she cannot be thinking in the words that Monica Ali uses for them.

The convention that everything is but a translation is one that seems easiest to accept with historical fiction—with John Banville's *Kepler* say, or Rose Tremain's *Music and Silence* (1999). The former is set in Central Europe in the early seventeenth century; the latter mostly in Denmark between 1629 and 1630. The former inhabits the thoughts of the great scientist and mathematician Johannes Kepler, a German speaker. The latter moves between the voices and the thoughts of various characters, most of them Danish, in the court of King Christian IV of Denmark. Both novels imagine worlds at such a distance in time from the contemporary reader that the use of modern English prose to represent German, in Banville's novel, or Danish, in Tremain's, is already a licensed liberty. The convention works smoothly in such cases because the reader can forget about it: neither novelist mentions that 'translation' is going on. *Brick Lane* does not allow such forgetting. It draws attention to the peculiarity of using one language to give access to another.

We cannot take the novel's English as some neutral medium, but are constantly reminded of it being a foreign tongue to the central character. You are made most aware of this at the borders between languages, where Bengali and English bump against each other. At first it is just the odd word, as when Nazneen hears her doctor's truculent, demanding daughter: 'She spoke in English. Nazneen caught the words *pub* and *money*' (111). The novel picks up the oddness of English phrases, suddenly entering another language. Eating a picnic with his family in St James's Park, Nazneen's husband, Chanu, comically tries out the true language of picnics. '"It's quite a spread," he said in English' (297). Hearing that a Bangladeshi teenager hangs around on the streets because his flat is full of his ten siblings, Chanu turns to what he fancies is a sociological vocabulary. '"Ah, it's *Overcrowding*," said Chanu dropping in the word in English. "*Overcrowding* is one of the worst problems in our community"' (330).

There are also disturbing collisions. Nazneen's daughter Shahana, born and educated in East London, speaks English at home against her father's stipulation—'his stupid rule' (193). '"*We* are not allowed to speak English in this house," said Shahana, transgressing at top volume.' When her father tries to introduce her to Bangaldeshi culture, she nettles him with the language of the country where she has been born. '"Bor-*ing*," sang Shahana, in English' (200). In a different collision of tongues, Nazneen's first conversation with Karim, the man who becomes her lover, takes place in clumsy alternations of Bengali and English (which is his first language). Ali's English prose must represent different characters' use of Bengali. Karim speaks urgently and self-confidently in English, usually about his hatred of Western values. When his speech stammers ('Y-y-yes, but t-t-too expensive') we know that he is trying to speak Bengali (211). When Nazneen's sister Hasina writes her letters from Bangladesh detailing her misadventures, they are phrased as in a broken, often incorrect English. 'Water coming through roof at home. Even it come through brick wall. When the plaster is finish then rain cannot come to the inside' (155). Yet this too is translation, intended to give the impression of Hasina's semi-literate written Bengali.

For years Nazneen picks up only scattered items of English vocabulary, but eventually her daughters teach her. 'Their method was simple: they demanded to be understood' (194). As she learns more English, we take in things around her that were inaccessible before. English is a language of weird official wisdom. It is also the language of cheek and obscenity. In the book's early chapters, the poor whites around her are beyond comprehension. Slowly, snatches of their conversations begin to enter the book and they seem even stranger, as when she overhears 'two white women discussing how to slim down their dogs' (206). Ali's interest in the collisions between languages also requires her to remind the reader that narrative itself is translation. This can be effective or problematic. Sometimes the narrative knowingly 'translates' a Bengali sentiment. When Nazneen's friend Razia 'sprawled over her chair in a manner unbecoming to a Bengali wife', we hear Nazneen's thoughts through those appropriately awkward English words ('a manner unbecoming') (127). At other times, the effect is uncertain. When Nazneen, in a 'reverie', gazes out of her flat at 'a coagulation of buildings', it is harder to believe that these are her words for what she sees (341). The awkwardness of words is one of Ali's chosen effects, a reminder that this is fiction-as-translation. Yet that awkwardness is itself awkward to manage.

PHONE CONVERSATION

Special conventions have evolved for the representation of phone conversations in novels. David Lodge has identified Evelyn Waugh as 'perhaps the first literary novelist to exploit this instrument on a significant scale to dramatise failures of communication, either deliberate or involuntary, between characters'.[4] In *The Art of Fiction* he piercingly analyses a phone conversation from *Vile Bodies* (1930), in which the characters reveals themselves in a dialogue 'presented without comment and even without speech tags'.[5] The omission of 'speech tags' (usually called *reporting clauses*) heightens the blank implicitness of speech. The technique has become common. Here is an example from Andrew O'Hagan's novel *Personality*, a snatch of phone conversation between the teenage celebrity Maria Tambini, in London, and her mother, who lives on the Hebridean island of Bute.

> 'You've only got one mother, and she knows how hard you've worked. Ignore them. D'you hear me, Maria? Those people are just doing a job. My God if I was down there I would take a strip off those people.'
>
> 'Never mind.'
>
> 'How do you think this makes me feel? Hundreds of miles away and there's nothing I can do. You never listen to me, I've said what people are like.'
>
> 'It's okay, mum.'
>
> 'I only want the best for you, Maria.' . . .
>
> 'That's the pips going.'
>
> 'What?'
>
> 'The pips. That's the money ran out.'
>
> 'Cheerio then.' (155–6)

The absence of reporting clauses mimics the distance between the speakers ('D'you hear me, Maria?'), the telephonic freeze on expression. Such dialogue is 'dramatic' in the sense that it is left entirely to the characters. They represent themselves to us.

Such conversation has become so conventional in novels that we hardly notice being admitted to an intimacy that is usually denied us. It is a jolt, I think, when Jonathan Coe's novel *The House of Sleep* (1997) gives us phone talk as we actually overhear it in life. Terry, a film reviewer, is staying in a clinic on the south coast and calls one of his employers.

> 'Hello, Stuart? It's Terry.'
>
> 'Not too bad. No ill-effects so far.'
>
> 'Listen—why haven't you asked me to write about the new Kingsley film? It's out on Friday.'
>
> 'Armstrong? What are you, out of your mind? He knows nothing about him. Nothing. He knows nothing about anything.'
>
> 'Of course I'm not on bloody holiday. I'm sitting down here in Arsehole-on-Sea with nothing to do all day, bored witless . . .' (60–1)

Only after a moment's confusion do we realise that we need to insert a silence after each passage of speech, while Terry listens to what someone is saying on the other end of the line. This is what we are used to from film and television: one side of a conversation whose other side we must infer (appropriate here because Coe wants to show Terry hustling his way in the world, without admitting any new character to the peculiarly enclosed world of his novel). Usually, in contrast, novels give us both sides of exchanges that are conventionally both intimate and distant.

Jonathan Franzen's *The Corrections* makes telling use of these conventions. The five disparate members of the Lambert family, scattered in various American cities, keep in touch by phone. The Lamberts are not good at communicating, and their not communicating is often clearest when one of them is on the phone. Franzen beautifully exploits the capacity of telephone dialogue to reveal misunderstanding, to focus incomprehension. There is a small, subtle example late in the novel, when Gary phones his mother, Enid, to tell her that, though he will be coming to the much anticipated Christmas get-together, he will not be bringing his son and the favourite grandchild, 8-year-old Jonah, who has a fever.

> 'See how he feels in the morning,' she said. 'Kids get twenty-four hour bugs, I bet he'll be fine. He can rest on the plane if he needs to. He can go to bed early and sleep late on Tuesday!'
>
> 'Mother.'

> 'If he's really sick, Gary, I understand, he can't come. But if he gets over his fever—'
>
> 'Believe me, we're all disappointed. Especially Jonah.'
>
> 'No need to make any decision right this minute. Tomorrow is a completely new day.'
>
> 'I'm warning you it will probably be just me.'
>
> 'Well, but, Gary, things could look very, very different in the morning. Why don't you wait and make your decision then, and surprise me. I bet everything's going to work out fine!' (542–3)

The phone makes Enid's characteristic self-delusion possible, as if the bad news in this call presages a lovely 'surprise' in the next call. Put the phone down, pick it up another day, everything is different. Meanwhile, you can sense something awkward in Gary's phone manner: 'Some bad news here . . . Believe me, we're all disappointed.' Soon we find out that Jonah is not 'really sick' at all, just manipulated by his mother (who resents all inclinations to gratify her in-laws) into staying behind with a new video game. In miniature, the dialogue enacts all that comes between Gary and his mother.

Earlier in the novel, there is a superb comic set-piece where Enid rings to try to pressure Gary into bringing his family for Christmas. It is a version of what most readers will recognize: the 'conversation' that takes place against the descant of domestic life. At Gary's end of the line, his sons talk loudly or ask him distracting questions, while his wife, Caroline, mimes her refusal to cooperate. Enid's dialogue with her eldest son—she, wheedling and aggressively pathetic; he, guilty and falsely reasonable—keeps being interrupted by his negotiations with his wife and sons (often requiring the primitive hand-over-receiver tactic). His mother wants him to bring his family 'for one last Christmas'.

> 'Hang on a second,' Gary said. 'I'll check with Caroline.'
>
> 'Gary, you've had *months* to discuss this. I'm not going to sit here and wait while you—'
>
> 'One second.'

> He blocked the perforations in the phone's mouthpiece with his thumb and returned to the kitchen, where Jonah was standing on a chair with a package of Oreos. Caroline, still slumped at the table, was breathing shallowly. 'I did something terrible,' she said, 'when I ran to catch the phone.' (165)

A cordless phone makes communication even more troubled. The phone can be taken into the press of any family dispute. As Gary carries the instrument into his kitchen, his son is stealing biscuits and his wife claiming (untruthfully) that she has injured herself in running to answer the phone. Enid has upset everybody just by ringing. The phone is ever peremptory, and Franzen exploits its capacity to insist on ill-timed family 'communication'. As Gary argues with Caroline about going to stay with his parents he must block out Enid at the other end of the line. 'Gary could feel the buzzing of his mother's voice against his thumb' (166).

Another time, Gary phones his sister Denise just as her female lover, Robin, is discovering her husband, Brian, in Denise's bed.

> 'Gary, hang on one second.'
> 'What's going on?'
> 'Let me call you right back.' (496)

Family members try to talk to each other with never an idea of the emotional chaos of each other's lives. Often phone conversation is talk being forced when something else should really be happening. The hopeless Chip, brother of Gary and Denise, has drug-fuelled sex with a student while she chats on the phone with her mother, gleefully conflating daughterly platitudes with encouraging messages to her lover. '"Uh-huh ... Uh-huh ... Sure, sure ... No, that's hard, Mom ... No, you're right, that is hard ... Sure ... Sure ... Uh-huh ... Sure ... That's really, really hard," she said, with a twinkle in her voice' (65).

Novelists keep rediscovering how phone conversation brings

people together just so that they can discover their distance apart. The phone conversation, we might say, is almost as old as the modern novel, for an early example can be found in *The Guermantes Way* (*Le Côté de Guermantes*; 1920–1), the third part of Proust's *A la recherche du temps perdu*. The narrator recalls waiting at the local post office for a pre-arranged phone call from his grandmother, for 'The telephone was not yet at that date as commonly in use as it is to-day' (vol. ii, ch. 1, 133). This sends him into a reverie about phone conversations.

> How often have I been unable to listen without anguish, as though, confronted by the impossibility of seeing, except after long hours of travel, the woman whose voice was so close to my ear, I felt more clearly the illusoriness in the appearance of the most tender proximity, and at what a distance we may be from the persons we love at the moment when it seems that we have only to stretch out our hands to seize and hold them. (135)

For Proust, a phone conversation can be 'a premonition also of an eternal separation'. In *The Corrections* too, though with brutal comedy, telephonic proximity is all about separation—all illusion or anguish.

CLICHÉS

A certain kind of novelist cannot afford to avoid clichés. Graham Swift's *Last Orders* is written in the voices of half a dozen characters, all of them elaborately involved in the events that they narrate. The novel expects us to imagine them as if they are speaking, though silently to themselves. They can be defensive or evasive or awkward, but they must seem unstudied. None of the characters should know that he or she is in a novel. We must not catch them sounding too original. Not only do we get clichés in the novel's dialogue, where we might expect them, we also get clichés in the narrative. 'I've heard it a hundred times before.' 'You've got another think coming.' 'He was putty in my hands.' These are not fragments of speech. These are all from the narratives of Swift's leading characters, their interleaved monologues.

Such clichés are often knowing, carrying the speaker's awareness that he or she is resorting to a formula. Ray tells us how the break-up of his marriage happened after the death of his father-in-law and his daughter's emigration to Australia. 'Never rains but' (59). He abandons the saying halfway. He knows that we know the words—but then, as the cliché has it, we know the feeling too. No need to say more. Clichés in this novel are not thoughtless phrases; they are the regretfully or sardonically repeated truths of life. 'It aint much to write home about,' says Ray to himself and to us when he sees Margate pier, from where he must scatter Jack's ashes (281). It is a ruefully appropriate formula, for also passing through Ray's thoughts are all the unwritten or undelivered messages of his life: the postcard that did not reach his father before he died, the letters he never wrote to his daughter. He thinks of her in Australia and of what she must think about his failure to keep in touch. 'Out of sight, out of mind' (282). But she is not out of his mind. This hackneyed formula is just what was not the case. Perhaps Swift has learnt from American fiction, often confident in its use of cliché. The novel to which *Last Orders* owes most, William Faulkner's *As I Lay Dying* (1930), is one in a line of now classic American novels that convince by their colloquial rhythms, from Twain's *Huckleberry Finn* to Salinger's *The Catcher in the Rye*. Their imagined speakers of these works are full of reanimated clichés, testing limited vocabularies on the unlimited perplexities of life.

Several of its first reviewers praised *Last Orders* for its imagining of 'ordinary' people and 'ordinary' lives. But clichés are not just the novelist's short cut to ordinariness—to colloquialism or authenticity. Different speakers use them differently. Vince, the car salesman, gets into resentful muddles with his clichés. When life is difficult, he says, you've always got your car. 'If it hadn't been invented, we'd have had to invent it' (73). Vic, the undertaker, artfully bends his truisms. Visiting the memorial to the Navy dead at Chatham he thinks, 'Even on land we're all at sea' (125). He calls retirement 'taking your nose from the grindstone' (82). Professionally speaking, his clichés are morbidly humorous. Reflecting on the unexpected meetings that 'come with the territory', he says, 'You never know who you might bump into, you never know whose toes you might tread on' (215). Common phrases are often apt in a novel about what is most common: mortality, the impermanence of 'flesh and blood' (85). Characters are brought to know that their sharpest pains are indeed but common, and all the sharper for being ordinary. Not even love is as hedged by clichés—desperate or consoling—as death. Near its end, the novel sums this up with a joke about a cliché, a piece of wisdom that Jack remembers from his trade as a butcher. 'What you've got to understand is the nature of the goods. Which is perishable' (285). True enough.

SWEARING

When I discussed Mark Haddon's *The Curious Incident of the Dog in the Night-Time* in *The Guardian*, I expressed surprise at not having read complaints about the language of a book that was originally marketed as children's fiction and continues to be sold in an edition 'for younger readers'. For it is unsparing in its use of four-letter words. The very first piece of dialogue in the novel contains an obscenity. Mrs Shears, a neighbour of the narrator, Christopher, comes out of her house in pyjamas and housecoat to find him hugging her dead dog, Wellington. 'She was shouting, "What in fuck's name have you done to my dog?"' (4). Christopher is himself chaste in his language, but dutifully records the swearing of other characters. '"Let go of the dog," she shouted. "Let go of the fucking dog for Christ's sake."'

These adult exclamations are simply what the narrator hears, and we might think that 'younger readers' will also hear people swearing in the street, or in their homes. Yet I was wrong to think that the book's language was uncontroversial. By the novelist's own account, one reader—or parent of a reader—even recruited their MP to complain. Swearing in novels can still be a live issue.

For most of its history, the Novel—despite being the genre of everyday life—has been peculiarly decorous about its use of oaths and its avoidance of 'obscene' words. Characters in Chaucer's *Canterbury Tales* are allowed to use items of vocabulary that only crept into novels in the latter part of the twentieth century. As well as the religious oaths that are likely to have shocked fourteenth-century listeners ('a Goddes name!', 'pardee!', 'for Goddes bones!') we can find *queynte* ('cunt'), *fart*, and *pisse*, words that have only been admitted to fiction relatively recently. Now that what TV announcers call 'strong language' is common on television, it is odd to recall that, fifty years ago and less, novelists were required simply to avoid certain words. Kingsley Amis remembered his publisher Victor Gollancz advising him in 1955 to alter the sentence 'I feel sorry for that poor bugger', spoken by one of the characters in a final draft of his second novel, *That Uncertain Feeling* (1955).[6] With 'bugger', he would certainly lose all sales to the Boots Booklovers' Library. Amis readily agreed on 'bloody fool' instead.

It was the 1960s, Amis thought, that made swearing no longer a matter for awkwardness or self-censorship. 'I have forgotten when I first said or made a character say *fuck* in print, but no one seemed to notice or care, any more than they did when my son Martin used the word several dozen times in one page in a novel published in 1978.' The novel to which he refers is *Success* (1978); the reference is implicitly dismissive (especially as one of his own 'rules for swearwords' will be, 'Use them sparingly'). He might have in mind the opening to the third section of his son's novel.

> You'll have to excuse me for a moment.
>
> Mouth-fuck, bum-fuck, fist-fuck, prick-fuck. Ear-fuck, hair-fuck, nose-fuck, toe-fuck. It's all I think about when I'm in my room. Bed-fuck, floor-fuck, desk-fuck, sill-fuck, rug-fuck.
>
> And in the streets. Tarmac-fuck, lamppost-fuck . . . (52)

And so, absurdly, on. All the *fuck*s purport to give you the uncensored monomania of the narrator's thoughts, though really you know little of what he has been thinking about.

Kingsley Amis regretted that, since the 1960s, swearing has ceased to be invigorating. 'An entire way of being funny, an entire range of humorous effects, has been impoverished.' Without widespread resistance to the use of bad language, it ceases to be, from the novelist's point of view, such a creative resource. Amis's own first novel, *Lucky Jim*, published in 1954, is peculiarly creative in its use of bad language. It was written when what were usually called 'four-letter words' were excluded from respectable fiction, and their occasional appearances in the novel do have a special power. Amis's unheroic hero Jim Dixon has curses and expletives running through his thoughts, but they are often idiosyncratic, or playful-sounding. Even interior monologue somehow belongs to an idiom of the early 1950s, when the barriers against saying something unrestrainedly rude are strong. After yet another frustrating conversation with his Head of Department, Professor Welch, Dixon meekly thanks him 'for their chat'. 'Going down the stairs towards the Common Room' (this is literally *l'esprit de l'escalier*), he says what he really feels 'behind closed lips'.

> 'You *ig*norant clod, you *stu*pid old sod, you *ha*vering, *sla*vering get . . .' Here intervened a string of unmentionables, corresponding with an oom-pah sort of effect in the orchestra. 'You *wor*dy old *tur*dy old scum, you *gri*ping old *pi*ping old bum . . .' Dixon didn't mind the obscurity of the reference, in 'piping', to Welch's recorder; he knew what he meant. (87)

This is the interior tune of heartfelt insults, a kind of exorcism of resentment with which any reader could identify. There are some ordinary rude words there, but woven into an inventive and personal vernacular. The mention of 'unmentionables' is the novel's acknowledgement that not everything can be said.

Now that everything can be said, swearing, by Kingsley Amis's logic, should lose its expressiveness. Yet the swearing in *The Curious Incident of the Dog in the Night-Time* is entirely droll. Christopher cannot imagine censoring the dialogue that he transcribes. He has a form of autism that makes empathy impossible. Facts are all he knows and recording is his ambition as a narrator. Unable to comprehend others' emotions, he can at least be exact. 'I put the dog down on the lawn and moved back 2 metres.' In the same spirit, without comment or selectiveness, he tells us just what adults say. Much of the book's comedy is in the contrast between the factual blankness of his narration and the exasperation implicit in the four-letter words he hears. Often he is himself the unknowing source of this exasperation. Utterly truthful, indefatigably logical, Christopher drives even the calmest adults to the edges of their linguistic resources. 'Jesus', 'God', 'Bloody hell', they exclaim (though Christopher, not registering their feelings, puts in no exclamation marks). Novelists usually use swearing as a sign of authenticity: being true to the way people speak means not keeping bad language out. Comically, adults in Haddon's novel try not to swear but are driven to do so by Christopher's innocent, pedantic pursuit of truth. Sometimes they try hard, like his mother's lover, Mr Shears, when Christopher turns up at their London flat.

> And I said, 'I'm going to live with you because Father killed Wellington with a garden fork and I'm frightened of him.'
>
> And Mr Shears said, 'Jumping Jack Christ.'
>
> And Mother said, 'Roger, please.' (234–5)

Having banned Christopher from interrogating their neighbours (he wants to be a detective and find Wellington's killer), his father discovers that he has been questioning the old lady who lives opposite.

> Then he said, 'Holy fucking Jesus, Christopher. How stupid are you?'
>
> This is what Siobhan says is called a rhetorical question. It has a question mark at the end, but you are not meant to answer it. (102)

Christopher notes some logical quirks of language, but records swearing without comment or comprehension. He cannot hear his devoted, linguistically dishevelled father being driven to distraction.

> He stood in the middle of the kitchen and closed his eyes.
>
> Then he opened his eyes and he said, 'I need a fucking drink.'
>
> And he got himself a can of beer. (104)

Have obscenities ever been used more pointedly in a novel? Swearing tells us of the real world of emotions out there, within Christopher's hearing but beyond his ken. It is a world not of higher rationality, but of bungling and distraction. Expletives tell us (but not the narrator) of all the comic moments of adult hopelessness. Wonderfully descending from authority to panic is the policeman who finds Christopher, running away from home, on board the London train standing in Swindon station. Christopher hates being touched and starts screaming as the policeman tries to usher him off.

> 'Now listen, you little monkey. You can either do what I say, or I am going to have to make . . .'
>
> And then the train jiggled and it began to move.
>
> And then the policeman said, 'Shitting fuck.' (198)

When Christopher's father enters his bedroom to find that his son has discovered the letters from his mother that he has been hiding, only the most uninventive swearing can express his sense of the terrible mess he has made of things.

> And he said, 'What the fuck are you . . .? That's my cupboard,

> Christopher. Those are . . . Oh shit . . . Shit, shit, shit, shit, shit.'
>
> Then he said nothing for a while. (143)

This is the kind of speech that Christopher would never use, for it is the direct expression of feeling. Yet it also stands for the linguistic incompetence of all those normal adults, inadequate in all their different ways.

6
Structure

BOOKS of narratology often contain diagrams of the narratives they analyse. Though these do not convey the literary qualities of a work that make it memorable to any reader, they can be useful. They often display clearly how the telling of a story has been arranged by its author—how a given narrative might be thought of structurally. This does not only apply to novels. A diagram is a rather good way of showing how the narratives of, say, *The Odyssey* or *Paradise Lost*, with their elaborate patterns of retrospect and inset narration, are structured. These epic narratives begin *in medias res*, telling us only later what happened earlier. It is the Novel, especially where it imitates biography or autobiography, that establishes a habit of beginning at the beginning. It is the habit memorably mocked in the opening sentence of J. D. Salinger's *The Catcher in the Rye*.

> If you really want to hear about it, the first thing you'll probably want to know is where I was born, and what my lousy childhood was like, and how my parents were occupied and all that before they had me, and all that David Copperfield kind of crap, but I don't feel like going into it. (1)

David Copperfield begins 'with the beginning of my life', narrating his birth and looking back 'into the blank of my infancy' (ch. 2, 12). Salinger's narrator, Holden Caulfield, begins with a kind of literary blasphemy against one of the most memorable of all fictional accounts of childhood and its pains.

Yet even novels that do begin with 'that David Copperfield kind of crap', and proceed forward chronologically, can have elaborate structures. Henry Fielding's *Tom Jones* may follow its 'foundling' hero from birth, through childhood and youthful adventure, to manhood and marriage, but the very fabric of its three parts, divided into eighteen Books with their subsidiary chapters, makes visible on its Contents pages the preconceived arrangement of the 'history'. Fielding wants the reader to notice his comically providential arrangement of things. The headings to Fielding's books—'Containing the time of a year' or 'In which the history goes forward about twelve hours'—let us see how he has divided up his narrative to establish the significance of its events. Indeed the questions of structure considered in this chapter can, for the most part, be reduced to two considerations: sequence and division. In what order are we told things? How is one part of a narrative divided from another?

Most novels have chapter divisions of some kind. The reader can be strongly influenced by the headings that a novelist chooses to give to his or her chapters. Some novelists are austere in this regard, declining to signpost their narratives. Jane Austen and Henry James, for instance, never use chapter headings, as if to do so would be to interfere in their ironical methods. (Though James does label the different parts of *The Awkward Age* by the names of the characters on whom he focuses in turn.) Others make their headings the stuff of their narratives: the example of Carol Shields in *Unless* is discussed below. There have been cases of authors who have changed their minds about whether to use headings or not. When Elizabeth Gaskell's *Mary Barton* was first published in 1848, chapters were headed only by sometimes enigmatic verse mottoes. In later editions chapter titles were inserted. A studious modern reader can see the difference by comparing the Penguin (based on the first edition) and Oxford World's Classics (third edition) texts. To take a simple example, the new heading to chapter xviii of the novel, 'Murder', lets the reader know in advance that John Barton will indeed kill the factory owner's son, a mission given him by his desperate fellow workers. Such foreknowledge can, of course, either strengthen or weaken a narrative, but must influence our reading of it.

Some of the structural variations and tricks described in this chapter are traditional. The use of inset narratives or of revelations in recent fiction, for instance, can helpfully be referred to the same techniques in classic novels. Some patternings of narrative, however, are relatively new. Though novels of the eighteenth and nineteenth centuries dealt with chronology in some subtle ways, there is no doubt that contemporary fiction feels able to play some potentially alarming chronological tricks. What is interesting here is that it is not only an avowedly experimental novelist like Don DeLillo, studied on university courses no sooner than he is published, who takes these structural liberties. The reverse chronology of DeLillo's *Underworld* is peculiarly challenging, but bestsellers like Zadie Smith's *White Teeth* and Andrea Levy's *Small Island* also fit their stories to unusual chronological patterns. The patterns are sometimes contrived with such a sense of design that we hardly notice the traditional business of a novel: its working up to a conclusion. In several of the sections below—'Plot', 'Prolepsis', 'Metanarrative'—I explore how the structuring of a novel, however sophisticated, depends upon something that is hardly new: the curiosity of the reader about how the story might end.

CHAPTER HEADINGS

Was it Fanny Burney who invented thematic chapter titles? Earlier novelists like Fielding had already used chapter headings in teasing ways—'Containing Matters which will surprize the Reader', 'Containing little or nothing', and so on (these are both from *Tom Jones*). Such titles, paradoxically, make us feel more keenly the shaping presence of the author, carefully arranging the plot. Dickens was to pursue the tactic in his early fiction. When chapter xxxvi of *Oliver Twist* declares itself 'A very short one, and may appear of no great importance in its place. But it should be read notwithstanding, as a Sequel to the last, and a Key to one that will follow when its time arrives', there is an odd mixture of playfulness and earnestness. The chapter features Harry Maylie's departure for London and his request to Oliver to keep him informed about the well-being of his mother and her ward Rose. It will prepare us for the eventual marriage of Rose and Harry, so far impossible because of the social chasm between them. He is setting out to sever his connections with all those who will not smile on their union. The chapter heading seems an attempt to turn into humour what is a structural requirement of Dickens's plot.

Burney produced titles that more explicitly, and less facetiously, detected some otherwise invisible pattern in her narrative. Her second novel, *Cecilia* (1782), had abstract nouns as chapter titles: 'A Supplication', 'A Provocation', 'A Perplexity', 'An Admonition'. *Cecilia* is a novel about a woman in an interesting and unusual situation: as an heiress, she has to survive the circling fortune-hunters and distinguish the benevolent from the parasitic. The chapter headings provide an agenda of what a polite young woman has to endure for hundreds of pages of her courtship by unsuitable men, while she is in love with an unavailable one. In *Camilla* (1797), Burney used didactic-seeming headings: 'Modern Ideas of Duty', 'Modern Ideas of Life', 'Specimens of Taste', 'The Danger of Disguise'. The impression fits the story: Burney's supposedly flighty heroine is given as a potential lover a young man, Edgar Mandlebert who is a constant and priggish monitor of her conduct and has a clergyman father who is always ready with teachings (one chapter is accurately entitled 'A Sermon').

It is appropriate that Burney should have pioneered the technique, for she was arguably also the first major novelist offering minutely to observe women's lives. Her headings wryly purport to detect shape in those lives. Burney is busy finding implicit patterns not always discernible to the characters themselves. An inheritor of this authorial habit is Carol Shields—a modern observer of ordinary women—in her novel *Unless*. This is divided up into thirty-seven short chapters, each with a title that is some unremarkable conjunction or adverb or preposition: 'Hence', 'Hardly', 'Yet', 'Next'. These are the small, unobserved words that string stories together. The structure of the novel draws attention to them, as if letting you see life's unnoticed stitching. In the novel's final chapter—which wryly fends off too happy an ending by being called 'Not Yet'—Shields's narrator, Reta Winters, herself a novelist, calls them 'little chips of grammar' (313). They cement isolated events into a narrative. They also enable a sentence to go off in some new direction. 'Nevertheless', 'Yet', 'Instead': words that leave behind what was being said. The headings allow the narrator to wander (but only apparently wander) away from the desperate fact that would 'Otherwise' (another chapter heading) drive her to despair. The eldest of Reta's three daughters has dropped out of university and become a silent beggar, sitting on a Toronto pavement all day, sleeping in a hostel for vagrants at night. Her unintelligible withdrawal from her family, and seemingly from life itself, is constantly at the narrator's heart. The novel is Reta's story of herself around, beside, or apart from that fact. Much of the time she worries instead (as in 'Instead') about the novel she is writing, and about how to manipulate the fortunes of its characters. The novelist's concerns compensate for reality.

The chapter headings that Shields uses encourage the reader to work out a logic beyond or behind the unfolding of events. There are chapters where the significance of the small word at the head of the opening page is apparent. The chapter entitled 'So' begins with that very word, drawn out long in Reta's memory by one of her daughters. 'So-oo-oo?' (69). 'So' is a child's prelude to a question that embarrasses a parent. 'Why exactly is it that you and Daddy aren't married?' 'So' is an adult's would-be casual opening to a painful enquiry. 'So' is a way, as Reta says, of 'clearing a little space' so that a story can be told (74). 'So, where do we go from here?' A chapter in which the narrator anxiously thinks of the future is headed 'Toward'; one where dangerous and trivial accidents coincide is called 'As'. You can see the point. More often the headings puzzle you to fit them to the narrative. You have to work to see that 'Every' reveals how a family fits even disaster into a weekly routine; 'Whether' shows Reta hesitating over the fate of her invented characters (while powerless to influence the actions of her own daughter); 'Notwithstanding' reveals the almost comic continuity of married life (thus that slightly, fittingly pompous conjunction).

Shields's opening epigraph is from George Eliot (taken, though this is not stated, from *Middlemarch*):

> If we had a keen vision and feeling of all ordinary human life, it would be like hearing the grass grow and the squirrel's heart beat, and we should die of that roar which lies on the other side of silence.

Unless is drawn to the ordinary, and especially the ordinarily unobserved. Its structure obeys this impulse, asking us to follow the logic of life's small connectives—which also mean the small jumps of distraction and digression that make life bearable. One of them is the very title of the book, what Reta calls this 'worry word of the English language' (224). 'Unless—that's the little subjunctive mineral you carry along in your pocket crease.' 'Unless you're lucky', there is despair. 'Unless' novels can 'provide an alternative, hopeful course, they're just so much narrative crumble. Unless, unless.' 'Unless' stands for all the slight, vital connectives of an ordinary life, captured in fiction. And the chapter headings of Shields's novels must connect as well as divide its parts.

CHRONOLOGY

Novelists sometimes highlight chronology by using dated sections to structure the narrative. An obvious example is Zadie Smith's *White Teeth*, whose four sections have as headings both the names of their central characters and the years in which they are set. 'Archie 1974, 1945' is the first, featuring Archie Jones's failed suicide and then successful marriage in 1974, but also going back to his experiences in the Second World War. 'Samad 1984, 1857' is the next, focusing on Archie's friend Samad Iqbal and the life of his difficult family. Set in 1984 it looks back to the Indian Mutiny of 1857, sparked, Samad becomes convinced, by the actions of his own great-grandfather. Smith's dates highlight her novel's interest in spanning the last twenty-five years of the twentieth century. When the novel was being written, this span corresponded to the author's own lifetime. Such a narrative moves in jumps, crossing gaps of time between these dated sections (as well as looking back to episodes in the historical past). From each part we are given the information to infer what has happened to particular characters in the gaps between the dates, allowing the novel to take them through changing times.

Contemporary readers have become used to elaborate chronologies. Don DeLillo's *Underworld* is unusual in having a structure that keeps shifting the reader back in time. After its prologue—the famous baseball game that takes place on the day in 1951 on which the Soviet Union first explodes an atom bomb—the novel's six major sections are dated in a reverse chronological order: 'Spring–Summer 1992'; 'Mid-1980s–Early 1990s'; 'Spring 1978'; 'Summer 1974'; 'Selected Fragments Public and Private in the 1950s and 1960s'; 'Fall 1951–Summer 1952'. Finally, an epilogue returns us to a date later than the first section, some kind of unspecific 'present day' (the book was first published in 1997). The structure is complicated by the insertion between these dated parts of much shorter sections of narrative labelled 'Manx Martin', the name of the father of the boy who gets hold of the baseball hit for a home run in the famous baseball game that opens the novel.

The backwards-shifting narrative is unconventional and

audacious. The novelist makes sacrifices by following the pattern: he loses not just the uncertainty about outcomes that can give a narrative its impetus, but also the sense of characters developing, changing because of what happens to them. What he can achieve, however, is a certain unsettling of perspectives. In the last chapter of the 'Spring–Summer 1992' section, Nick, as a birthday present to his wife Marian, takes her on a balloon ride over the Arizona desert. Husband and wife—he in his fifties, she in her forties—are elated and affectionate. The chapter ends with the easy intimacy of their bedroom conversation. Yet in the next section, several chapters later but a few years earlier, Marian is in a borrowed apartment having sex with one of Nick's friends and business associates.

Her adultery is truly surprising, for the marital contentment we have just seen enacted seemed genuine. Now we know that Marian has cheated on Nick. In the next section, further on in the novel but further back in time, we witness Nick's own infidelity, and his confession of it to his wife. Later still in the novel, now back in the 1960s, we see Nick and Marian again, when they were first lovers, both uncertain if they will marry—or drift apart in search of other partners. Marriage has been built on, or over, all this. As the novel has gone on, what began as permanent has seemed more and more accidental. Narrating such personal histories in reverse generates dramatic irony. The reader knows what the characters cannot. In the 'Spring–Summer 1992' section, Nick tells of meeting Klara, a woman now in her seventies and a famous artist, with whom he had a brief, intense affair four decades earlier. They talk for a while of family and friends, their most important shared memories remaining tacit. Nick has a brief glimpse of their younger selves—a recollection of 'the younger woman's turned mouth', a once thrilling imperfection, her special 'erotic flaw' (75). And then the two go their different ways. Hundreds of pages later, but all those years earlier, we see, this time from her point of view, their original, hurried, passionate coupling. This is what it was once like, heedless of consequences; this is what the characters could not talk about.

Given later outcomes before earlier actions, we keep sensing how little foreseen by characters are their lives—how reliant on accident or arbitrary decision. Characters follow in uncertainty narrative paths that are already clear to the reader. There is something extraordinary and melancholy about this. The chronological shifts give a provisional quality to human choices. We are told that, as a teenager, Nick killed a man. Only at the end of the novel's last (but therefore earliest) section are we given that terrible, long-before moment of violence. Seeing how Nick has lived after this act—successfully, perhaps happily—makes it the more shocking. A normal chronology would plot consequences and reverberations; instead, the reverse chronology undoes the effects of forgetting and repression.

In matters of character and personal destiny, the chronological complexity is often intriguing. DeLillo himself does not always seem to recognize the potential of his own narrative method. Those critics who have found him a coldly brilliant writer, interested in ideas rather than people, have not acknowledged the subtle dramatic effects of his technically elaborate chronology in *Underworld.* Yet they still have a point. DeLillo is most interested in the historical utility of his narrative structure—not in human individuality but in the 'underground network' of a society. Looking backwards is his way of investigating America through its cold war. So instead of a plot there is an uncovering of causes and connections. (Or perhaps a demonstration of how characters must invent 'connections', a word used over and over again in *Underworld.*) The reverse chronology can make poignant or ironical our view of characters' strivings, but DeLillo has his eye on a bigger goal. Here is a novel concerned, in the end, not with time, as humanly experienced, but with *the times*, a topic for intellectual investigation. Characters have to take second place.

INSET NARRATIVES

Jonathan Coe's *The Rotters' Club* includes an interesting allusion to a habit once common in novels, but now rare. A guide to one of Coe's own narrative predilections is provided by his main character's enthusiasm for Henry Fielding (unusual reading material for a 16-year-old schoolboy). In his first-person account of a family holiday in Denmark, Benjamin Trotter recalls being gripped first by *Joseph Andrews* and then by *Tom Jones*. He hardly notices the dangerous quarrels taking place around him. Rolf, the German boy with whose parents the Trotters are staying, is involved in some dark feud with the Danish teenagers living next door. Benjamin, however, is buried in Fielding and oblivious to the violence in the air. When Rolf returns with Benjamin's brother Paul from an evidently traumatic bicycle trip to the sea, he is preoccupied. 'I was deeply immersed in the Story of the Man of the Hill, that curious, lengthy digression which seems to have nothing to do with the main narrative but is in fact its cornerstone' (127). He only finds out later that, in revenge for Rolf's anti-Semitism, the Danish boys, Jorgen and Stefan, have tried to drown him. He has been saved by Paul.

The reference to the tale that gripped Benjamin is to a story within the story—an inset narrative—in *Tom Jones*. As they wander through England, Tom and his companion Partridge meet a singular, misanthropic gentleman, who lives in solitude on a hill in Gloucestershire. Over the course of a night, and five chapters of the novel, he tells them his 'history' of disappointments and defeats. Setting out hopefully on life, he has been variously cheated, traduced, and betrayed. Affluent and able, he was befriended by a rich young rake at Oxford, a man who 'had a great delight in destroying and ruining the youth of inferior fortune, by drawing them into expenses which they could not afford so well as himself' (bk. VIII, ch. xi, 392). He fell in love with a woman who ruthlessly betrayed him. Alienated from his benevolent father, he tried to make his way in London, where he was seduced into gambling. Eventually he became a propertyless wanderer through Europe, where he found everywhere 'the same hypocrisy, the same fraud; in short, the same follies and vices, dressed in different habits' (ch. xv, 417). Disgusted at the world's knavery, he has become a recluse. The good-hearted Tom tries to persuade him of human goodness, but the Man on the Hill's 'history' has served as a cameo of human 'baseness'.

The Fielding allusion comes within Coe's own inset narrative. An opening section of his novel has introduced us to a group of Birmingham teenagers, and their families, in the 1970s, and has ended with the death of Lois Trotter's boyfriend in one of the IRA pub bombings of 1974. Now we are suddenly plunged into a first-person narration concerning events two years later. Benjamin tells us how Rolf was bullied by the Danish boys, and how their grandmother eventually offered the explanation. This is a story within the inset narrative. Jorgen and Stefan are half-Jewish; their mother, Inger, fled Denmark in 1943 but her Jewish fiancé was arrested by a German officer who was her admirer. He perished in the Holocaust and Inger never recovered. Eventually, years later, she killed herself. Her sons, by the husband she met after the war, are exacting vengeance for her torment. Within this notionally comic novel, the inset narrative is a splinter of something different. It becomes darker still when Rolf, who has heard the grandmother's tale, turns on Jorgen and Stefan, who are mocking his mother's incompetent driving, to say 'an appalling thing': 'Well, at least my mother isn't a filthy Jew, like yours was' (126). There is a terrible scene, tears, apologies, apparent reconciliation. But a few days later the Danish boys try to kill the German.

This inset narrative is included by awkward means. At its end we are told it is an unpublished story 'found among Benjamin Trotter's papers by his niece, Sophie, in 2002' (129). Inset narratives invariably have this artificial aspect. In the past we would be supposed to be listening to a character telling his or her tale, as in *Tom Jones*. Tobias Smollett's *Adventures of Peregrine Pickle* (1751) included the entertainingly scandalous 'Memoirs of a Lady of Quality' by having the hero encounter a lady in a stage coach who then told her story. Such insertions run counter to our expectations that a novel have a formal unity. They are remnants of pre-novelistic prose fiction, where—as in Cervantes' *Don Quixote*—any overarching narrative contains a miscellany of individual stories. The habit lingered on into the nineteenth century and is alive in early Dickens. His first sustained work of fiction, *The Pickwick Papers* (1836–7), shows us how it will proceed by ending what was its first instalment with the preamble to an inset narrative that begins its second. In a roadside inn Mr Pickwick and his friends have met a 'dismal man' who duly tells them a story (ch. 3, 32), 'The Stroller's Tale'. This grim vignette, the dismal man's eyewitness account of the harrowing death of an alcoholic former clown, is but the first of series of inset narratives, usually told by characters Pickwick meets on the road. As here, they often introduce to this buoyantly comic novel material that is incongruously unsettling or even gruesome.

What about Jonathan Coe's inset narrative? Why is it there? It is not randomly included, but designed to have consequences: in the novel's sequel, *The Closed Circle* (2004), Rolf reappears as a wealthy but glum adult, apparently cursed by that teenage 'indiscretion'. He is one of the BMW managers who take over the car factory in which some of the characters in the earlier novel worked. But this point of future plotting lies outside *The Rotters' Club* itself. While we are reading it, the inset narrative seems more like the novelist's way of introducing to his tale of adolescent follies and pleasures a kind of descant. This is, as in *The Pickwick Papers*, incongruous material. Fielding's *Tom Jones* featured an infallibly good-hearted hero, but his inset narrative told of the bitterness into which an intelligent person might be forced by the world's vices. Similarly, *The Rotters' Club* tolerantly chronicles the earnest frolics of youth, but his inset narrative tells you of the fear and loathing that youth can incubate.

PARALLEL NARRATIVES

Novels with several narrative strands are common enough, but only rarely are these strands completely separated by time. The children's writer Alan Garner used such parallel narratives in his experimental and mystical *Red Shift* (1973), a novel usually categorized as 'teenage fiction', though its structure is more demanding than most 'adult' novels. It takes place in three different narrative times: the present day, some time during the Roman occupation of Britain, and the time of the Civil War. The novel has no chapters, and the parallel narratives are separated only by white spaces on the page. What they have in common is location, a particular hill in Cheshire. Indeed, novels with parallel narratives often use location to hold them together. Peter Ackroyd does so in both *Hawksmoor* and *The House of Mr Dee* (1993). A more recent example is *The Dream of Scipio* by the writer of historical mysteries, Iain Pears. Set in Provence, this has three interleaved narratives in three different times (the fifth, fourteenth, and twentieth centuries). 'Mystery' is quite often what such novels are after in keeping their narratives discrete, providing satisfaction by bringing them together only at the end.

Michael Cunningham's *The Hours* tells three stories of the events of three particular days, held apart by time. They are held together by the book from which Cunningham's novel derives, Virginia Woolf's novel *Mrs Dalloway*. In New York at 'the end of the twentieth century' Clarissa Vaughan, a writer, prepares a party for a dying friend (9). In Los Angeles in 1949 Laura Brown, a mother pregnant with her second child, suffers from anomie and solaces herself with snatches of *Mrs Dalloway*. In Richmond in 1923 Virginia Woolf tries to write this very novel. Woolf talks to her husband, she has tea with her sister, she fights back the despair that afflicts her. The sections of the three narratives alternate, inviting the reader not only to make connections between them, but to sense the characters' separateness. It is a method suited to narratives of isolation. The women after whom Cunningham names each of his three strands are caught up in their intensely private thoughts. Both the self-doubt and self-vaunting passion of Cunningham's 'Mrs Woolf' have to be kept from her husband. 'Mrs Brown', the Los Angeles housewife, dreams of non-being, of suicide, but tells no one of this. 'Mrs Dalloway', Clarissa's nickname, keeps to herself the sharp pleasures she takes from life even while her dearest friend is dying. All imitate Woolf's Clarissa Dalloway, whose isolation—from husband, daughter, former lover—is delighted as well as melancholy.

Such parallel narratives show that coherence is to be grasped by the reader alone. We follow the thoughts of Woolf, as imagined by Cunningham, while she ponders her new work, sometimes while she 'feels powerful' as a writer (69), sometimes as she becomes certain that it 'will prove arid and weak, devoid of true feeling; a dead end' (163). The rhythms and phrases of Woolf's novel-to-be reappear in Cunningham's other two stories. Yet she cannot imagine the echoes of her inventions spreading down the years. She cannot know those parallel narratives, in which her fiction is reanimated beyond her own death. In *The Hours* there is the pleasure of seeing this happen in a process of transplantation. Where stranger to take Woolf's restrained, fey English characters and her politely whimsical cadences than Los Angeles and New York? In the heads of readers whom she can never know, Woolf's sentences renew their life. There is both sparkle and sadness here. In suburban Los Angeles Laura Brown finds that Woolf's novel imparts some kind of poetry to what is ordinary. In the present, with death all around her, Clarissa Vaughan, like Clarissa Dalloway, finds unexpected delight in the weather in the streets, the oddness and noisy accident of city life.

Cunningham's novel does likewise, though, as in Woolf's original, delight is alongside death. Richard, Clarissa's AIDS-stricken friend, kills himself in front of her. His aged mother comes to New York for the funeral and stays with Clarissa. This woman is none other than Laura Brown, the same person who was grasping at Woolf's vivifying sentences in 1940s California. It is a plot contrivance, but a fitting one. The narratives have been held together by those constant references to *Mrs Dalloway*, a novel that looks back to the First World War and that is shadowed by deaths, including the suicide of Septimus Smith. Cunningham has Laura wonder at Woolf's own suicide, given the love of the momentary in *Mrs Dalloway*: 'life; London; this moment in June' (4). In parallel, the narratives in *The Hours* borrow a little of Woolf's energy of life against death.

PLOT

Does every novel have a plot? Colloquially the word 'plot' is often used as if it were synonymous with 'story' or 'narrative', as if it were the substance of any novel. Yet not all novels require us to uncover some hidden design. Some novels are not much interested in plot at all. 'I have never troubled myself much about the construction of plots,' confessed Anthony Trollope, with no appearance of guilt.[1] Some novelists have suspected that plot is inherently unrealistic, unlifelike. Others, meanwhile, are enjoyed especially for their plots. A good example is John le Carré. All his novels involve the uncovering of secrets, the investigation of a mystery or a puzzle. His protagonists, therefore, as well as his readers, are required to connect disconnected events. In any one of his cold war novels, the plot, we might say, has been hatched by Soviet spymasters. We are invited to read for this plot.

It is useful to distinguish between *plot*, *narrative*, and *story*. We can think of a novel's *story* as the material of its events and characters—what happens in it. Take the example of le Carré's

The Constant Gardener. It is the story of a minor diplomat, Justin Quayle, whose young, idealistic wife is murdered because of her investigations into pharmaceutical experiments on Africans, which have been sponsored by powerful commercial interests. The bereaved husband tries to track down those responsible. He is thus drawn into his wife's investigations and discovers what she was trying to expose. The *narrative* is the way that this story is told. Describing the narrative of *The Constant Gardener* involves explaining that Tessa, Justin's wife, is dead on the novel's first page, and that everything we see or hear of her, including passages of quoted dialogue, is given in flashback in the thoughts of other characters. The same story might be narrated in different ways. Le Carré might have chosen to begin with Tessa and Justin's first meeting (this episode is narrated later, in wistful retrospect). He might have made Justin the narrator. He might have had a different first-person narrator. And so on. *Plot* is something else again. We sometimes talk of a plot being 'unravelled', for it is the causal chain that connects events and characters. We discover the plot as we read, so the plot-driven author must conceal connections as well as eventually reveal them. A plot has clues or hints in one part of the narrative, suggesting that something will be explained in another part. If plot is paramount, a novelist must foresee the end before finalizing the beginning. (If we look at Dickens's surviving chapter plans for the monthly parts of his novels, we can illuminatingly see this business of foreseeing at work in the mind of a plot-driven novelist.)

Initially, in *The Constant Gardener*, we know there is a plot because Woodrow, a British diplomat in Nairobi, does. The news of Tessa Quayle's murder makes him remember visiting her in hospital and seeing a mysterious man in a white coat, arguing with Bluhm, her fellow campaigner against the depredations of the giant pharmaceutical companies. Woodrow cannot forget him. 'His eyes, round with hurt, are haunted by a horror that both men seem to share' (86). Woodrow, a man who prefers the quiet life, knows that something wrong is going on in that hospital. Later, when Quayle is being interrogated by the British police officers investigating the murder, he too mentions white-coated attendants, but withholds something. 'With three golden bees embroidered on the pocket of each coat, he might have added, but his resolve held him back' (174). If he does not tell them, we know it must be important. The ThreeBees company is ubiquitous, its products oddly noticed in passing. When the British police officers questioning Woodrow about Tessa's murder ask him about the company because one of them 'wanted to watch your face while I talked about them', we must sense that there is a plot beneath (127). The ThreeBees logo keeps cropping up in the narrative, the signal of a buried conspiracy. Justin, leaving Africa determined to find his wife's killers, is stopped in his tracks at the airport by a ThreeBees poster, its large, thick lettering replicated in le Carré's text.

> The poster held him.
>
> Exactly as it had held Tessa. (148)

We should know from these emphatic, unnecessary paragraphs that we are seeing the outlines of a plot. Sure enough, we will find that Tessa was investigating this company's lethal drug-testing, and that her discoveries got her killed.

In le Carré novels, the characters themselves sense plots (paranoia is a wise state of mind in his fiction). Quayle's pursuit of the truth takes him, and the reader, from Kenya to London to Italy to Switzerland to Canada and back to Kenya, tracking down each witness, interviewing each guilty character. While beating the path of this plot, the intriguing patterns of causation are discovered in what the operatives of le Carré's cold war novels called 'tradecraft': how Quayle discerns pursuers, how he conveys messages without detection, how he works out who has betrayed him. In all these the reader is his collaborator. There are also disappointments about the plot that are a consequence of le Carré's own convictions about the behaviour of multinationals. In his spy novels, elaborate plotting was made possible by moral and psychological complexity. Motives were mixed, individuals were compromised, it was not easy to see right and wrong. *The Constant Gardener*, in contrast, has a campaigning, polemical energy that simplifies its larger plot. From very early on, the author can allow no doubt about what has happened. He cannot find it in himself to hide things. Only at the novel's end, where we are unexpectedly made to share the helplessness of one individual up against a huge drug company, is there a pre-arranged twist. It makes you realize that, through most of the novel, the novelist would rather his plot be inevitable than surprising.

REVELATIONS

Few novels are complete without revelations. These are the moments when the surface of things suddenly changes its meaning, when what we have already read shifts its significance. Revelations can be satisfying or irritating—narrative fulfilment or narrative trickery. When, near the end of Fielding's *Tom Jones*, the hero is revealed to be the illegitimate son of Squire Allworthy's sister Bridget, there is an aspect of trickery. The rash but good-hearted Jones, unjustly disowned by Allworthy earlier in the novel, must be rewarded for his virtues. As at the end of many a novel, he must get an appropriate inheritance, as well as the hand of the woman he loves. The foundling—*The History of Tom Jones, A Foundling* was Fielding's original title—becomes a propertied gentleman. Yet the revelation is fulfilment too. It allows the reader to recognize clues that have been artfully scattered through the novel. From the moment that the normally uncharitable Miss Bridget advocates that the bastard left at the Allworthys' door should be taken into the family, there is puzzling behaviour that only the final revelation explains. Now we understand why Blifil, Bridget's legitimate son, has been so determined to destroy

Jones (and we recognize exactly the moment earlier in the novel when Blifil discovered the facts that are now openly declared). However improbable, the revelation is fair: the truth that is uncovered has been encoded into the novel.

Except in narratives written in letters or diaries (*Clarissa*, say, or *Dracula*, 1897) a narrator must already know all that he or she unfolds to us. Fielding has made the withholding of vital information into a game between himself and the reader, but also a part of the novel's plot. Blifil acts to try to keep the information secret; the revelation is his come-uppance. Comparably, in first-person narratives, revelations are only possible if narrators have kept things back from us. Logically speaking, as he begins his story, Pip, the narrator of Dickens's *Great Expectations*, already knows that the convict Magwitch will be revealed as his own benefactor and the father of Estella, the woman he comes to love. The plot relies on his withholding this knowledge from us until just the right moment. Yet we do not feel cheated, because Dickens has carefully allowed his narrator's ruefulness, his sense of his own ignorance, to seep into the narration. Surprises are sprung on us, but the withholding of information lets us see how Pip himself was also surprised. A stranger case is Charlotte Brontë's *Villette*. Here the narrator, Lucy Snowe, reveals that 'Dr John', the physician employed by the Belgian girls' school where she teaches, is in fact Graham Bretton, the son of her godmother and a friend from her childhood. (He has not recognized her.) When she reveals the fact, Lucy also tells us that she knew his identity at a much earlier point in her narrative than she chose to say. 'The discovery was not of to-day, its dawn had penetrated my perceptions long since' (ch. xvi, 219). She has kept her knowledge from us, as she kept it from him; the revelation is manufactured, though true to the secretive, suspicious character of Brontë's narrator.

Carefully managed revelations work backwards to reshape the narrative that has gone before. A good example is Graham Swift's *Last Orders*. The four men who set off in Vince's leather-upholstered Mercedes to scatter Jack's ashes know plenty about each other. We do not. In the course of the novel we discover hidden facts, matters of history that shape their exchanges. Why is there something needling, for instance, in Lenny's habit of calling Vince 'Big Boy'? In one of Lenny's interior monologues we find that Vince got his daughter pregnant and then dumped her. Twenty years of resentment lie behind his each little gibe. Swift manages the revelations of his novel by making his reader feel like an outsider, allowed to glimpse knowledge that his characters share. Taciturnity and jokey evasion govern their dialogue. Revelations are necessary to explain its emotional voltage. Ray's friends prod him for his feelings about his daughter, who has emigrated to Australia. Late in the novel we discover that in twenty-five years he has not told her of his separation from her mother. 'I'm a small man but I've got my pride' (281). Even confessing to the reader seems to go against the grain.

The most important fact withheld from us is that Ray, the central character, has had an affair with Amy, Jack's wife. At the beginning of the book we have seen Ray and Amy alone together, through Ray's narration, with no mention of this history. He tells us, 'I let my hand move up to give her arm a little squeeze' (16), but only much later will this intimacy take on a special meaning. More than halfway through the novel, he recalls how, over twenty years earlier, he and Amy had weekly trysts in his camper van, when she was supposed to be visiting her brain-damaged daughter in her 'home'. Now the duty that he is performing for his dead friend Jack, scattering his ashes, suddenly changes its meaning. We have to adjust to what Ray knew all the time. And it turns out others have known too. Later we discover that Vic, the undertaker, another in the party to Margate, found out about Ray's affair with Amy. He saw them together once on one of his outings to collect a body. 'You shouldn't judge. What you learn in this business is to keep a secret' he says, to no one except us (219). Meanwhile, Lenny, the 'stirrer', keeps hinting that he suspects something. 'Seems I'm the only one here who aint in the know' (30).

By the end of the novel, Ray has become convinced that Jack himself had long lived with the knowledge. On his deathbed he revealed to Ray his debts, hidden from his wife, and asked him to pay them off. It is 'like a blessing' on the relationship between Ray and Amy (283). 'But *he* knew all along. That's the long and short of it.' It seems Jack, a man who kept everything to himself, was the person who knew everything. A dead man, living on in each character's recollections, reaches back and prompts each reluctant revelation.

SPLIT NARRATIVES

Reviewers of the 2002 film *Ripley's Game*, adapted from the novel by Patricia Highsmith, complained that, while they were allowed to relish the antics of John Malkovich's Ripley, they were given little understanding of Dougray Scott's Trevanny, the ordinary man whom Ripley leads into murder. Here the film could not match the logic of Highsmith's novel, which requires us to believe that, in special circumstances, a good man might be made into a killer. The novelist makes this credible in a manner that a film could not imitate, by splitting her narrative between Ripley and Trevanny. The novel is consistently narrated in the third person, but we are always in the head of one of the two men; the narrative is divided between the corrupter and the corrupted. There is a symmetry between them. Both are connoisseurs of art, though Ripley is a collector and an arranger of forgeries, while Trevanny ekes out a living as a picture framer. Both are foreigners in France (Highsmith's own adopted home): Ripley is American, Trevanny English. As outsiders they are both more susceptible to the temptations of crime, as if neither is properly rooted in the respectability of the provincial French society. Both have attractive, distant French wives. Trevanny's wife is so principled and religious that he can confess nothing to her; Ripley's is so blithely unprincipled that she wants to know nothing.

The novel's narrative structure follows this symmetry. The book's opening behaves as though it will be like the two previous Ripley novels: *The Talented Mr Ripley* and *Ripley Under Ground* (1970). We are seeing things through Ripley's eyes. The earlier novels were notorious for inviting an intimacy that felt close to complicity with Highsmith's resourceful, amoral antihero. In this third Ripley novel we seem to be going the same way. So easily are we taken into his mind in the first chapter that we end by being told exactly his thoughts as he lies in bed at night. He has had an idea. He is planning to recruit Trevanny as an assassin. Then, at the beginning of the second chapter, something odd happens. It is ten days later, and Jonathan Trevanny has just received a letter from a friend implying that his rare blood disease is worse than previously thought. 'What was Alan talking about?' (13). This is no narrator's question; it is what Jonathan himself wonders (we now shift from calling him by his surname to using his Christian name). We have moved from Tom's plans to the thoughts of his victim. The move is the more marked as we surmise that the letter is somehow Ripley's doing. He is the cause of the anxieties that ripple through Trevanny's mind and through the narrative. 'Had his doctor, Dr Perrier, said something to his *friends*, something he wouldn't tell him? Something about not living much longer?' The novel will continue to record Jonathan's lonely awareness of his approaching death. His fatalism is what most makes him persuadable to murder.

At first, chapters alternate between the points of view of the two men. Then Ripley disappears and we have only the narration of Jonathan's experiences and thoughts. Ripley has set events in terrible motion, though Jonathan does not know this. Manipulated by Ripley's criminal friend Reeves, who offers him a large payment that he can leave to his wife and son after his death, he shoots a Mafia hood. When we return to Ripley, it is for the first meeting of Highsmith's dual protagonists, more than a third of the way through the novel. Crucially, for this first encounter we see things through Ripley's eyes, as the two men have a drink together. Our sympathy with the anti-hero predominates. 'Trevanny wanted to ask him something, Tom felt. What?' (95). In this scene, we know no more than Ripley. When the men next meet, Highsmith plays the trick in reverse. We are with Jonathan on the Munich to Paris express as he prepares nervously to attempt his second assassination, the garrotting of another Mafia man. Just as he is thinking that the task is impossible, he sees a figure walking down the corridor of the swaying train. 'Then he blinked. The man coming towards him was Tom Ripley' (110). The surprise is the reader's as well as Jonathan's. Unknown to us, Ripley has decided to help out the man who has been his dupe. As they do the killing together, Highsmith moves back and forward between their points of view. 'Tom yanked the garotte viciously—one of Marcangelo's own weapons in his prime, Tom supposed—and Tom saw the nylon disappear in the flesh of the neck . . . Jonathan was thinking that Marcangelo's friends would appear at any moment' (114).

It is a hazardous technique and only possible because Highsmith saves it for critical episodes, when both characters are acting under pressure and the action can move us, as if naturally, from one viewpoint to another. The next time that the novel gives us a chapter where this happens is when the two men are in Ripley's chateau, preparing to be attacked by vengeful Mafiosi. Ripley is cool and intelligent, Jonathan appalled but cooperative. Ripley will survive; Jonathan will only be severed from Ripley by his death. Highsmith's splitting of the narrative makes possible her manipulation of our sympathies. Access to Ripley's inner world reveals him as a thoughtful and discriminating criminal and killer. Letting us see Jonathan's doubts and fears from the inside makes his weakness seem reasonable and, ironically, saves Ripley from seeming merely an irresistible and sinister predator.

METANARRATIVE

When Ian McEwan's *Atonement* was first published, reviewers, not wanting to spoil a surprise, failed to mention its metanarrative—the story about how its story comes into being. On page 349 of the British edition, we reach the end of Briony's wartime visit to her sister Cecilia and Cecilia's lover, Robbie, in Balham, South London. Briony parts from the couple at the tube station, having promised that she will write to her parents and to lawyers admitting that she lied some six years earlier when she testified to Robbie being a rapist. 'She knew what was required of her. Not simply a letter, but a new draft, an atonement, and she was ready to begin.' What is this 'new draft', this 'atonement'? At the foot of the page is printed

> BT
> London 1999

The first-time reader is likely to be puzzled for a moment. But then the place and date are repeated as the heading for the next section of the novel, 'London, 1999'. Here Briony is the first-person narrator, on the day of her seventy-seventh birthday. You realize that those initials at the foot of the previous section ('BT' is Briony Tallis) mean that the whole of the rest of the book was Briony's story—her work of fiction. She has been writing it and rewriting it for the previous fifty-nine years. We find out that it has gone through 'half a dozen drafts' (369). The latest one is what we have just read. The novel is composed of this story and the metanarrative—the short final section—that accounts for its existence.

It is perhaps something like the discovery near the end of the film *The Usual Suspects* (1995) that all that has gone before has been the invention of one of the characters. Except that even on first reading we might notice the clues McEwan has given to the provenance of the narrative. Young Briony is an aspirant novelist, always 'writing stories' (7). Her sharpest experiences are simply those that seem worthy of being turned into writing. When she imagines anything it is always to think 'how she might describe it' as a writer (156). The novel's catastrophe, for which she is largely responsible, is all the more numbing because she is always dreaming up little catastrophes that she might turn into writing. Wandering off to the swimming pool, she imagines finding her 9-year-old twin cousins drowned, and how she might turn what she found into words, 'the way they bobbed on the illuminated water's gentle swell, and how their hair spread like tendrils and their clothed bodies softly collided and drifted apart'. Working as a trainee nurse, she finds secret moments to fill her foolscap notebook with fictionalized elaborations of her experiences on the ward, as if the experiences were not enough. McEwan's device is time-honoured. Cecilia Tallis, Briony's elder sister, is whiling away the hot summer after leaving university by reading Samuel Richardson's *Clarissa*. Robbie keeps asking her how she is getting on with it. Richardson's novel too tells the very story of its own existence: you find out at its conclusion that the 'letters' between the main characters that comprise the book are Clarissa's 'legacy' after her death. The heroine commands in her will that they be published. Indeed, Richardson was somewhat fanatical about his metanarrative, publishing his novel anonymously and writing, as an 'editor', as if he were arranging and making public real letters. Did McEwan have this in mind when he decided to make his own novel the novelistic testament of one of its characters?

Metanarrative should not be confused with *metafiction*, though the latter often contains versions of the former. *Metafiction* has become a label for novels about novel-writing. Often it is attached to supposedly postmodernist fiction, though much earlier works seem to fit into the category. A notorious case is Laurence Sterne's *Tristram Shandy*. Metafiction is persistently self-referential, like Italo Calvino's *If On a Winter's Night a Traveller*, which from its first sentence makes a story out of how reader and writer conspire to make a story. McEwan's metanarrative, however, is, at least on first reading, withheld from the reader. Some have felt cheated by it, like viewers of *Dallas* who were suddenly shown by desperate script-writers that the traumatic events of the previous series were just Pam Ewing's 'dream'. The test of the trick is perhaps in the rereading. Even knowing what is to come, it is, I think, impossible the second time around not to believe in the characters and situations as thoroughly as on the first reading. If it works, the novel compels you not to treat it as mere fiction. Unlike writers of metafiction, McEwan wants you to identify with characters, to succumb to narrative illusion, to believe in it for the moment. For Briony to undertake her 'atonement', her work of fiction must make up for and confess the wrong that she has done. In a novel, she can make the world better than it truly is. She can make Cecilia and Robbie survive and meet again. And we must be allowed to believe it.

MONTAGE

Don DeLillo likes cinematic analogies and so do his characters. When Nick Shay in *Underworld* thinks forty years back to the night of the famous Giants–Dodgers baseball game, which he heard on his radio on the roof of his apartment block, it is 'a day now gone to black and white in the film fade of memory' (134). This is Nick's own metaphor as much as DeLillo's. When Nick himself narrates a brief, extramarital sexual encounter, he cannot help seeing the opening exchanges of the adulterous courtship as if filmed. 'These were movie scenes, slightly elliptical in tone, with the shots maybe a little offhand, slurred by incidental action' (292). As a parallel to its narrative methods, *Underworld* even offers, at its structural mid-point, the screening of a 'lost' Eisenstein film (invented by DeLillo) called *Unterwelt*. Klara

Sax, who watches the film, knows all about 'the undeniable power of the montage' that makes Eisenstein's films gripping even when they are 'comically overwrought' (425). Her pretentious boyfriend knows 'inside and out' the director's famous sequences of shots, the intercut images from *Battleship Potemkin* that make you feelingly imagine violence that is not actually shown. 'The deadly cadence of black boots. The white jackets of the soldiers. The mother clutching weakly at her waist. The rear wheels of the baby carriage rolling out of the frame.'

DeLillo has talked of the influence of cinema on his narrative technique, his attempts to find literary equivalents for 'the strong image, the short ambiguous scene . . . the artificiality, the arbitrary choices of some directors, the cutting and editing'.[2] *Montage* (from the French *monter*, 'to assemble') refers to the editing of different shots and sequences to make a film narrative. It has come to mean a style of 'cutting and editing' that calls attention to the jumps and clashes between sequences. *Underworld* edits together images and episodes in a comparable way, relishing 'the juxtaposed shots, the sense of rhythmic contradiction' (429). Montage also characterizes the novel's cutting from one scene or character to another. Narrative is footage. Nowhere is this clearer than in the novel's opening section, describing that baseball game in New York in 1951. The abrupt, unannounced switching between characters and actions, a narrative method learned from film, is used to represent the experience of a crowd. We move from one character, to the game—a momentous American drama of triumph and disaster—to another character. There is Russ Hodges, the radio commentator, there is Cotter Martin, the black teenager who has gatecrashed the game, there are various 'personalities' including Frank Sinatra and J. Edgar Hoover (the latter will reappear in the novel). All perspectives are separate; one replaces another.

Later we even cut between one time and another. A lengthy section of the novel, 'Better Things for Better Living through

Chemistry', applies the montage method across time. Subtitled 'Selected Fragments Public and Private in the 1950s and 1960s', it is composed of narrative snatches, each headed only by a date, mostly from the lives of characters we have already met. In amongst these are fragments from the routines of the radical stand-up comedian Lenny Bruce, a character to voice the anxieties of the times. A long penultimate section, 'Arrangement in Gray and Black', arranges fragments from the earlier lives of several of the main characters, in the Italian section of the Bronx in the early 1950s. These vivid cameos—two boys sneak into a funeral parlour to see a dead body, a teacher tells his bored class about the wonderful power of atoms, a woman seduces the teenager who delivers crates of soda—are significant only because of what we already know of the characters' later lives. In their passing assortment we seem to see fate following patterns invisible to the characters.

The liking for montage works its way down into the very arrangement of sentences and staccato paragraphs. Here is Marian (Nick's future wife) at home in Madison, Wisconsin, in 1967 on a day of student protests against the Vietnam War at the local university.

> She wanted to call Nick but knew he wouldn't be there.
>
> The radio played recorded gunfire, car crashes, lines of gritty dialogue from old war movies.
>
> Her mother called her remiss and indifferent. She suffered from disambition, said her mother.
>
> Faculty Document 122 authorizes force against students. Faculty Document 122 authorizes force against students. (600)

Private desires, radio broadcasts, parental refrains, and, somewhere nearby, loudspeaker warnings to a crowd: all are simply interleaved. This jumpy narrative method is best suited to juxtaposition and incongruity—to representing differences. We must take it on trust that the fragments belong together. Klara Sax searches *Unterwelt* for its 'politics of montage' and DeLillo takes it that his reader will have the faith to attempt a similar activity of interpretation.

PROLEPSIS

Prolepsis is the rhetorical trick of anticipation. It refers to the strange business of a narrative letting us know in advance what will happen later. Prolepsis has been an element in the development of the Novel since its earliest days. Daniel Defoe's narrators constantly say, 'as you shall hear' and 'as shall appear by and by'. They can hardly tell us anything without thinking of what is to come. Once these hints at what comes next were thought to be signs of primitive technique, like some incompetent raconteur robbing his own anecdotes of surprise. In fact, prolepsis is the fitting habit of Defoe's penitent sinners, who know all too well just where their stories are leading. Here, for instance, is the narrator of his *Roxana*, recalling how her maid enjoyed being 'merry' with the man who was to become Roxana's own seducer. 'I had always found her a very modest Wench, as any I ever saw in all my Life; but, in short, the Mirth of that Night, and a few more such afterwards, ruin'd the Girl's Modesty for ever, as shall appear by and by, in its Place.' (44). The narrative is always reaching forwards—'. . . afterwards . . . as shall appear . . .'—for the moral consequences of its episodes. Moralizing novelists are drawn to prolepsis. Dickens is another who likes proleptic narration, shaped by intimations of future events. (This was not least because writing novels in instalments required him to keep suggesting that the reader was encountering parts of a larger whole.) In the first instalment of *Dombey and Son*, where he tells the reader of Mr Dombey's neglect of his daughter Florence, he also indicates that Dombey will be self-punished for this failure of fatherliness. Florence is taken under the wing of her baby brother's nurse Polly, who, in her tenderness, 'could have brought a dawning knowledge home to Mr Dombey at that early day, which would not then have struck him in the end like lightning' (ch. 3, 29). Dombey is rejecting the one person in the world who will love him, and by his cruelty making a hard fate for himself. This 'end' will come, in a chapter bluntly called 'Retribution', hundreds of pages and some fifty-six chapters later.

There can be good reasons why a novel should risk smothering curiosity by telling us of what is to come before we reach it. Ian McEwan's *Atonement* does so to unsettling effect. On the novel's second page we hear how the 13-year-old Briony has written a play, which she intends her cousins to perform. She proudly shows it to her mother, who tells her it is 'stupendous' (4). Then some all-knowing narrator adds, as if in an aside, 'Briony was hardly to know it then, but this was the project's highest point of fulfilment.' The comment is so unnecessary that it draws attention to itself. Can the novelist not resist letting us glimpse the future that he has plotted? Briony's creative dreams will be frustrated—this is significant, as she will later vent her imaginative urge by claiming falsely to recognize her sister's lover, Robbie, as her cousin Lola's rapist. As we read further into *Atonement* we see that the narrative has a pattern of these glances at the future. Later, for instance, Briony witnesses unseen a mysterious tableau in which her elder sister, Cecilia, strips and plunges into a fountain, watched by Robbie. She feels an 'elusive excitement at a prospect she was coming close to defining'. What is this 'prospect'? 'The definition would refine itself over the years' (40). We are suddenly taken into the future; she will learn how this scene in fact inspires a work of fiction. We are told that this child will become a novelist.

> Six decades later she would describe how at the age of thirteen she had written her way through a whole history of literature, beginning with stories derived from the European tradition of folk tales, through drama with simple moral intent, to arrive at an impartial psychological realism which she had discovered for herself, one special morning during a heat wave in 1935. (41)

The episode will become significant, just as the budding novelist would wish. The irony is that it will thereby allow the novelist of the future 'to produce a story line' about her own development. Everything becomes convenient narrative material.

Prolepsis—the reader's 'premature' knowledge of eventualities—enacts some loss of innocence. 'In the years to come he would often think back to this time, when he walked along the footpath that made a shortcut through a corner of the oak woods' (90). This is Robbie, walking to the Tallises' house on the evening when he and Cecilia are to make love, and he is to be wrongfully arrested for rape. Naturally, the innocuous prelude will lodge in the memory. The short span of time will become charged with its own innocence. But at this stage of the novel, 'the years to come' belong to the reader, not the character. It seems the puzzling privilege given us by an omniscient narrator, but our discovery near the end of the novel that this is all Briony's story-making, her telling of the story of her 'crime', changes what the prolepsis means. These glimpses of the future come from her. The forward glances are, after all, not McEwan's but his character's. The preservation of an innocent moment in Robbie's recollection is created by the pressure of Briony's penitent imagination. She imagines this; she re-creates it. It is her anticipation guiltily or wishfully intruding into the narrative.

So an oddity of the narrative is revealed to be a logical part of it. The future for McEwan's characters is contained within the frame of his novel. In unusual cases, however, a narrative might refer proleptically to what will occur beyond its own ending. A peculiar example is Jonathan Coe's comic novel *The Rotters' Club*, which ends with an unusual 'Author's Note': 'There will be a sequel to *The Rotters' Club*, entitled *The Closed Circle*, resuming the story in the late 1990s' (403). (This is some twenty-five years after the opening of the earlier novel.) Many novels have sequels, of course, but it is unusual for the first work to point forward to an as yet non-existent follow-up. Louisa M. Alcott did so at the end of *Little Women* (1868), though without Coe's decisiveness. 'So grouped, the curtain falls upon Meg, Jo, Beth, and Amy. Whether it ever rises again, depends upon the reception given to the first act of the domestic drama called "LITTLE WOMEN"' (pt. 1, ch. 23, 228). She would like to follow her characters into married life, but will only do so if the original novel is popular. It was, indeed, hugely successful and its continuation, *Good Wives*, was written, and published the next year. Similarly, Daniel Defoe's *Robinson Crusoe* reached forward to the future with a final sentence that anticipated another commercial opportunity for the author. 'All these things, with some very surprizing Incidents in some new Adventures of my own, for ten Years more, I may perhaps give a farther Account of here after' (306). *Robinson Crusoe* sold well on publication in 1719 and Defoe evidently got rapidly to work. A few months later, *The Further Adventures of Robinson Crusoe* (1720), in which our hero crosses Russia and Friday gets killed, was for sale.

Often the novelist does not know that he or she is going to revive a group of fictional characters. When Anthony Trollope wrote *The Warden* (1855), he did not know that its success would prompt him to write its sequel, *Barchester Towers* (1857), and thereafter a sequence of loosely connected novels that came to be known as his Barsetshire Chronicles. Coe not only knew that he was to return to his characters, but inserted into *The Rotters' Club* hints as to what would happen to them in a later fictional life. In the novel's third chapter, characters whom we hardly know yet, pupils from the matching boys' and girls' grammar schools in suburban Birmingham, are on the bus home. We see Philip Chase getting off at the same stop as Claire Newman and following her 'at an unnaturally slow pace', too shy to overtake her (28). Then the narrator intervenes. 'At this point it would have been hard to imagine that one day they would become friends or even, briefly and unsuccessfully, husband and wife.' It is a weirdly rueful look forward, justified by the endless preoccupation of the teenage characters with finding a desired partner. The two characters keeping a distance from each other are the two destined to marry each other.

Coe likes prolepsis because he is writing about teenagers, who live with their thoughts and fantasies about what will happen to them. They spend their time imagining brilliant futures and happy consummations. They are always recognizing 'fateful moments', hinges on which their lives will turn (296). But you are to know that outcomes will not be as hoped. Philip, lusting after Lois Trotter at a sublimely awkward dinner party, mishears and offends her. They exchange no more words, 'not only for the rest of that evening, but for the next 29 years, as it happened' (54). Their next conversation, in fact, will be the one that concludes *The Closed Circle*, the novel that followed *The Rotters' Club* as Coe said that it would. Coe stores up materials for this later comedy of disappointments (his sequel is a notably jaundiced book). In *The Rotters' Club*, prolepsis involves the deliberate leaving of loose ends. What would be unsatisfactory in a self-contained novel—and had to be evaded in the TV adaptation of *The Rotters' Club*—are the strands of narrative left unresolved. What happened to Claire's sister Miriam, who unaccountably disappeared? Was Richards, the only black boy in the school, drugged before his vital A level exam by a jealous rival? Is Benjamin right to think that Cicely, the love of his life, will return to him? All these questions are indeed answered in *The Closed Circle*, though answers too can prove disappointing. Looking back from its sequel, the undecidedness of *The Rotters' Club* appears part of its appeal. It then seemed possible that Coe had not made his mind up about recent history, and that he could not close down the future fantasies of his characters. Its undecidedness seemed true to their hopes. In the sequel, which is a lament for the end of political idealism, he is too obviously decided and illusions are all dispelled. (The strain of anti-New Labour complaint is loud and unvaried.) The closure announced in the second novel's title may have been made necessary by the prolepses of the first novel, but it risks deflating our expectations rather than satisfying them.

7
Detail

IN David Lodge's novel *Small World* (1984), two characters whom we have first met in his novel *Changing Places* (1975) encounter each other once again. The academics Philip Swallow and Morris Zapp are on a plane together and Philip is about to tell Morris the story of the one time in recent years that he has known 'intensity of experience' (67). Morris, a high-powered American literary professor, throws in comments on the logic of Philip's narrative. This involves a British Council visit to Genoa, where he is looked after by a Council representative, with whose wife, it transpires, he has a brief, passionate encounter. Mentioning that her husband had to get up early the next day to drive to Milan for a meeting, Philip adds, 'That comes into the story.' '"I should hope so," said Morris. "There should be nothing irrelevant in a good story."' A few lines later he is contradicting his own tenet. Philip recalls taking off in a plane from Genoa.

> 'It was a British plane. I was sitting next to an English businessman, a salesman in woollen textiles I think he was . . .'
>
> 'Is that relevant?'
>
> 'Not really.'
>
> 'Never mind. Solidity of specification,' said Morris with a tolerant wave of his cigar. 'It contributes to the reality effect.' (68)

As Morris indicates, there are sometimes things in a narrative that have no 'relevance' and that make it believable. This is particularly so in novels, often made probable by circumstantial details. Thomas De Quincey made the same point about Defoe's 'solidity of specification' that Morris Zapp makes. Defoe's narrators, he acutely observes, like to gives us facts that 'seem, by their apparent inertness of effect, to verify themselves':

> for, where the reader is told that such a person was the posthumous son of a tanner, that his mother married afterwards a Presbyterian schoolmaster, who gave him a smattering of Latin, but, the schoolmaster dying of the plague, that he was compelled at sixteen to enlist for bread—in all this, as there is nothing at all amusing, we conclude that the author could have no reason to detain us with such particulars but simply because they were true.[1]

Novels have always been intrigued by odd details, by the clutter of life. Early novels were thought by many good literary judges to be vulgar for their devotion to petty details. The protagonist and main narrator of Samuel Richardson's groundbreaking novel *Pamela* worries a good deal about her soul, but also (as befits a 15-year-old servant girl) thinks about clothes.

> Since my last, my Master gave me more fine Things. He call'd me up to my old Lady's Closet, and pulling out her Drawers, he gave me Two Suits of fine *Flanders* lac'd Headcloths, Three Pair of fine Silk Shoes, two hardly the worse, and just fit for me; for my old Lady had a very little Foot; and several Ribbands and Topknots of all Colours, and Four Pair of fine white Cotton Stockens, and Three Pair of fine Silk ones; and Two Pair of rich Stays, and a Pair of rich Silver Buckles in one Pair of the Shoes. (Letter VII, 19)

With psychological exactitude, Richardson has his heroine so fussed by all this stuff that she cannot notice what her would-be seducer is up to. Such details seem to make probable the world that we come to inhabit when we read a particular novel. A latter-day confirmation of this vulgarity would be the readiness of some novels to tell us about products and purchases (see 'Brands', below). Novels can be minutely worldly. Historical novels demonstrate this in what has become a respectable manner. In the section in this chapter entitiled 'Research' I examine the enjoyment that a writer, quite as much as a reader, may derive from recovering the little bits and pieces from some past time.

The 'reality effect' that Morris Zapp describes requires the inclusion of life's circumstantial facts. Yet the sections here entitled 'Weather' and 'Meals' show how such details readily become charged with significance. In Jane Austen's *Emma*, a change in the weather, from 'cold stormy rain' to sun, and wind from 'a softer quarter', changes the mood (vol. iii, ch. xiii, 384). The 'melancholy' that 'seemed to reign at Hartfield' gives way to 'summer'. Emma, 'with spirits freshened', takes to the garden. After the gloom of the previous chapter, with Emma convinced that Mr Knightley would marry Harriet, the meteorological relief cannot but be symbolic. Providential even, for the suddenly seasonal weather allows Emma and Mr Knightley to take a couple of turns around the Hartfield grounds, giving him the opportunity to clear up Emma's misconceptions about Harriet and to declare his feelings. If the wind had not shifted, would she have been condemned to spinsterhood? As well as discovering the fictional importance of weather, Austen used meals, notably in *Emma*, for narrative ends. They become occasions for teasing out undeclared tensions, especially between neighbours or family members. The section entitled 'Meals' below shows how the very business of describing dishes and ingredients can reveal the truth about the relationships between those who are eating.

So 'relevance' and 'the reality effect' are not quite the mutually exclusive alternatives that Morris Zapp implies. We can see this when we consider a novel's sense of place, discussed in 'Location' and 'Setting'. The exactness with which a location is seen can certainly contribute to a novel's credibility, and is as important in certain kinds of popular fiction, like crime novels, as it sometimes is in so-called literary fiction. Yet location and setting easily become metaphorical. The most powerful example is Wessex in Thomas Hardy's novels. We must believe that, however renamed, every place in the novels—every village, or hill, or road—is taken from a real place. Yet fiction makes these locations into a map of aspirations and disappointments. We might say something similar about James Joyce's *Ulysses* (1922), which turned a particular city into a universally known place of the imagination, while taking a single day as the story of an epic journey through life and death.

Ulysses, famous for shattering conventions of novelistic realism, actually grasps its circumstantial details quite as firmly as any novel ever has and might have provided examples for any of the sections in this chapter. Some of the most innovative novels of the twentieth century remained greedy for the small, true details of ordinary life. *Ulysses* is full of the particularities, the quiddities, of a Dublin day. Think of what Leopold Bloom sees and, especially, smells as he walks the streets. 'He approached Larry O'Rourke's. From the cellar grating floated up the flabby gush of porter. Through the open doorway the bar squirted out whiffs of ginger, teadust, biscuitmush' (69). Then he is at the window of the butcher's. 'The shiny links packed with forcemeat fed his gaze and he breathed in tranquilly the lukewarm breath of cooked spicy pig's blood' (70). Soon he will be getting hungry, what with all these odours. 'Hot mockturtle vapour and steam of newbaked jam-puffs rolypoly poured out from Harrison's. The heavy noonreek tickled the top of Mr Bloom's gullet' (198). And then there are the novel's noises. '—Mkgnao!' goes Bloom's cat (65). And a little later, with the tiniest difference in sound, '—Mrkgnao!' 'Pwfungg!' goes the gas jet (683). Or 'Pooah! Pfuiiiiii!' (627). Somewhere a train whistles, 'frseeeeeeeefronnnng' (894). The novel is exuberantly true to sense impressions, to the small, noticed details of the day. Quite as pedantically as any novel by Daniel Defoe will it list domestic items, when the unheroic wanderer Bloom returns to his home:

> On the middle shelf a chipped eggcup containing pepper, a drum of table salt, four conglomerated black olives in oleaginous paper,

> an empty pot of Plumtree's potted meat, an oval wicker basket bedded with fibre and containing one Jersey pear, a halfempty bottle of William Gilbey and Co's white invalid port, half disrobed of its swathe of coralpink tissue paper, a packet of Epp's soluble cocoa . . . (788)

and so on. There is almost poetry in it, life's details.

FACTS

Facts do not have to have some hidden significance. Circumstantial details included in a work of fiction do not have to be symbolic or metaphorical. A writer who beautifully exploits the inertness of facts is William Trevor. Near the beginning of the first story in Trevor's 2004 collection *A Bit on the Side* is a detail that epitomizes this writer's way with closely observed details. 'Sitting with the Dead' is about a man's death and its effects on his wife, Emily. At its opening, mortally ill, Emily's husband is struggling out into the farmyard, his overcoat over his pyjamas. 'A stitch was needed where the left sleeve met the shoulder, she noticed' (1). Why are we being told this? Is it the tender concern of a wife who is otherwise helpless in the face of her husband's illness? Is it the housewifely fussiness of a woman who tries to avoid facing his impending death? Neither. The observation, we will soon find, is more to do with Emily's lack of feeling for her husband, the grieflessness that is the subject of the story. The detail resists the significance we would attach to it. You would think that the brevity of a short story allowed for no details that were not significant. Everything must matter. Yet Trevor's stories often take the time, like this, to ascertain facts that appear utterly circumstantial.

In 'Three People', the first story in Trevor's collection *The Hill Bachelors*, the middle-aged Vera and the taciturn handyman Sidney perform some unexpressed courtship, watched by Vera's aged father, and the narrative supplies details to fill the spaces.

Invited to stay to lunch, Sidney says he will light a fire. 'She takes a box from a cupboard, swinging back the door that's on a level with her head, reaching in. *Cook's Matches* the label says. She hands them to him, their fingers do not touch' (19). In the charged absence of contact, we notice, as they might, the detail of the label. The essentially meaningless facts are there because there is so much not being said, as if the narrative has to latch on to these little particulars. Anything else would be speculation. Domestic detail is often a kind of solace for Trevor's characters. As the young wife in 'Death of a Professor', fearful of her resentful, older husband, waits for his return home, the narrative tells us how the table is laid and what is for lunch. Why? Because this she can safely think about. Narrative enacts her nervous focus on detail. Similarly, in the collection's title story a widow wonders whether her son will return to her lonely hill farm after her husband's death, and, as we wonder with her, the story carefully describes just what she is cooking him for breakfast.

Some writers would squeeze symbolism from a story's small, charged facts, but Trevor lets them acquire merely accidental significance. This helps each story to live in its own small world. In 'The Telephone Game', when Tony recalls falling in love with Liese he thinks of the different kinds of glove manufactured by her family—for this was what she spoke of when they first shared a taxi together. '00178 was the number on the back of the driver's seat in the first taxi they sat in together, black digits on an oval of white enamel' (208). The details mean nothing, yet have been made resonant by association. And perhaps it is only association that makes facts meaningful. 'A Friend in the Trade' tells the story of a married woman who is aware that a foolish family friend has always secretly loved her, and Trevor delights in filling in merely accidental details of their encounters. The absurd acquaintance is a bibliophile and acquirer of literary manuscripts, and much space is given to detailing the 'scraps' that he pointlessly collects and endlessly describes. He would rather say anything than what really brings him on his visits. So perhaps no detail is truly inert. As soon as it is included, it signifies. As a person's memory makes life's small accidents take on meaning, so Trevor's short stories uses their circumstantial details to focus his characters' hardly spoken passions.

LOCATION

The British Novel took a long time to discover a sense of place. In eighteenth-century novels, characters like Fielding's Tom Jones and Smollett's Humphrey Clinker roamed the nation, but they were not shaped by the places from which they came. They did not belong to anywhere. Bath and London were the places for novels to visit, while the countryside was much the same everywhere. It was not until Walter Scott that particular places, known to the novelist, formed characters. Scott made the Scottish Borders and the city of Edinburgh into locations recognized by readers throughout Europe. These locations were not just convenient because known well by the author. In the early Scottish novels, Scott took his stories and some of his characters from local history and legend. Later novelists are now better known for their sense of place: Dickens for London, Hardy for Wessex, Joyce for Dublin. Yet it was Scott who first traded on the reader's certainty that he had frequented the scenes of his fiction. In fact, he was prone to assure the reader of this. In a characteristic aside in *The Heart of Midlothian,* he concludes a picturesque description of Salisbury Crags, near Edinburgh—where two of his characters will have a surreptitious meeting—with a personal reflection. 'This path used to be my favourite evening and morning resort, when engaged with a favourite author, or a new subject of study' (ch. viii, 74).

Many contemporary novelists attempt to conjure a particular sense of place. It is particularly important for crime and thriller writers (think of Colin Dexter's Oxford or Ian Rankin's Edinburgh). Location contains the information that the detective must decode. Detection begins from a 'crime scene'. Only a few novelists, though, rely on our sense that they have, like Scott, walked the very ground. One is Ruth Rendell. You feel that she might do the research for each new novel simply by fixing on some locality and then tramping round it, noting those details of topography that can only ever be recorded, never just imagined. This is the trick of it, getting the place right. For *The Keys to the Street* (1996) she must have done just such scouting around. The book's knowledge of the paths and streets around London's Regent's Park—and the observation of the fences and gates and alleys that appear in no A–Z—is so disturbingly precise. The reader is taken to just where the novelist imagined things. My hunch is that Rendell often starts with the place rather than the characters. If the location can be particularized, the psychology takes root. Grubby London is her forte, though she is also drawn to East Anglia (she has a rural retreat in Suffolk) and has wandered as far as Alaska (*No Night Is Too Long*, 1994). London is best for her. It allows strange, frighteningly accidental collisions of characters.

Several of the key relationships in her *Adam and Eve and Pinch Me* are between neighbours. The main location in this novel is Kensal Green in north-west London. Minty Knox lives there in an invented street: 'Syringa Road' (Rendell must have enjoyed that grim-sounding, faux exotic name). But everything else about the locality seems to have been observed, not least the nearby Kensal Green Cemetery, where Minty performs her odd rituals of expiation to the 'ghosts' that haunt her. Very late in the novel we encounter the neighbourhood through the eyes of an outsider, a smart woman journalist, who is taken aback by its unloveliness. Minty, however, inhabits her locality as if it were the only possible place in the world, worried about the increasingly threatening young people in the street, but unable to conceive of living anywhere else. Her odd habits are expressed through her locale: the routes she follows, the places she visits.

Location matters in a special way to 'thrillers' such as Rendell's, which set out to discover what is threatening and violent in ordinary places. To this end, Rendell relishes catching the peculiarity of some run-down London suburb, some unobserved corner not far away. A sceptic would say that location is what anchors otherwise implausible events in a probable world. Oddly, Rendell attaches herself to traditional literary topography by mixing real and pseudonymous locations in this novel. The outer reaches of the Harrow Road exist, as do her other London locations. Jarringly, however, when we go down to Dorset where Jims, a Conservative MP whose story becomes weirdly entangled with Minty's, has his constituency, things are different. We encounter not only invented villages, but also a place called 'Casterbridge'. This is, of course, the name given in Thomas Hardy's novels to Dorchester, his home town. Her reuse of the name feels coy, an implicit confession that the real Dorset is not known to her. She needs a country place for her plot, but nothing more. Perhaps only London can give her locations that are both real and strange. And just as she must know her places, she surely realizes that any reader who half-recognizes the scenes of her research will gain more of a frisson from the novel. This is, after all, her game: making something frightening from what is banal, suggesting that her weird and fatal plots might have their foundations in a world that we know and, like her, can visit.

SETTING

It might be useful to distinguish between a *location*, which a novel makes exactly known, and a *setting*, which a reader can treat as 'foreign'. There is, for instance, a striking Anglo-American tradition of novels with European settings, where any sense of place is also a sense of being out of place, a tourist. It was begun by Laurence Sterne, whose *A Sentimental Journey* (1768) is set in France and from its first sentence, '—They order, said I, this matter better in France—', exploits the mutual strangeness of the English and the French. A foreign setting became something like a structural principle of fiction with Henry James and E. M. Forster (and others like Ford Madox Ford and Edith Wharton). They were interested in the unsettling transformations that can occur when characters are away from home. The foreignness of their settings was not only a function of contemporary habits of travel, it was also a matter of fictional logic. Florence in *A Room With a View* (1908), say, corresponds to an actual place, and sometimes Forster even sounds as though he assumes that we, fellow tourists, will recognize it. 'Accordingly they drifted through a series of those grey-brown streets, neither commodious nor picturesque, in which the eastern quarter of the city abounds' (ch. 2, 39): '*those* grey-brown streets'. But the place is also the necessary setting for the fictional action, the stage for a release of its English characters' restraints.

Patricia Highsmith's *Ripley's Game* is a peculiar addition to the tradition of Anglo-American novels with 'Continental' settings. Most of it takes place in France, where the beguiling murderer Tom Ripley has chosen to live. Why did Patricia Highsmith transplant him here after the first of the five novels in which he featured, *The Talented Mr Ripley*? In the opening paragraph of that book, we met him in a bar in New York, uneasily aware that another drinker was 'eyeing him carefully' (5), though soon he was on the Italian Riviera, paid by a millionaire to track down his errant son. When he next appeared, in *Ripley Under Ground*, he was ensconced in a lovely French chateau, though travelling to commit his crimes in England, Switzerland, and Germany. The foreign setting is crucial to the Ripley novels. In the first two, Ripley's schemes involve impersonation: firstly, of Dickie Greenleaf, the rich young man whom he has killed; secondly, of Derwatt, the dead artist whose paintings he is having forged. It is all so much easier abroad. Ripley is morally untethered and freed from social ties, able to create the identity (charming, cultured, cosmopolitan) that he feels he deserves. France is perfect because he is a connoisseur: of art, food, music, gardens. To his delight, no one quite understands him. He moves easily amongst all those respectable people.

Being displaced is what Ripley relies on. He is sealed off from everyone except the reader. His loyal housekeeper Mme Annette, 'bless her soul, didn't understand English' (7). His wife, Heloise, is 'not comfortable in English', though she understands enough to make Tom cautious when she can hear him talking on the phone (8). His marriage is founded on mutual deceit: he pretends that his activities are legitimate, and she pretends that she has no suspicions to the contrary. In a neat symmetry, Jonathan Trevanny, the Englishman whom Ripley corrupts, also has a French wife who can hardly understand English. In his case, being an exile isolates him and make him the more vulnerable. The two men are brought together, with terrible consequences, by their equal foreignness. Jonathan thinks that 'Ripley looked un-French', without quite knowing why (141). Tom listens to Jonathan dealing with a customer in his shop and notes, 'Trevanny's accent was quite good' (93). Both men are sharply aware of what makes someone an outsider. Jonathan has emigrated to France in pursuit of 'dreams of freedom' (21). Ripley will introduce him to a new freedom: the freedom from moral restraint.

In the 2002 film of *Ripley's Game*, the setting is shifted to northern Italy. Instead of the bourgeois local town of Fontainebleau, we are given a delightful, if geographically nonsensical, composite of baroque towns of the Veneto. Ripley lives not in the pleasant country house that his in-laws have given him in Highsmith's book, but in a full-blown Palladian palazzo. As ever, things have to be grander on screen. In a novel, the distinctiveness of a setting is often tacit. In a film, the camera gazes at what is picturesque. Highsmith makes her setting concrete with a hundred trivial French details: the attention to dress, the strange opening and closing times of businesses, what people eat and drink (all these little things actually matter at different times to the novel's plot). It seems first-hand. While it is formally necessary that Ripley be an émigré, there is also a more ordinary explanation for this. Highsmith wrote much of the first Ripley novel while living in Italy. Later, she emigrated to France. Perhaps because a crime writer cannot have first-hand experience of the novel's deadly actions, he or she tends to require a lovingly observed setting. Highsmith chose provincial France because she needed a place to whose special foreign features she could be true and where Ripley, her émigré from morality, could come alive.

WEATHER

'I love England in a heat wave,' says Leon Tallis in Ian McEwan's *Atonement* (128). 'It's a different country. All the rules change.' There is some dramatic irony in his complacent small talk. Restraints have already begun to collapse. Robbie and Cecilia have become fumbling lovers and have been interrupted in their first coupling by the appalled Briony, Cecilia's sister. The weather is suffocating. In 'an aroma of warmed dust from the Persian carpet' the characters try to eat their sweltering roast dinner (125). Very English. Very English too because nothing can be adapted to really hot weather. The adults want a glass of cool water, but propriety condemns them to dessert wine at room temperature. None of the dining room windows will open. The very fabric of the house has been put together without a thought of a heatwave. 'The effect of suffocation was heightened by the dark-stained panelling reaching from the floor and covering the ceiling.' But Leon has more of a point than he thinks, for the heat will also release something. Before the evening is out, the shocking and mysterious act of violence at the novel's heart will have been committed. And Briony will have committed her crime of false testimony.

Heat hangs over the first part of McEwan's novel and shapes its action. Emily Tallis, Briony's mother, lies nursing her migraine and thinks of 'the vast heat that rose above the house and park, and lay across the Home Counties like smoke, suffocating the farms and towns' (64). Later she jokes that her parents thought that 'hot weather encouraged loose morals amongst young people' (128). They were right. Unknown to her, sexual passion and resentment are brewing. 'Fewer layers of clothing, a thousand more places to meet. Out of doors, out of control,' she goes on. Perhaps they were wise to something, that they should want to keep their English daughters indoors. No wonder hot weather fascinates English novelists. In some novels there is the heat of foreign places: Conrad's Africa or East Indies, Forster's Italy or India, Greene's colonial outposts. It transforms or saturates European characters, overcoming their defences, draining them of self-assurance. It is a received truth that foreign heat undoes repression. The heat of an English summer, of a country not used to such things, is strange in a different way. The characters in *Atonement* themselves realize this, storing up meteorological observations as if they sense that something extraordinary is happening. Robbie notes the 'improbable' effects of light on a baking evening (78); Briony records the smells of 'the hard-fired earth which still held the embers of the day's heat and exhaled the mineral odour of clay' (156).

It is odd that the Novel, the genre committed to life's circumstantial aspects, did not discover the weather until the nineteenth century. In eighteenth-century fiction, storms or balmy days are merely convenient for the story. Real weather is more intrusive. One of the earliest novelists to be interested in weather was Jane Austen, ever attentive to the small comforts and discomforts of her characters. There is a memorable heatwave in *Emma*, a novel in which the weather is several times important to the plot. During the party at Mr Knightley's Donwell Abbey, heat erodes gentility. Amidst irritation and tactlessness, even the saving manoeuvres of politeness fail. 'Some people were always cross when they were hot', Emma observes (vol. iii, ch. vi, 286). The appalling Mrs Elton is defeated by the sun as she never was by any rival lady, her very language melting into nonsensical mutterings. After Austen, hot weather becomes a useful condition for many a novelist of manners. The country house summer swoon of *Atonement* recalls most obviously the long heat of L. P. Hartley's *The Go-Between* (1953). Animation is suspended, the habits of every day are halted, but suppressed passions brew.

Sometimes disastrously, heat in fiction releases the English from restraint, and novelists have often used it for episodes of sexual awakening. The natural and unnatural stirrings of adolescent sexual instinct in McEwan's first novel, *The Cement Garden* (1978), take place during a heatwave (the famously hot summer of 1976). The extraordinary chapters of Hardy's *Tess of the d'Urbervilles* set at Talbothay's Dairy, charting the growing attraction between Tess and Angel Clare, rely on hot weather. In 'Ethiopic' heat, the air of the novel becomes 'stagnant and enervating' (ch. xxiv, 164). 'And as Clare was oppressed by the outward heats, so was he burdened inwardly by the waxing fervour of passion for the soft and silent Tess.' Perhaps there are also memories of the old-fashioned children's story (of Enid Blyton or Arthur Ransome) in long days of fictional heat. *Atonement* trades effectively on the importance of weather to recollection, the idea that summers were always hotter in the past. The structure of the novel—the events of its first part compulsively recollected in the following three parts—makes the hot, suffocating days of its opening seem to belong to another time: distant, past, yet palpably there in the memorable, inescapable sense of the weather.

MEALS

What kinds of novel feature meals? Sometimes the satirical, but invariably the familial. A meal is a focus of ordinary social and family life. Courtship might happen at a dance, flirtation in a drawing room, but mealtimes are for the essential chemistry of a group. 'Your family has a diseased relationship with food,' Caroline tells her husband, Gary, in Jonathan Franzen's *The Corrections* (211). We know that family life depends on eating together; we know from novels that communal eating is where you can see everything going wrong. The unspoken anguish of growing up in the Lambert household is incarnated in the very food on the plate. Enid serves up meals that mock comfort and pleasure.

> Brown grease-soaked flakes of flour were impastoed on the ferrous lobes of liver like corrosion. The bacon also, what little there was of it, had the colour of rust . . . A dollop of mashed rutabaga at rest on a plate expressed a clear yellowish liquid similar to plasma or the matter in a blister. Boiled beet greens leaked something cupric, greenish. Capillary action and the thirsty crust of flour drew both liquids under the liver. When the liver was lifted, a faint suction could be heard. The sodden lower crust was unspeakable. (293–4)

The precision of the description comically mimics the horror with which Enid's youngest son gazes at what is on his plate. It is as punishing as the vividly recalled burnt porridge in *Jane Eyre*.

Ironically, Denise Lambert escapes family expectations through food. She becomes a trendy chef. While her mother dishes up failed meals in her Midwest kitchen, Denise flees only as far as her own fashionable concoctions of 'fennel relish' and 'good bitter wholesome rapini' (460). She becomes expert at cooking, but no better at satisfying her family. On a parental visit, she hands out 'Parmesan shards packed in an excelsior of shredded arugula', and 'crust-bottomed vehicles . . . paved with minced olive meat and olive oil, and covered with a thick red tarp of pepper' (75). With shaking hands her Parkinsonian father duly deposits the frail things on the carpet. Meals can be how you try to make things seem better than they are. Chip Lambert goes through a brief phase when he has a girlfriend and a job, and entertains colleagues and occasional precocious students; he 'surprised them with langoustines, or a rack of lamb, or venison with juniper berries, and retro joke desserts like chocolate fondue' (39). It cannot last. He takes the girlfriend to his family's Thanksgiving dinner, thereby ensuring her swift exit.

A meal is never just food. Novelists have long known what anthropologists discovered relatively recently: social eating means something. Dickens perfected the art of the meal as a fictional set-piece. His meals can signify small human hopes being strangled (*Oliver Twist*), or the gusto of life valued for its ordinary pleasures (the tuck-ins in *The Pickwick Papers*), or the chill privilege of mean luxury (any meal chez Dombey). As a specimen of the latter, here is the repast at Paul Dombey's christening party: 'a cold collation, set forth in a cold pomp of glass and silver, and looking more like a dead dinner lying in state than a social refreshment' (ch. v, 63). Dickens does not hesitate to keep repeating the word 'cold'. This cold food chills all the guests, their spirits frozen by their host's warmthless hospitality. Dombey, proud of his display, asks a guest what he has on his plate:

> 'I have got a cold fillet of veal here, Sir,' replied Mr. Chick, rubbing his numbed hands hard together. 'What have *you* got there, Sir?'
>
> 'This,' returned Mr. Dombey, 'is some cold preparation of calf's head, I think. I see cold fowls—ham—patties—salad—lobster. Miss Tox will do me the honour of taking some wine? Champagne to Miss Tox.'
>
> There was a toothache in everything. The wine was so bitter cold that it forced a little scream from Miss Tox, which she had a

> great difficulty in turning into a 'Hem!' The veal had come from such an airy pantry, that the first taste of it struck a sensation as of cold lead to Mr. Chick's extremities. Mr. Dombey alone remained unmoved. He might have been hung up for sale at a Russian fair as a specimen of a frozen gentleman.

Only discomfort is possible at a gathering presided over by Mr Dombey, a rich man whose human spirits have frozen. The enjoyment of a meal is something special for Dickens, the sign of good-heartedness as well as good fortune. Franzen too believes that a meal will reveal what is wrong amongst those who eat it. The meals in *The Corrections* have an especially painful quality because the novel is set in a land of plenty, its pages full of readily available comestibles. Traditionally, meals have been satisfying to novelists when plenty and pleasure have been unusual. One of the most famous examples is Evelyn Waugh's *Brideshead Revisited*, a novel of wartime deprivation which relishes its plovers' eggs and lobster Newburg and strawberries and champagne. At home Charles Ryder dines with his misanthropic father, who reads a book during meals. There is 'a white, tasteless soup, over-fried fillets of sole with a pink sauce, lamb cutlets propped against a cone of mashed potato, stewed pears in jelly standing on a kind of sponge cake' (66). His wonder at being admitted to the bright world of the Marchmains is caught in his amazed delight at their terrific meals. Graham Greene recalled that Evelyn Waugh 'once wrote to me that the only excuse he could offer for *Brideshead Revisited* was "spam, black-outs and Nissen huts"'.[2]

Franzen gives us the reverse of this. Rich Gary Lambert, depressed, drunk, and deep in a cold war with his wife, produces a memorably appalling 'mixed grill' to celebrate the privileged life of his family in their Philadelphia suburb. In the past, he has been able to do this with aplomb. 'He did partridge breasts, chicken livers, filets mignons and Mexican-flavoured turkey sausage. He did zucchini and red peppers. He did eggplant, yellow peppers, baby lamb chops, Italian sausage' (188). But now he is feuding with his wife and is on the bottle. His children are learning to regard him as a depressive. He has learned the word 'anhedonia': 'a psychological condition characterized by inability to experience pleasure in normally pleasurable acts'. So the pleasure of the barbecued feast disappears and, with the booze and the self-pity kicking in, Gary's culinary expertise evaporates. Franzen describes in a detail that will resonate with any occasionally incompetent cook the consequences of forgetting about the barbecue, pouring water on the flames, and then trying to complete the cooking on the damp coals. 'He flipped all the meat scraps, exposing their charred, glossy undersides. There was a smell of wet burnedness such as firemen leave behind' (263). But the food must be consumed. 'He sat with the unchewed bird-flesh in his mouth until he realized that saliva was trickling down his chin—a poor way indeed to demonstrate good mental health. He swallowed the bolus whole.' His family watch him. It is getting hard to pretend all is well. At mealtime, it is impossible to keep up appearances.

BRANDS

When James Bond first enters *From Russia With Love*, it is with an assertion of his tastes. We are to understand that he knows what he likes. His 'treasured Scottish housekeeper', May, hands him a tray with his breakfast and *The Times*, 'the only paper Bond ever read' (ch. 11, 96). Why should we be we told this? In a different kind of novel it would signify that he was reactionary or narrow-minded. Here it means that he is an exacting man, unswayed by fashion. The newspaper is the first of the novel's brands. Soon Bond's breakfast is being itemized in a manner that assures us of his qualities of character. Brands mark decisiveness and sagacity. Once Bond has discovered what is best, he never veers. When in London, his breakfast is 'always the same': coffee from De Bry in New Oxford Street, brewed in an American Chemex, drunk from Minton china; toast with Norwegian heather honey from Fortnum's; a single brown egg, from a French Marans hen. Even the chicken sounds like a luxury brand.

As he travels, the brands vary, signifiers of cosmopolitan choosiness. In *From Russia With Love* he goes to Turkey, where he smokes delicious Diplomate cigarettes and drinks Kavaklidere with his first Turkish meal: he knows it is 'a rich coarse burgundy like any other Balkan wine' (ch. 15, 139). Other novels feature a huge variety of wines and champagnes; only in the films does he stick to vodka martini, 'shaken not stirred'. The brand names are also there for the novels' machines. Bond cannot board a plane without remarking its exact make and specifications. His car is a Continental Bentley, 'the "R" type chassis with the big 6 engine and a 13:40 back-axle ratio'. Fleming originated this tactic. Now we are habituated to novelists' use of brand labels, often lazily, to persuade us of the credibility of a character, or a way of life. Some of it bolsters what has been called 'recognition fiction': novels that require the readers to recognize a lifestyle that they share. Brands are key signifiers here. But Bond's brands are different. They constitute a language that would scarcely have been more foreign to Fleming's first readers than it is now. They are calculated to intrigue a British audience that in 1957, when *From Russia With Love* was first published, had only recently struggled out of post-war austerity.

A later age of novelistic product placement is represented with satirical excess in Brett Easton Ellis's *American Psycho*. This novel's psychopathic yuppie narrator, Patrick Bateman, cannot separate character from object of consumption. 'Courtney opens the door and she's wearing a Krizia cream silk blouse and Krizia rust tweed skirt and silk-satin d'Orsay pumps from Manolo Blahnik' (8). There is a kind of absurd poetry to it. Even in solitude, Bateman clutches at his brands.

A visit to his own bathroom becomes a celebratory materialistic catalogue.

> I stand in front of a chrome and acrylic Washmobile bathroom sink—with soap dish, cup holder, and railings that serve as towel bars, which I bought at Hastings Tile . . . Then I squeeze Rembrandt onto a faux-tortoiseshell toothbrush and start brushing my teeth . . . Then I use the Probright tooth polisher and next the Interplak tooth polisher (this is in addition to the toothbrush) which has a speed of 4200 rpm and reverses direction forty-six times per second . . . I rinse again with Cepacol . . . (25)

And so it goes on. Fleming also likes luxurious bathrooms. In *Dr No* (1957) Bond enters the villain's lair, where he finds himself comforted with just the right products. 'There was everything in the bathroom—Floris Lime bath essence for men and Guerlain bathcubes for women . . . The soap was Guerlain's Sapoceti, *Fleurs des Alpes*' (ch. 13, 187). Yet we know that all this, down to the Lenthéric aftershave lotion, is to soften Bond before the kill. The chapter is, after all, titled 'Mink-Lined Prison'. The luxury products are seductive, but they are tricks of the villain's trade. Bond is an epicure, for sure, but one who must finally escape temptation. 'The blubbery arms of the soft life had Bond around the neck and they were slowly strangling him' we are told on his first appearance in *From Russia With Love*. All those brands can best be savoured by the man who is not beguiled by them.

RESEARCH

The writer who invented the historical novel, Sir Walter Scott, also introduced research into fiction. Like many who have followed him, Scott became addicted to the fact-finding. Eventually he came to annotate his own novels, adding notes identifying the experts on folklore who had assisted him, or explaining how he had come by his knowledge of military history. The research that went into fiction was there to be noticed and relished by the reader. Ever since, one possible role for the novelist has been letting us see how the past might be reconstructed. It has recently become common for novelists to append bibliographies to their novels, showing where they have got their information. We might expect Colm Tóibín's *The Master*, a novel about Henry James, to list its sources, but less obviously researched novels do so too. Amongst the recent novels examined in this book, five—Jonathan Coe's *The Rotters' Club*, Michael Cunningham's *The Hours*, Andrea Levy's *Small Island*, David Mitchell's *Cloud Atlas*, and Andrew O'Hagan's *Personality*—end with reading lists. The supportive list of sources is evidence of the writer's scrupulous attention to detail. This is a new habit, which tells us something of how novelists have come to present themselves, and perhaps see themselves, as historians or intellectual detectives. It is not unprecedented. Georgette Heyer, a romantic novelist sometimes praised for her care with historical detail, provided a bibliography for just one of her many novels: *An Infamous Army* (1937). Covering the Battle of Waterloo (as well as the romantic exploits of the head-strong young widow Lady Barbara Childe), the novel is dense with minute diplomatic and military detail. Heyer evidently felt, as she did not with any of her forty or more other historical novels, that she needed to display her research work. The book 'realized an ambition which, though I fear it may have been presumptuous, I could not resist attempting' (Author's Note).

So even the most populist of novelists can want to advertise the research behind a novel. Michel Faber acknowledges in an afterword to *The Crimson Petal and the White* that hard study has gone into the writing of his novel of Victorian London, but cheerfully declines to provide a bibliography. 'Mindful of the necessity to keep this book nice and slim, I can't list all the publications I've consulted.' He does name the Internet discussion group where he has had many of his questions about nineteenth-century life answered (and some academic specialists in the nineteenth century recall the stream of enquiries that he sent out via the Internet). He does name one book, telling us about his reliance on Jennifer Davies's *The Victorian Kitchen*[3] (invaluable for this novel, in which social aspiration or deprivation are realized in diet). The research is not invisible. On the contrary, we are to feel reassured that when a street scene is described, a season's theatrical repertoire enumerated, or the books that a lady reads in bed listed, we are being given a credible texture of impressions. It should intrigue the reader to find out, thanks to Faber's research, that in the early 1870s a passionate argument was taking place about the desirability of cremation as opposed to burial. It also fits a novel so much concerned with the palpability of men's and women's flesh. We can enjoy the description of a department store of the 1870s or of Verdi ('an impish old rogue') conducting his own *Requiem* at the Royal Albert Hall, dazzled as the eager punters are dazzled (368). Faber has said that he spent years in libraries preparing for this book and we are supposed to notice the fruit.

Henry James doubted that one could get into the mind of a person from the historical past.

> You may multiply the little facts that can be got from pictures & documents, relics & prints, as much as you like—*the* real thing is almost impossible to do, & in its absence the whole effect is as nought; I mean the invention, the representation of the old *consciousness*, the soul, the sense, the horizon, the vision of individuals in whose minds half the things that make ours, that make the modern world were non-existent.[4]

But a novelist can certainly attend to the externals, those 'little facts', and can take a kind of delight in doing so. First there is the place. The rookeries of St Giles were graphically enough described in a series of contemporary campaigning investigations, some of which Faber has clearly read. Indeed, he makes one of his characters, Henry Rackham, an amateur explorer of these slums, enabling the reader to be informed along with the character. He also exactly arranges the suburban spaces of affluent Notting Hill, where William Rackham lives, carefully checking the omnibus routes that link the two. His narrative attempts no Ackroyd-like imitation of historical language; our sense of this world's pastness must come from what we see.

Research can be a problem. One of the high Victorian novelists whom Faber most admires, George Eliot, transposed so much of her research into Judaism into *Daniel Deronda* that her audacious exercise in sympathy—a novel whose heroine marries a vicious man for mercenary reasons—became weighed down with her findings. At one point Faber seems to recognize this risk, making two of his philanthropists discuss their reading of Mayhew's *London Labour and the London Poor* as if awkward about his own reliance on this work (404). When his characters argue about Darwinism, you can sense a striving after period specificity. When they are innocently preoccupied with matching just the right weird-seeming hairstyle for the season, however, you can more easily believe the ridiculous detail. Faber is best and most enjoyable on the little things that puzzle and convince the modern reader, and these are perhaps the most reliable pleasures of historical fiction. You are shown, in passing, how an affluent Victorian household prepares for autumn (changing the curtains, scouring the chimneys, bulk-buying the choicest tinned condiments). You find out what a lady keeps in her bathroom cabinet or her reticule. Agnes Rackham opens her purse and 'removes, from amongst the face-powder shells, smelling salts and button-hooks, a much creased and tarnished prayer card' (386). Here are the items that no Victorian novel would find it worth mentioning. The book is full of such feminine impedimenta, for its central male character is a manufacturer of perfumes and sundry toilet products. You discover, as Faber must have done, about the constituents of rose cold cream. You sniff Lavender Milk and Poudre Juvenile. You are told of the properties of sulphur soap and the advertised powers of Aureoline hair treatment. Henry James might be right and Victorian psychology may be obscure to us, but not what was offered in its chemists' shops.

8
Style

HERE we are at the heart of what makes a novel or a novelist distinctive. The way that a book is written is sometimes called a novelist's 'tone of voice'. An author's particular tone can be what makes the telling of the story seem unmanufactured, inimitable—in Henry James's highest term of praise, 'sincere'. With some novelists, tone is all; it is the hardest thing to catch, yet what often matters most to readers. It is what makes you think that a Jane Austen sentence could not have been written by anyone else, as if, like stylistic DNA, the smallest element of a writer's prose carried within it the essence of his or her singularity. Publishers frequently talk of finding a new novelist who has his or her own 'voice'. Academic critics are more sceptical. When tough-minded literary theory arrived in the English departments of British universities at the beginning of the 1980s, 'tone' began to be frowned on as a descriptive term, sure evidence of a woolly and impressionistic approach to textual analysis. It was particularly shunned as a metaphor taken from speech (implying that when we read we hear a *voice*). 'When I am reading a book, whether wise or silly, it seems to me to be alive and talking to me,' wrote Jonathan Swift.[1] Perhaps we all know this impression, which literary theorists began to call an illusion. Jacques Derrida, in particular, had influenced many to believe that it was a cardinal error to think of language as essentially spoken (personal, spontaneous) rather than always written (systematic, second-hand).

Yet there are novelists whose success stems largely from the finding of a distinctive tone, even if this might be an elaborately artificial achievement. Take Nick Hornby, a writer whose narrators seem to address the reader with a colloquial familiarity. Reviewers invariably speak of the 'tone' of Hornby's narratives and it is surely as good a word as any for his special appeal. Here is something like a typical Hornby sentence from *How To Be Good.* Katie, the novel's narrator, is telling us about a row with her husband, David.

> It begins with something about a plastic bag with a hole in it (I didn't know it had a hole in it, and I told David to use it to . . . Oh, forget it); it ends with me telling David that he's a talentless and evil bastard, and with him telling me that he can't hear my voice without wanting to throw up. (21)

David hates the sound of Katie's voice, but the sound of her voice is what we are being given too. The very banalities and exaggerations that a true stylist might want to avoid are the point of this style. The intended effect is of a voice (Hornby's, to all intents and purposes) ruefully admitting to the ordinary, self-administered disasters of life. That interrupting parenthesis is very Hornby: his narrators often lead you part of the way down an absurd explanation before saying, as Katie likes to, 'I will spare you any further details.'

In his invaluable, now neglected, book *Practical Criticism* (1929), I. A. Richards defined 'tone' as a speaker's '*attitude to his listener*'.[2] 'He chooses or arranges his words differently as the audience varies, in automatic or deliberate *recognition of his relation to them*. The tone of his utterance reflects his awareness of this relation, his sense of how he stands towards those he is addressing.' Richards was thinking of poetry, but his definition is more generally useful. It catches at the knowingness of a speaker who is alert to our expectations or judgements. Hornby does not address a 'reader', as some novelists have done; he makes his narrators tell their stories with a *listener* in mind. Familiarly, they agree, concede, admit. 'Tone' is entirely separate from story. In a first-person, confessional narrative, tone is even separate from the actual content of the narrator's thoughts. In the example from *How To Be Good*, tone is how Katie thinks about what she is thinking, what she says about what she is saying. She is always stopping herself, correcting herself, not quite liking what she has just told us. She finds herself privately appalled by her daughter's 'charitable' friendship with an obnoxious, 'deprived' schoolmate.

> So. To recap: I wish to be forgiven for my trespasses . . . and yet I will not forgive those who trespass against me, even if they are eight-year-old girls whose only real trespass is smelling bad. And having grey skin. And not being terribly bright. Right. OK, then. Let me think about that, and I'll come back to you. (184)

The tone always has to be anti-solemn, even if melancholy is sometimes allowed. Self-mockery is the sign of candour.

Each section of this chapter examines a particular aspect of a novelist's style. It goes into some of the minutiae (paragraphing, say, or the linking of sentences, or the choice of words) by which a distinctive tone is produced. Style does not need to be sincere; it can be parodic, as in the types of narration dealt with in the first two sections. In the first, I show that even tonelessness can be a kind of stylistic effect; in the second, that novelists have long liked to imitate antiquated aspects of English prose. In both cases a writer has had to strive to adopt peculiar stylistic habits, to write in an unnatural way. Though there is no term for it in literary analysis, there is a fundamental difference between a style that is native to a writer, even while writing in the person of an invented character, and a style that is achieved by study and contrivance. With the exception of pastiche and heteroglossia, the aspects of style discussed in this chapter could be used either sincerely or parodically. Some, like streams of consciousness, are technically demanding and highly literary. Others, like hyperbole, are forms of rhetoric familiar from everyday language which can be put to inventive fictional use. As I hope we can see by looking at Woolf's use of parentheses or

Don DeLillo's employment of parataxis, the most ambitious of novelists can rely on the simplest of stylistic effects. Some of these thrust themselves at us, and of others we are hardly conscious. The section here on paragraphs presents perhaps the best example of the latter, a matter that is elemental to a writer's style, governing the very rhythm of his or her prose, but unnoticed in most literary criticism.

PLAIN PROSE

In his hugely influential book *The Rise of the Novel* (1957), the critic Ian Watt described one of the distinctive features of the novel form, in its first eighteenth-century experiments, as 'a prose which restricts itself almost entirely to a descriptive and denotative use of language'.[3] Its 'realism' committed the novelist to a plain style, avoiding ornamentation and figurative extravagance. The pioneers of whom Watt writes with most enthusiasm, Daniel Defoe and Samuel Richardson, were both mocked for their failures of elegance. They both favoured narrators whose stylistic abilities were designedly curtailed: Pamela, the pious servant girl; Robinson Crusoe, the matter-of-fact adventurer. Yet plainness in prose is as artificial and as difficult to achieve as figurativeness. In order to write *The Curious Incident of the Dog in the Night-Time*, Mark Haddon must have made great efforts to keep figures of speech at bay. For, as if with Ian Watt's formula in mind, here is prose reduced to its most literal patterns. Christopher Boone, Haddon's narrator, is autistic. Without any ability to interpret the signs of feeling in others, he must merely describe their behaviour. His is a language of unselective reporting. Doggedly accurate himself, he complains about how people insist on using metaphors. 'They had a skeleton in the cupboard'; 'We had a real pig of a day'. 'I think it should be called a lie because a pig is not like a day and people do not have skeletons in their cupboards' (20). When Christopher tries to picture such phrases, 'it just confuses me'. He is disturbed when Mrs Shears, a neighbour who—we infer—is having a somewhat desperate affair with his father, says things like 'I'm going to hit the hay' or 'It's brass monkeys out there.' 'And I didn't like it when she said things like that because I didn't know what she meant' (55).

For Christopher, all language's indirectness (metaphor, irony, understatement) is mysterious. Rhetorical tricks are unimaginable. His narrative allows for some similes, but only, as Christopher himself tells us, to show us some literal resemblance. When he says that a policeman with a very hairy nose 'looked as if there were two very small mice hiding in his nostrils', it is because 'it really did look like there were two very small mice hiding in his nostrils' (22). A simile is not a lie, 'unless it is a bad simile'. Christopher does not use language ornamentally or indirectly, because he cannot. He reports things. He collects observations and strings together statements. Never can there have been a novel in which so many sentences begin with the word 'And' (see 'Parataxis', below). Christopher's weird plainness is there in the very appearance of any page of his narrative. Many readers will have their experience of Haddon's novel shaped by a technical peculiarity of which they might not be conscious. *The Curious Incident of the Dog in the Night-Time* uses a sans serif font. This is highly unusual in any published book; the conventional wisdom is that serifs help the brain's visual apparatus as a line of print is scanned. The tiny thickenings and thinnings of the limbs of every letter give the eye something to catch on to (they are doing so for you in this book). Sans serif fonts may be used in advertisements, headlines, and the like, but their simplicity is almost physically uncomfortable in any lengthy text. The font's discomfiting simplicity is perfectly suited to Haddon's narrator, in all his pedantic veracity, with his cataloguing and enumerating. Reading a page printed like this is, I think, visually disconcerting. Graphically speaking, we are in Christopher's nuance-free world from the start. (Only the A level maths question that he gives us—'And this was my favourite question' (259)—is in a normal font with serifs.) We are unsettled by a sans serif font's lack of variation, just as we will become conscious of Christopher's flat-voiced failure to sense the emotions and tones of the novel's other characters.

One of several reasons why this plainness is intriguing in a novel (as it would not be in life) is that it comes close to parodying what the novel as a genre originally set out to achieve: to be true to the world of circumstantial facts. Christopher's narrative is prose reduced to its most literal patterns, accuracy its only standard. He duly provides us with lists and measurements, and sometimes even pictures and diagrams, as if these fulfilled the purposes of narrative in a more satisfactory way than sentences. His descriptions are collections of 'things I noticed', unsorted by significance or priority (176). 'I see everything' (174). Travelling on his own to London for the first time, he must describe exactly the condition of the lavatory on the train. He tells us things because they are true, and we begin to realize what a strange standard the plain truth truly is.

ANTIQUE PROSE

Enfolding all the other stories in David Mitchell's *Cloud Atlas* is the old document with which we begin and end: 'The Pacific Journal of Adam Ewing'. Its supposed author is an American lawyer, Adam Ewing, travelling in the South Seas in the 1850s. We can arrive at its date from clues gradually given: we are in an age of sail, yet also of steam trains; there is mention of a gold rush in San Francisco; Herman Melville is a contemporary writer. But it is a matter of form as well as content. We can tell that the document is antique from the way it is written as well as from its subject matter. The matter of form is pressed on us by a kind of visual conceit. The journal's title and daily headings are printed in the facsimile of what looks like an antique handwriting. More importantly, Ewing's style and diction are throughout fabricated in order to sound as though they come from another time.

Mitchell has said that it took him a year and a half to get this part of the book right, and certainly he has conscientiously larded it with the curlicues of an antique prose. 'To wit', 'whene'er', 'loath as I was', 'ere our departure', 'peradventure'. More subtly, he had contrived a dated stylistic formality that clashes expressively with the 'uncivilised' scene that Ewing surveys. 'I vouchsafe he is the only other gentleman on this latitude east of Sydney,' he writes when he meets an English surgeon 'upon a forlorn strand' (5). As he writes this, he is in as remote a spot as can be imagined: the Chatham Islands, off the eastern coast of New Zealand. Here, at the edge of things, colonizing Westerners erect their frail structures of self-belief and our narrator learns to doubt their good influence. 'I recall the crimes Mr Melville imputes to Pacific missionaries in his recent account of the Typee', a reference to Herman Melville's 1846 novel of 'Polynesian Life' (511). Is civilization good? 'I know not the answer, nor whence flew the surety of my younger years' (512).

Ewing's account must physically exist in its oldness because it is to be discovered by Robert Frobisher, the narrator of 'Letters from Zedelghem', the next of the six stories that compose *Cloud Atlas*. He finds a published version in the library of the reclusive English composer whom he visits in Holland in the early 1930s. The narrative baton is handed on. Oddly enough, from Ann Radcliffe's Gothic fiction in the 1790s to A. S. Byatt's *Possession*, plots of novels have not infrequently depended on discovering antique manuscripts. It is how present and past get connected. In some cases, as in *Cloud Atlas*, the old texts are given us to read, their prose embodying their antiquity. A specialist in this has been Peter Ackroyd. Having mimicked the style of Oscar Wilde in *The Last Testament of Oscar Wilde* (1983), he included in *Hawksmoor* the narrative of Nicholas Dyer, written in what appeared to be late seventeenth-century prose. 'And so let us beginne; and, as the Fabrick takes its Shape in front of you, alwaies keep the Structure intirely in Mind as you inscribe it' (ch. 1, p. 1). The father of such experiments was perhaps Thackeray in *The History of Henry Esmond, Esq.* (1851), which copied, as its dedication declared, 'the manners and language of Queen Anne's time'. This story of an eighteenth-century adventurer, 'Written by himself', was even printed in a special type designed to mimic the appearance of a book of that period.

Thackeray was after historical verisimilitude, but Mitchell's purposes are rather different. He gives Adam Ewing the moral earnestness of a nineteenth-century man, believing in the beneficent influence of progress and troubled by 'that casual brutality lighter races show the darker'. While more humane than his fellow colonizers, his own racism has an ingenuousness that is itself antique. 'She has a tinge of black blood,' he says of a maid servant, '& I fancy her mother is not far removed from the jungle breed' (5). In a novel whose six stories are all parables of human predatoriness, this enfolding journal is an original test of human decencies. In expression as well as attitude, Ewing in the South Seas is made an anthropological version of Darwin in the Galápagos. The irony of his story is that the worst predators are the Maori, who ruthlessly exploit the peaceableness of 'the aboriginals of Chatham', the Moriori. Ewing helps one of the last of this people to escape the genocide visited on them by the Maori. It is this 'savage' who saves him in turn, when the 'gentleman' surgeon whom he has befriended turns out to be another predator. There is a moral here about how 'humanity may transcend tooth & claw'; only a nineteenth-century writer, someone speaking with an antique voice, can be so candid as to state it (528).

PARATAXIS

You cannot imagine Henry James beginning several consecutive sentences with the word 'And'. Only the most primitive of narratives, we might think, would just keep adding one statement to another. Indeed, before children learn the uses of different conjunctions and the arts of subordinate clauses, they sometimes write in this way: 'And . . . And . . . And . . .'. Paratactic style is common in oral literature and in stories intended for the young. In histories of English we find it associated with an undeveloped state of the written language. It becomes less frequent after the sixteenth century, when 'the loose association of clauses (parataxis) gives way to more precise indications of logical relationship and subordination (hypotaxis)'.[4] It might seem characteristic of linguistic immaturity, yet its has long had expressive uses. It will be familiar to many from the King James Bible. The story of the Creation and the Fall in Genesis is a masterpiece of parataxis, leaving it widely open to interpretation. Take Eve and Adam eating the forbidden fruit.

> And when the woman saw that the tree was good for food, and that it was pleasant to the eyes, and a tree to be desired to make one wise, she took of the fruit thereof, and did eat, and gave also unto her husband with her; and he did eat. And the eyes of them both were opened, and they knew that they were naked; and they sewed fig leaves together, and made themselves aprons. (Gen. 3: 6–8)

Did Adam take the fruit readily or only after much persuasion, gladly or despairingly? The narrative refuses to say. In this translation, the openness to interpretation of much of Genesis is a consequence of the paratactic style (much altered in more modern translations).

There is something lacking in paratactic narration, a fact rather brilliantly exploited in Mark Haddon's *The Curious Incident of the Dog in the Night-Time*. Its 15-year-old autistic narrator Christopher Boone is autistic, recalls dialogue without registering reactions or emotions. 'And I said . . . And she said . . . And I said . . .'. The reader must infer the other characters' feelings, omitted by the narrator. We might expect this style from a novel with such a naive narrator, but parataxis can also be used in a novel that is narratively highly sophisticated. In *Underworld*, Don DeLillo often places sentences and clauses one after another without indicating by connecting words (beyond 'and') the relations between them. Here the artist Klara Sax recalls a teenage trip to Manhattan with her mother and her best friend.

> And they stood outside a skyscraper on Fifth Avenue, it was probably 1934 and the Japanese were entrenched in Manchuria and they looked straight up the face of the building and walked through the polished lobby and it was the Fred F. French Building, which intrigued the girls because who on earth was Fred F. French, and Klara's mother . . . did not have a clue to the identity of Fred F. French, and this intrigued the girls even more, intrigued and amused them, they were thirteen and fourteen and everything amused them. (398)

Forty years on, recollection evens out the historical and the circumstantial. There is no obvious logic to what is remembered and why. By chance and the habit of memory, fragments of the past, private and public, belong together. DeLillo's parataxis tells us how his characters remember or how they think. This can include how they avoid thinking, as in this characteristic sentence about American nuclear weapons researchers.

> They came to do science in New Mexico during the war, an overnight sprawl of trailers and hutments, and they ate the local grub and played poker once a week and went to the Saturday square dance and worked on the thing with no name, the bomb that would redefine the limits of human perception and dread. (421–2)

In the very syntax, the 'bombheads' (as they are called) devote themselves to refining apocalyptic weaponry as readily as they adopt local pleasures and pastimes.

Parataxis often gives DeLillo's prose its particular rhythm, sometimes blankly reporting the hardly intelligible facets of urban life. Here is Albert, Klara's former husband, surrounded in his Bronx apartment by pushers and junkies.

> And when he went out they were on the front stoop muttering something that sounded like Wall Street and Albert finally surmised this was a brand of heroin for sale, Wall Street, Wall Street, and he could hear them in the halls, strangers in the building, breathing in and out . . . He heard them breathing in the halls and knew he had food for two days easy and when the milk went sour he could open a can of peaches and dump the fruit and syrupy juice on the breakfast cereal . . . He heard them late at night and knew he could stretch the chopped meat, bulk up the tomato soup with macaroni, and they didn't live in the building and would find another place. (230–1)

There is a logic here: Albert thinks of how he might improvise rudimentary meals because he is frightened to leave his apartment. Yet the mere addition of the statements also seems to enact his numbed fatalism.

But there is not always logic. *Underworld* wants to give a sense of 'the sand-grain manyness of things', all those details that make actuality, and brings to the task a prose of accumulation. Here is a paragraph from a chapter describing Nick and his friends in the 1950s, sunning themselves on rooftops ('the tar beaches') in a hot New York summer.

> The tar softened and fumed and the heat beat down and the green gnats stuck to their bodies and across the way the pigeon kid sent his birds into spiral flight with a bamboo pole, and waved a towel at times, and whistled like a traffic cop, and his flock mixed in midair with a rival flock from a roof three blocks away, a hundred-birded tumult and blur, and younger birds flew with the wrong flock and were captured and sometimes killed, dispatched within the rules by the rival flyer of the other roof, and after a while the girls had to leave because the sun was just too smoking hot, singing lyrics as they rolled their blankets up. (771)

One thing and then another. The paratactic prose is fashioned to act like memory, simply collecting the details that are vivid. In many places this habit of collecting produces sequences of verbless sentences, simply presenting us with the elements of a scene. Here is the stadium at which the novel's opening baseball game takes place, seen by the radio commentator Russ Hodges. 'The big square Longines clock that juts up from the clubhouse. Strokes of colour all around, a frescoing of hats and faces and the green grandstand and tawny base paths. Russ feels lucky to be here' (15). While concerned with hidden connections and beguiling conspiracy theories, down at eye level it is disconnected 'manyness'. Parataxis performs the disconnection, catching at fragments. You have to make a narrative to connect what the prose does not connect. No wonder that, for DeLillo's characters, paranoia, which always supplies a story, is such a solace.

PARAGRAPHS

The keen student of fiction might read many books of narratology or guides to the work of leading novelists and never find any account of this most elemental element of fiction: paragraphing. Yet what most fundamentally determines the very rhythm of reading? The passionate conviction of a stretch of *Jane Eyre* is enacted in the pulse of its short, emphatic paragraphs. The experience of reading late Henry James is of the length of his paragraphs. He expatiates for 500, even 1,000, words without drawing breath, tirelessly subtilizing his analyses. Franz Kafka's *The Trial*, while a short novel, has paragraphs that stretch to 4,000 words and more (see, for instance, the chapter entitled 'The Uncle—Leni', which has a paragraph that runs to over eleven pages in the Penguin Classics edition). The reader is indeed trapped in these blocks of narrative, unrestfully required to pursue the strange logic of Josef K.'s experiences, with no escape. Any reader of Kafka's novel is likely to find him- or herself, on occasion, looking for some intermission. You too are caught up in 'Der Prozeß', as Kafka's German title has it.

Often what is most distinctive of a writer's style in a particular novel can be caught if we characterize his or her use of paragraphs. In Carol Shields's *Unless*, the first-person narrative of Reta Winters, her ordinary heroine, has a rueful or self-deprecating rhythm. Speculations stop short; wishfulness is curtailed. Three or four paragraphs build to an anticlimax or a reversal: a very brief paragraph that waves away what was being said. Musing on the supper that she has ready at home for her family, the narrator becomes sarcastic about her own wifeliness: 'such a good woman, so organized too', the paragraph ends (47). 'Enough of that!' is the next paragraph in its entirety. She will not let herself drift into unrestrained resentment. 'Oh, loosen up, Ms. Winters' is a whole paragraph that follows her ruminations on how to avoid sex scenes in her novels (188). Frequently we know that a paragraph has been cut short, because the next one begins 'No', or 'Stop it', or (Shields's favourite paragraph opener) 'But'. Danielle Westerman, the famous feminist intellectual whose works Reta has been translating, is the opposite. 'She has arrived in her old age at a gorgeous fluidity and expansion of phrase.' We can only imagine her self-proliferating style, 'inviting us, her readers, to believe in the totality of her abandonment'. Reta breaks off from her description of this 'rapturous' prose to add her descant, in one of her bathetic little paragraphs.

> Either that or she's gone senile to good effect, a grand loosening of language in her old age. The thought has more than once occurred to me. (15)

The collapsing of paragraphs into single sentences is a favourite device in *Unless*. When she finds herself thinking that her mysteriously traumatized daughter will be forever excluded from life, Reta fends off her fears with a one-sentence paragraph:

> No, I am not ready to believe this (179).

She dare not say more. After the opening two paragraphs of the novel—the first squarely telling the reader of the narrator's unhappiness, the second conceding all the things for which she should be grateful—we get this complete paragraph:

> And I have my writing (2).

It is a kind of joke. When her daughter becomes a catatonic drop-out, this is the consolation that Reta is offered by her culture-respecting friends:

> But you have your writing, Reta.

The single-sentence paragraph pretends to be weighty with significance, but the implication of presenting it as a self-sufficient paragraph is different. Reta's novel-writing is more like an airy diversion. The thing that keeps being said to her as a consolation is blank and banal.

The ordinariness of the terrors and hopes that Shields depicts requires a reining-in of sentences. Truthfulness means a refusal of eloquence. Other novelists of domestic life have found different rhythms, allowing for the elaborate tracing of ordinary motivations. *Unless* has an epigraph from George Eliot, the spaciousness of whose fiction is often enacted in the span of her lengthy paragraphs. Look at the opening paragraph of *Middlemarch*, which describes Dorothea Brooke's peculiar beauty, her 'plain' style of dress, her social status, her intellectual and Christian fervour, and her situation as an orphan living with her bachelor uncle. It is about 600 words long, and this is typical of the novel, especially when Eliot has a complex or subtle explanation to include. She always has such room for further exact, tolerant explorations of her characters' motives. Comparably, Virginia Woolf's *To the Lighthouse* (1927) sometimes employs paragraphs that, in closely printed paperback editions, are two or three pages long. In the stream of one of her characters' thoughts, reveries unspool, unbroken by any conventional requirement of 'units of meaning'.

In general, paragraphs have become shorter in novels over the last century. It is tempting to think that short paragraphs are for short attention spans, and it is true that popular fiction usually uses short paragraphs. Yet there is also the example of authors who made a stylistic achievement out of a spare prose. Ernest Hemingway is the most influential. Here is a characteristic fragment of 'Indian Camp', from Hemingway's *In Our Time* (1925). Nick is a boy accompanying his father, who is a doctor, to an isolated Indian reservation. Nick's father has to perform a Caesarian delivery without an anaesthetic. Nick's uncle and three Indian men hold the woman down and she bites his uncle's arm in her agony. The baby is born and Nick's father stitches the woman up.

> Nick did not watch. His curiosity had been gone for a long time.
>
> His father finished and stood up. Uncle George and the three Indian men stood up. Nick put the basin out in the kitchen.
>
> Uncle George looked at his arm. The young Indian smiled reminiscently.
>
> 'I'll put some peroxide on that, George,' the doctor said.
>
> He bent over the Indian woman. She was quiet now and her eyes were closed. She looked very pale. She did not know what had become of the baby or anything. (17–18)

The staccato pattern of statements mimics the boy's perceptions. Apart from the biting, everything about the woman's ordeal is left out. We can infer the elemental business, but nothing like sentiment or empathy is going to be given to us. Distantly, Hemingway's example is behind the liking of Shields's narrator for the bare, unelaborated statement of fact. The reader is asked to recognize significance where little, apparently, has actually been said. In one typical instance in *Unless*, a brief paragraph tells us about Reta's housework.

> With my dampened dust cloth in hand I'm keeping myself going. I reach under the sink and polish that hard-to-get-to piece of elbow pipe. Tomorrow I'm planning to dust the basement stairs, swiftly, but getting into the corners. (61)

All her despair, all her angry belief in the consolations of ordinary life, are implied. But she breaks off before telling us of them.

DICTION

Do novelists sometimes use special words just because they are writing novels? Jane Austen evidently thought that they did, and that they should not. When her niece Anna sent her draft chapters of her own would-be novel, Aunt Jane encouraged the author but subjected her work to detailed criticism. Amongst other things, she warned against novelistic vocabulary. 'Devereux Forester's being ruined by his Vanity is extremely good,' she said encouragingly, 'but I wish you would not let him plunge into a "vortex of Dissipation". I do not object to the Thing, but I cannot bear the expression;—it is such thorough novel slang—and so old, that I dare say Adam met with it in the first novel he opened.'[5] Austen was all too used to the hyperbolic diction of the novels of her day, and especially their hyperbolic words for virtue or vice. One point of her joke is that, when she writes, novels have not been around for very long, yet 'novel slang' already seems as old as can be.

Alan Hollinghurst's *The Spell* features a good deal of dissipation and, Austen would have been glad to know, one mention of a 'vortex'. Alex drives through the English countryside on a summer's day, roof down, 'in a private vortex of wind and sunlight' (158). Perhaps Austen would have forgiven this apparently literal usage ('vortex': 'a whirling motion forming a cavity at the centre', *Chambers Dictionary*), though the excitable old metaphor is there too: Alex is hurrying to meet his new lover Danny and is suitably over-stimulated. To express the 'racing fuddled sense of surrender' to entrancement by lust or drugs (throughout the book, chains of adjectives come without commas, as if punctuation would take away their immediacy) Hollinghurst does sometimes use special words—'fuddled' itself being one. It is as if the vocabulary itself goes a little woozy. Drugged on ecstasy, Alex feels 'etherised regret' (173). Justin thinks of his ex-lover Alex with 'whoofs of lust'—no dictionary will help you identify these (89). Equally there is a peculiar vocabulary of negation to match the deflated mood after a trance has passed. One man acquires an 'unlasting aura' (198), an ex-partner has an 'unlifelike voice' (202), a character sees only 'eventlessness' (142).

Hollinghurst is a writer who likes out-of-the-way words: torchere, epiphytes, finials, Orchidaceae, oculus. Such diction reflects his characters' special knowledge, their appreciation of architecture or botany or antiques. There is a certain kind of novelist who collects recondite vocabulary. The classic English novelist of whom one thinks is Thomas Hardy. A browse through *Tess of the d'Urbervilles*, that most accessible of his novels, will turn up words like 'dolorifuge', 'pachydermatous', 'niaiseries', 'carking', 'drachm', 'temerarious', 'prestidigitation', 'flexuous', 'vitalizations' and 'boreal', over which generations of sixth-form readers have passed without comment. In Hardy's case these might point us to the author's inferiority complex about his own education, or lack of education. He wished to show his learning. Yet the vocabulary also serves to treat what it describes with the precision of philology or natural history. As well as telling a story, the novelist is revealing organic or historical processes. A popular exemplar of unusual diction is Patrick O'Brian, whose historical tales of nautical adventure are sprinkled with words like 'auscultation', 'fulvous', 'grego', 'grigs', 'horchata', 'leet', 'mumping', 'sillery', 'wariangle', and 'xebec' (these all from *The Yellow Admiral*, 1997). The recondite diction is essential to his appeal. The unusual words are not there just because he writes stories of the sea, full of salty slang and names of the parts of ships. Only the last of the words above is specifically nautical: 'xebec': a small three-masted Mediterranean ship, lateen-rigged but with some square sails. (Two of them, however—'horchata' and 'sillery'—are alcoholic drinks: another of O'Brian's interests.) It is rather that the unusual words are prominent signs of the novel's appetite for peculiar lore and encyclopedic detail.

Except in their casual sexual encounters, which are usually speechless, Alan Hollinghurst's characters are a word-relishing lot. No wonder that Justin and Robin have an ill-tempered game of Scrabble, in which Robin proudly produces PROEMS ('which came to a timid twenty-six') when, as his calculating opponent sees, 'TEMPORISE was waiting to be deployed' for some huge score (207). The lovers quarrel when Justin tries PIRRENT ('It means . . . sort of *vainglorious*') and the board ends up on the floor. Epicures of one kind or another, the characters naturally attract rare or delicious diction. Robin enjoys a 'monkish kind of aestivation' in his country cottage (182): 'aestivation': 'the passing or spending of the summer', a word unrecorded by the *OED* since Johnson's *Dictionary* in 1755. When asked if his book is sexy, Danny makes 'a moue of uncertainty' (219): 'moue' was apparently introduced into English by Thackeray, and is a Hollinghurst favourite. The 'whoosh of tonic-water' into a glass of gin is also called a 'susurration' (227): 'a rustling murmur', *OED*, from *susurratio*, the Latin for 'whispering'.

Henry James, a lover of recherché words whom Hollinghurst greatly admires, replied to an enquiry about whether he invented words with the assertion that he tried to write only 'in a language already existing & consecrated'.[6] English already provided the novelist with a 'superabundantly' demanding vocabulary. Hollinghurst, however, edges towards new coinages. *The Spell* emphasizes uncertain perceptions, its description often qualified by 'oddly' or 'rather' or 'strangely'. Adjectives acquire *-ish* endings: not just 'oldish', 'smallish', 'heavyish', but also 'straightish' (sexually speaking), 'invalidish', 'gypsyish' or 'Mick Jaggerish'. This is made the diction of a self-contained gay group. An attractive young man squeezes Alex's arm 'with a sweet spivvish suddenness' (29); party guests crammed in the back of a car make 'sluttish jokes about the tight squeeze' (117).

There are also the playful words ending in -y: 'dotty', 'pansy' (as an adjective), 'sarky', 'cruisy' ('He raked the beach with a cruisy steadiness'; 213). Sometimes the diction's oddness—Danny recalls a restaurant with a 'chorus-line of cow-licked young waiters' (220)—is nicely comical and, it has to be said, entirely camp.

Usually writers who want different words get them from other languages. The English novel has always accommodated words not from English, and some of the most influential non-American novelists in English of recent decades have been creative importers of words. Salman Rushdie is an influential example. Look back on *Midnight's Children* and you can sense his consciousness of his diction by the consistency with which he translates the strange words that he introduces. 'Young goondas, that is to say hooligans' (408); 'During the nikah, the wedding proper' (415); 'at the valima, the consummation ceremony' (416): these phrases are characteristic. Rushdie's narrator is aware of a British reader. So too is Monica Ali in *Brick Lane,* though times have changed and the instant explanation of 'foreign' diction is only rarely provided. In *Brick Lane,* Nazneen's bravest rebellion against her circumstances hinges on a word that few readers will ever have encountered before, a word whose strangeness to most readers the novel well knows.

Alone in her East End council flat, Nazneen is visited by the baleful Mrs Islam, who styles herself a wise adviser to younger women but is really a bullying moneylender. She brings her two threatening sons; they demand more money and begin smashing up Nazneen's home. Nazneen has paid her husband's debt many times over. '"I'm not going to pay any more . . ." She hesitated. "Any more riba"' (444). 'Riba'. The word has a strange power. '"You bitch," said Son Number One.' Yet his mother, irresistible until now, is stunned. '"Riba," whispered Mrs Islam. "Riba, she says." Her head lolled around as if the word had given her fever.' The women are speaking in Bengali, but 'riba' is picked out, as if untranslatable into English. It must mean something like 'interest', the word that appears in Mrs Islam's defensive response. 'Do you think, before God, that I would charge interest? Am I a moneylender? A usurer?' But 'riba' is nothing so bland as 'interest': it is a forbidden thing, and a word that, as Nazneen's hesitation tells us, is not easy to say. Muslims are forbidden to make profits from charging for the loan of money. Nazneen offers to pay if Mrs Islam will swear on the Qur'ān that she is not a usurer. She will not, and she and her sons are driven away. Until this moment none of her victims has dared give its true name to the 'riba' that she collects. The word carries into Ali's immigrant narrative its special power of prohibition.

Some novelists (Henry James, Will Self) use larger vocabularies than others (Daniel Defoe, Samuel Beckett), but a few reach beyond dictionary English altogether. Laurence Sterne's *A Sentimental Journey* and Charlotte Brontë's *Villette* variously stitch French vocabulary into English prose as their English narrators are cast loose in, respectively, France and Belgium. Saul Bellow peppers his American narratives with the untranslated Yiddish words—'schlemiel', 'kvetch', 'goy'—that seem to express the rough candour of his characters. The Novel as a genre is remarkably accommodating to foreign words that have not yet been accepted elsewhere in the language. *Brick Lane* is full of words transliterated from Bengali (their English forms are, of course, merely approximations of their proper pronunciation—signposts to sounds beyond our hearing). You have to stick with a foreign word if what it names is untranslatable, un-English. There are the food words, for instance, that conjure contentment for Nazneen: 'ghur' and 'shimai' and dried 'hilsha'—the latter being what her husband, Chanu, decides to buy when their Westernized elder daughter has provokingly asked for 'Birds Eye burgers' (195). Shop windows display pyramids of 'ladoos' and towers of 'shondesh'. After her son is born, Nazneen goes out walking with Chanu and her child to buy sweetmeats with gratifying names: 'milky roshmolai, sticky brown gulabjam, golden whirls of jelabee' (91).

We take the novel's alien diction as Nazneen's way back to her life in Bangladesh. She looks at the heroine on a film poster and sees how 'the kohl around her eyes made them smoke with passion' (55). She sits on a bench on an East End patch of grass like 'a maharanee in her enclosure' (58). She thinks it odd that her friend Razia wears 'a baggy jumper' and trainers with 'her salwaar kameez' (the words hardly go together) (69). When she is distraught at the illness of her son, she has a 'jinn' in her head (143). When Chanu tries to discipline his insubordinate daughters he puts all his force into 'the niyyah—the making of the intention' rather than the punishment (181). The last of these belongs with the many words imported into Monica Ali's narrative that speak of special cultural or religious practices. Nazneen thinks that the imams must have compassion for women because they allow them, when pregnant, to 'do namaz' from a chair (234). Her prayers are disrupted when she drops her 'tasbee' under a radiator (130). Her lover, Karim, is 'taqwa' (255). 'More God-conscious than her own husband' is the gloss on this word. Yet these three usages, like others, are not just there to widen many readers' knowledge of another culture. Each of these three is being used humorously. The fact, for instance, that Karim is 'taqwa' is one of the reasons that Nazneen gives herself for being drawn to him—that, and his beautiful neck. The humorous use of the diction suggests something else: that the words that Nazneen has been taught are becoming foreign to her too.

AMPLIFICATION

When reviewers and critics try to describe what is special about Philip Roth's late fiction they say something about the style. Everyone refers to the passion, the urgency, of the prose. These are the right words, but they make the writing sound like an outpouring of feeling. In fact it is all carefully arranged. A great writer of speeches, Roth is a rhetorician amongst novelists, and the terminology of rhetoric often best describes his persuasive patterning of words. The traditional name for one of Roth's favourite rhetorical devices in *The Human Stain* is *amplification*. You say something, and then you say it again in a different way. And again. You make a sentence, then you make another with the same beginning but a different ending. And another. Expressiveness comes with repetition, with the sheer accumulation of words. Roth follows the advice of Thomas Wilson's *The Art of Rhetoric* (1553), a Renaissance manual of style. 'Sentences gathered and heaped together commend muche the matter.'[7] So whole paragraphs consist of sentences that start with the same words. When Coleman Silk is telling his mother that she will never be allowed to meet his wife and children, we see how he hardens himself against her. 'It was not a moment for him to be recalling his childhood' (138). There is his thought. But this sets off another. And then another and another.

> It was not a moment for him to be admiring her lucidity or her sarcasm or her courage. It was not a moment to allow himself to be subjugated by the all-but-pathological phenomenon of mother love. It was not a moment for him to be hearing all the words that she was not saying but that were sounded more tellingly even than what she did say. It was not a moment to think thoughts other than the thoughts he'd come armed with. It was certainly not a moment to resort to explanations . . .

Half a dozen sentences begin the same way. The prose amplifies all that he must not do—all the natural feelings that he must fend off—and reproduces the sheer energy of his renunciation.

Such prose is often more like drama than narrative. Over the phone, Coleman tells his disapproving son Jeff that his affair with a much younger woman, Faunia, is over. 'Is it? How come?' the son asks.

> He thinks, Because there's no hope for her. Because men have

> beaten the shit out of her. Because her kids have been killed in a fire. Because she works as a janitor. Because she has no education and says she can't read. Because she's been on the run since she was fourteen. Because she doesn't even ask me, 'What are you doing with me?' Because she knows what *everybody* is doing with her. Because she's seen it all and there's no hope.

The heaping-up of unspoken reasons, the vehemence of this, is more important than any of the reasons themselves. The amplification shows us why the affair is not over at all. As the character thinks of why he should leave, he knows why he cannot. Similarly, visiting his daughter's class for children with learning difficulties, he associates them with the apparently illiterate Faunia. 'What do you do with the kid who can't read?' (163). We are swept up in the gale of his thoughts, nine long sentences each beginning 'The kid who . . .'. It is both a résumé of her misfortunes and an angry expression of his attachment.

As here, the muscular variation on a theme is often a property of free indirect speech (see Chapter 2). In both sympathy and mockery, this technique lets us understand Coleman's academic enemy and nemesis Delphine Roux. Reiterated phrases perform her self-obsessed, passionate dissatisfaction. She has come from France and understands only 'academic American',

> which is hardly American, which is why she can't make it *in*, will never make it in, which is why there'll never be a man, why this will never be her home, why her intuitions are wrong and always will be, why the cozy intellectual life she had in Paris as a student will never be hers again, why for the rest of her life she is going to understand eleven percent of this country and zero percent of these men . . . (276)

One clause detonates another in anguished repetition. When she thinks of Coleman's affair with Faunia, the sentences amplify her conviction. 'He settles on this broken woman who cannot possibly fight back' (198). It is not true, but she is away. 'He settles on a woman who has never defended herself . . .

settles on her for the most transparent of reasons.' He hates Delphine 'because he considers all women inferior and because he's frightened of any woman with a brain. Because I speak up for myself, because I will not be bullied, because I'm successful, because I'm attractive, because I'm independent-minded, because I have a first-rate education, a first-rate degree . . .'. In fevered self-righteousness, thoughts become refrains, the repetition of a pattern becomes its self-evidence.

Amplification also expresses the unsatisfied insistence of the narrator himself. Witnessing Coleman Silk's tragedy, he only has to wonder 'why . . .?' for us to get a stream of urgently unanswerable 'why? . . . why? . . .' questions (208). Recalling Coleman Silk's funeral, Nathan Zuckerman cannot remember the gap between the last movement of Mahler's Third Symphony that ended it, and finding himself in the cemetery by the graveside.

> One moment we were immobilized by the infinite vulnerability of Mahler's adagio movement . . . one moment we were immobilized by that exquisite juxtaposition of grandeur and intimacy . . . one moment we were immobilized by the swelling, soaring, climaxing, and subsiding of an elegiac orgy . . . one moment we were, at Mahler's mounting insistence, inside the coffin with Coleman . . . and then somehow or other sixty or seventy of us had got ourselves over to the cemetery to watch as he was buried. (312–13)

The amplification is the narrator's own return to the terrible, numbing experience, the rhetorical trope, as often in Roth, chosen to match the narrative's emotional truthfulness.

PARENTHESES

Literary mimicry is sometimes thought of as a low art, but the writer who catches the superficial peculiarities of another writer often lets us see surprisingly deep into them. Michael Cunningham's *The Hours*, described by its author as a 'rewriting' of Virginia Woolf's *Mrs Dalloway*, has latched onto one small yet special feature of Woolf's prose in that novel: her use of parentheses. A reader of *The Hours* who is not familiar with *Mrs Dalloway* might find strange the novel's constant emphatic asides. Cunningham's narrative appears to be addicted to brackets. Here is the opening of the first chapter: 'There are still the flowers to buy. Clarissa feigns exasperation (though she loves doing errands like this), leaves Sally cleaning, and runs out' (9). The aside makes Clarissa's unexpressed enthusiasm a conscious secret—the unstated truth that runs underneath the ordinary exchange. She thinks about how much she loves simply walking the streets on a June day. 'If she were to express it publicly (now, at her age), this love of hers would consign her to the realm of the duped and simpleminded' (12). That parenthesis is the character's own rueful reflection, a private reflex of self-mockery, alongside her simple pleasure.

In *Mrs Dalloway*, parentheses are everywhere, giving us life in its layers and consciousness in its contradictoriness. One simple effect is of the poignant bathos when actions are set amongst thoughts. Take this sentence from Woolf's novel: 'But this question of love (she thought, putting her coat away), this falling in love with women' (28). Clarissa muses on her long-ago lesbian flirtation (one kiss) with Sally Seton, but as she does so the parenthesis lets us see her as the elegant, respectable lady of the house. The unspoken and the ordinary, what is thought and what is done, are simultaneous. Here is Peter Walsh, who is just leaving Regent's Park and recalling his love for Clarissa: 'A terrible confession it was (he put his hat on again), but now, at the age of fifty-three, one scarcely needed people any more' (67). What an observer might see is in the brackets. Everything else is the unguessed tragicomedy of consciousness. Unlike commas or dashes, brackets seal off a reflection or fact and so let characters digress from their own thoughts. Here is *The Hours*: 'She, Clarissa Vaughan, an ordinary person (at this age, why bother trying to deny it?), has flowers to buy and a party to give' (10).

What the parentheses enclose is not Cunningham's intervention, but the straying thoughts of his character. Clarissa, in her enjoyable whirl of activity, suddenly and lightly confesses her ordinariness (in brackets), even though she has led a life in which she imagined herself extraordinary. But no dwelling on this, for there is shopping to do. When Clarissa visits her dying friend Richard, a parenthesis captures her suppressed fastidiousness. 'Here are his cardboard boxes, his bathtub (filthier than she'd realized). The dusty mirror and the expensive coffeemaker, all revealed in their true pathos' (195). She cannot forget that she likes things to be clean, though the parenthesis seems to acknowledge that she should be thinking of more important things.

In Woolf's parentheses, minds wander. Peter Walsh recalls the summer day more than thirty years earlier when he imagined marrying Clarissa. 'He had twenty minutes of perfect happiness. Her voice, her laugh, her dress (something floating, white, crimson), her spirit, her adventurousness' (53). The mind clutches at that dress, irrelevantly yet significantly. It cannot quite be seen, though two colours flash back on the memory. 'For himself, he was absurd. His demands upon Clarissa (he could see it now) were absurd.' The aside is a private acknowledgement, as if we were to hear a man stiffly talking to himself, trying to push away a possibility that he cannot quite forget. Cunningham has copied this trick of the parenthesis as a way of catching two things, two thoughts, happening at once. Richard kills himself, and Clarissa finds herself with his body, frozen. 'She feels (and is astonished at herself) slightly embarrassed by what has happened' (202). In the brackets is a second feeling, no truer than the first, an inescapable trick of self-consciousness. Faced by something shocking, terrible, Clarissa finds herself an observer of her own reactions.

Critics have, as far as I know, not written in any wide-ranging way on the uses of parenthesis in novels. There is a weird and wonderful book on parentheses in English, John Lennard's *But*

I Digress, but it is mostly about its use by poets. Amongst novels, only Laurence Sterne's *Tristram Shandy* is truly admitted, its parentheses being essential to its art of digression. Sterne uses parentheses in 'a reaction against standards of propriety . . . asserting that the human personality is beyond the range of fashionably regulated writings'.[8] Certainly the parenthesis is nicely suited to the enactment of a person's idiosyncratic habits of thought. For the rendering of the oddity of consciousness, of the way the mind can insert one incongruous thought into another, it can be one of a novelist's most subtle resources.

HYPERBOLE

Only a certain kind of fiction accommodates hyperbole. For many novelists, their genre's best ambitions are exemplified by George Eliot's analogy for its duty of verisimilitude. In *Adam Bede* (1859) she proposes as a model the 'rare, precious truthfulness' of 'many Dutch paintings'. The novel must be faithful to the ordinary proportions of life. But it is not necessarily so. There is a comic tradition of exaggeration in the English novel. Take these sentences, which a realist in Eliot's mode could never have written: 'Mr and Mrs Veneering were bran-new people in a bran-new house in a bran-new quarter of London. Everything about the Veneerings was spick and span new.' They come from Dickens's *Our Mutual Friend* (1864–5) (vol. i, bk. i, ch. ii, 17). The Veneerings, absurd worshippers of wealth, are brought to grotesque life by the buzz of cliché and the insistence on the hyperbole. So mad for the polish of affluence are these two that 'everything' (no, really, *everything*) about them must be new. In Dickens, hyperbole is a fundamental impulse of the imagination. Parody and simile and caricature all become different kinds of exaggeration. The hyperbole is often, as with the Veneerings, an expression of satirical exuberance, taking its energy from the absurdity of what it mocks.

Martin Amis's *Money* has a satirical bent that makes hyperbole its natural rhetorical tendency. It is a novel that has little to do with moderation. It is all much too much. Just think of the food and the booze. Sick and jet-lagged on his arrival in New York, John Self drops in at Pepper's Burger World. 'I had four Wallies, three Blastfurters, and an American Way, plus a nine-pack of beer' (29). He feels a little sleepy, but 'ready for anything'. It is horrible to imagine just what those dishes might be, but we know they are surely more than a mortal could ingest. The drinking is, literally, unbelievable. Before meeting Fielding Goodney at his club (the Pluto Room) he consumes six glasses, 'or vases', of Californian wine, 'a quart' of Chablis, a pint of rum, and 'a drink or two' of spirits (44). En route, 'I bought a joint, a popper, a phial of cocaine and a plug of opium from a fat spade in Times Square and snuffled it all up in a gogo bar toilet' (46). The boasts are themselves a self-indulgence. 'I was in capital fettle' (48). At the club he gets through a couple of bottles of champagne before collapsing into narrative amnesia.

'I am a vitamin addict, I am a penicillin addict, I am a pain-killer addict' (72). Faced by a newspaper story of a girl wasting away because she is 'allergic to the twentieth century', he responds, tastelessly, 'I am addicted to the twentieth century.' The addiction is there in the sour relish of his exaggerations. Can his local (Bayswater?) off-licence really vend 'tubs of Nigerian sherry, quarts of Alaskan port', or 'a product called Alkohol, sold in cauldrons of label-less plastic' (70)? Reality is stretched to make us see it. Hyperbole is the appropriate ploy in a novel so gripped by excess. *Money* also lets Self's narrative voice follow the habits of colloquial hyperbole that we do not usually allow into writing. Think of them: 'I feel like death'; 'I haven't seen her for ages'; 'I've got millions of things to do'. Like Dickens, Amis enjoys exaggerations that are extensions of cliché. When he has to play tennis with Fielding Goodney, he faces a superior being, 'tanned, tuned, a king's ransom of orthodonture having passed through his mouth' (31). Taking an economy flight from

Heathrow, Self does justice to the ordinary hell of air travel and our ordinary apocalyptic diction. 'Terminal Three was in terminal chaos, the air and light suffused with last things, planet panic, money Judgement' (91). The opening cliché is just Self's way into a thoroughly modern glimpse of damnation.

This narrator has a figurative momentum that is itself excessive. He likes to take a thought and take it too far. Musing xenophobically on the 'foreigners' who fill his part of town, he wonders if 'they even speak Earthling?' 'They speak stereo, radio crackle, interference. They speak sonar, bat-chirrup, pterodactylese, fish-purr' (87). The narrative habit is like the narrator himself: feverish, bloated, mostly very funny. The brutish extravagance of Self's language, deliberately giving up its grasp on reality, is suited to the novel's almost non-existent plot. Self eventually finds that he has been conned by Fielding Goodney. He was living a self-delusion, tricked by his appetites—but carried along also by his own gift for hyperbole.

PASTICHE

Many people have read A. S. Byatt's *Possession*, but how many of them have read the verse by its two fictional Victorian poets, Randolph Ash and Christabel LaMotte, that is supplied with the novel? Some have been almost proud to claim that they have not done so, even while saying they have enjoyed *Possession*, as if the commonsensical reader would know better than to pause over this mock-Victorian literary charade. Byatt's American publishers initially wanted her to cut large parts of it, fearing purchasers would be put off. Certainly the novelist has taken an odd sort of gamble with her pastiches. Most readers will surely not be able to recognize the genres she imitates, the verse forms she mimics, the habits of diction and imagery that she follows. And those who do appreciate these will see that the faux Browning blank verse credited to Ash is ploddingly regular stuff compared to the original; that in LaMotte's creations Christina

Rossetti's fable-mongering is often awkwardly blended with Emily Dickinson's short-winded, staccato stanzas. The gamble seems the greater as the poetry has no obvious narrative function, except to serve as a kind of authentication device, hinting at a larger imagined world. Formally, indeed, it is not even part of the narrative. It is given without explanation or interpretation.

'Pastiche' originally means a medley of different styles, being derived from the Italian word *pasticcio*, which referred to a pie containing numerous different ingredients. Byatt has fabricated a variety of texts from which the past is to be pieced together. There are other elements of pastiche in the novel besides the imitation Victorian verse. Some of these—bits of the 'diary' of Ellen Ash, or of the academic biography of Ash written by Mortimer Cropper—do serve the plot. The enjoyable parodies of feminist or post-structuralist literary criticism have sharply satirical purposes. The pastiches of Victorian poetry, however, just sit there, as if suggesting the gap between the modern narrative of 'explanation' and the still-mysterious voices of the literary past. Yet, on closer examination, these 'quotations' do set the mood for what follows. So, for instance, LaMotte's sub-Dickinson lyric about the violence pent 'behind the blinds' of domesticity, where 'walls break outwards—with a rush—' heads the chapter where Maud and Roland visit the house LaMotte once shared with her jealous 'companion' Blanche (210). We find in the course of the novel that the two women's companionship, idealized by later feminist critics, was torn by jealousy and resentment that were hidden from the world. Similarly, the poems provide clues to the relationship between Ash and LaMotte: read rightly, the imagery of *Melusina* in fact shows that the poets were in Yorkshire together, where their illicit affair was consummated (266). They also trigger mistaken interpretations. Byatt relishes showing how, before Maud and Roland get digging, academics have found all the wrong biographical suggestions in the verse. She provides a parody of academic criticism by the American feminist intellectual Leonora Stern, who irresistibly demonstrates that LaMotte's poem 'The Fairy Melusine' is a work of lesbian eroticism (244–6). In fact, as we discover, it has been inspired by LaMotte's secret love affair with Ash.

The custom of opening sections of a novel with fragments of poetry that Byatt adopts itself has a peculiar history. It was pioneered by Ann Radcliffe. In her fiction, every chapter begins with its epigraph, usually a passage of verse. She especially favours Shakespeare, notably *Macbeth*, Milton, and eighteenth-century poets of sensibility—Thomson, Beattie, and Collins—in their melancholy moments. She also makes her characters poets, and inserts into her novels, especially *The Mysteries of Udolpho*, moody verse that she had written for them. Other Gothic novels, like Matthew Lewis's *The Monk*, followed her lead in the use of quotations at the heads of chapters. Later, Sir Walter Scott took to the fabricating of appropriate, antique-sounding, fragments of verse, meaningfully placed at the heads of chapters. 'I believe that, in some cases, where actual names are affixed to the supposed quotations, it would be to little purpose to seek them in the works of the authors referred to,' Scott disarmingly admitted at the beginning of *Chronicles of the Canongate* (1827).[9] 'I drew on my memory as long as I could, and, when that failed, eked it out with invention.' A few Victorian novelists pursued the trend, most teasingly George Eliot, a favourite of Byatt. *Middlemarch* is full of mock fragments of verse and drama, carefully forged by Eliot (and invariably passed over without comment by annotators and critics). She clearly delighted in manufacturing these perplexing or gnomic morsels of literature, running through various styles and periods, at once 'discovering' wisdom and mocking sententiousness. She surely offered a model for the invention of old verse in *Possession*.

For pastiche means mimicry that we enjoy without being fooled. Byatt's versions of Browning, given to Ash, are more satisfying in this way than some of LaMotte's verse, where the poetry sometimes seems intensely in earnest. Browning was a ventriloquist, a great writer of dramatic monologues and personae. Ash is allowed to be the same, so pastiche playfully reflects the original. Byatt invents an 1856 entry from Crabb Robinson's diary describing Ash's newly published 'dramatic poems', including 'those purporting to be spoken by Augustine of Hippo, the ninth-century monk, Gotteschalk, and "Neighbour Pliable" from *Pilgrim's Progress*' (23). These could easily be voices from Browning. She provides at the heads of some chapters poems that follow his method of dramatic monologue. There is 'Swammerdam', the monologue of the great seventeenth-century Dutch microscopist Jan Swammerdam (202–9), and 'Mummy Possest', a poem spoken by a fictional nineteenth-century spiritualist, Sybilla Silt (405–12). The latter specifically echoes Browning's 'Mr Sludge, "the Medium"', lines from which, likening a fraudulent medium to a creative writer, Byatt has taken as an epigraph for her novel. Her pastiches are emphatically not wonderful poetry, yet display considerable technical skill (how many academic critics could produce such things?) and function as a kind of homage to the poetry she admires. They work best while they remain merely amusing copies of the surface qualities of nineteenth-century verse, flattering the attentive reader. It is only when her imitations get serious that we have reason to feel uncomfortable.

HETEROGLOSSIA

You could accurately tell the 'story' of Andrew O'Hagan's *Personality* without giving any sense of what it is actually like to read the novel. The reader's experience is formed above all by the variety of kinds of writing that the author employs. One could list some of these: third-person narration, monologues by different characters, newspaper articles, song lyrics, letters, dramatic dialogues, interview transcripts. There is no master narrative organizing these (as when, in *Pride and Prejudice* say, the narrator will introduce a letter before quoting it, and then explain how its recipient reacted to it). The various elements are simply gathered together for us by some silent editor. Newspaper articles are inserted without comment, and we are left to measure their accounts against what we know from other parts of the novel. 'OPPORTUNITY KNOCKING FOR ROTHESAY TEENAGER' (86) gives way to 'CHILD STAR'S SECRET ORDEAL' (207). Maria's payment for being a 'personality' is that her life is also to be narrated, sentimentally or impertinently, in newsprint. The letters of an obsessive fan are simply laid before us, without any comment on him or on Maria's reactions. The dangerous oscillation between foul-mouthed abuse and sentimental adoration is left to speak for itself. 'I've moved address so you can call the police all you like I'm not worried you fucking bitch . . . On Des O'Connor you were the loveliest person in the world tonight and I am proud of you' (290–1).

It is not just a matter of sheer stylistic variety, as when Dickens might turn in the space of a sentence from pathos to sarcasm, without your once losing the sense that you hear his voice. These different kinds of writing have different origins and are, in some sense, irreconcilable. They are designed to clash. This is the case not least with the lyrics of the songs that Maria sings. They are baldly transcribed, their happy or sentimental assurances incongruous given the life that Maria leads.

Over and over, my friends say I'm a fool
But oh-oh-over and over
I'll be a fool for you. (171)

Yet perhaps they do express the singer's 'personality' better than anything that she can say in her own words. Only singing, beyond anything that the printed page can convey, is she fulfilling herself.

Even the list above hardly does justice to the different kinds of writing contained in O'Hagan's novel, for within the third-person narrative itself there are unpredictable switches. When we follow Maria to her debut at the London Palladium, for instance, the narrator adopts a swooping view of the city. In Dickensian manner, we see through walls and windows.

> An eye, passing this, passing St Mary's Hospital, its yellow windows and damp brick, the unwell captured in their beds and the smell of fruit and stewed tea hanging about the wards ... A woman goes up in the lift to see the mother she has never met. Porters smoke on the stairwell and remember the worst and the best of Friday night. (160)

Suddenly Maria's big night shrinks to one small part of a teeming urban world. The novelist seems determined to test out different writings, though as he does so he risks the virtuosity becoming the only object of the reader's attention.

The Russian critic and literary theorist Bakhtin coined a useful (if overused) term for such variety. 'Heteroglossia' is the translation of his Russian word *raznorechie*—literally, 'many-voicedness' (from *raznyi(o)*, 'various', + *rechie*, 'speech'). He believed that the special power of the Novel as a genre was to assort together different voices and types of language. Bakhtin privileged heteroglossia: works that make present the clashes and incongruities of different voices were to be preferred to those that create a 'unified' narrative surface. So determined was he to pursue this line of argument that he was led to the absurd conclusion that the Novel was inherently superior to poetry, the latter being 'monologic'. Yet, descriptively, he was onto something. Many would feel that there is a difference between novelists with some kind of consistent voice and those who like to make novels from colliding different voices. At the extreme are works like Joyce's *Ulysses* or Sterne's *Tristram Shandy* that stitch together different kinds of writing, many of them parodic. (The latter, published in the 1760s, is a useful corrective to the idea that this is a particularly 'modern' tendency.)

Certainly there is nothing politically subversive—as Bakhtin would have wished—in the heteroglossia of *Personality*. What it offers, more simply, is the mere pleasure of variety and surprise. You feel that it offered this to the author too—as if each new part was a new kind of writing exercise. And this, of course, is the disadvantage of the method, for it highlights the author's command of style and mimicry and pushes the people in the novel away from us. The author may not be speaking, but, as in O'Hagan's novel, his stylistic virtuosity never lets you forget him.

STREAMS OF CONSCIOUSNESS

Mrs Dalloway, the novel to which Michael Cunningham's *The Hours* is a homage, is often cited as a prime example of a 'stream of consciousness' narrative. Such a narrative is supposed to follow not just the unvoiced thoughts of a character (Jane Austen's *Emma* does that), but the leaps of association that connect those thoughts. The narration sets out not to tell us what a character thinks, but to follow *how* he or she thinks. In particular, it aims, as in the bravura opening of *Mrs Dalloway*, to be true to the way memories keep bursting into the present. Clarissa Dalloway thinks of the preparations for her party and the freshness of the morning.

> What a lark! What a plunge! For so it had always seemed to her when, with a little squeak of the hinges, which she could hear now, she had burst open the French windows and plunged at Bourton into the open air. How fresh, how calm, stiller than this of course, the air was in the early morning; like the flap of a wave; the kiss of a wave; chill and sharp and yet (for a girl of eighteen as she then was) solemn, feeling as she did, standing there at the open window, that something awful was about to happen; looking at the flowers, at the trees with the smoke winding off them and the rooks rising, falling; standing and looking until Peter Walsh said, 'Musing among the vegetables?'—was that it?—'I prefer men to cauliflowers'—was that it? (3)

Here is the path of a mind at work (semi-colons make Woolf's syntax possible). Narration follows the activity of memory, but without actually returning us to the past. For the prose is full of the later consciousness, reaching back: '. . . which she could hear now', 'stiller than this of course', 'was that it?' This is not memory but the activity of remembering.

In imitation of Woolf, here is a single characteristic sentence from *The Hours*. We are being shown Clarissa Vaughan, out buying flowers like Woolf's Clarissa Dalloway, pausing on a particular street corner in Greenwich Village, New York, remembering her brief affair, many years before, with Richard, whom she is about to visit.

> Here on this corner (in front of what had been a head shop and is now a delicatessen) they had kissed or not kissed, they had certainly argued, and here or somewhere soon after, they had cancelled their little experiment, for Clarissa wanted her freedom and Richard wanted, well, too much, didn't he always? He wanted too much. (52)

It is 'this corner' because we see things from her point of view; the comment about the delicatessen is in the present tense because it catches her stray observation (even amongst poignant recollections she cannot help noticing what happens to shops). Yet it is not conventional free indirect speech, for it follows the indirection of consciousness: she thinks they kissed, but perhaps not; that confusion of place and time in 'somewhere soon after' is hers, as is that silent 'well', where the character expressively checks herself; the final colloquialism ('didn't he always?') is her hustling the train of thoughts to its end. The last sentence is an emphatic repetition: she has reached her conclusion, her judgement on the past.

What is striking is that this kind of narration, once radically experimental, is now quite ordinary. Traces of the stream of consciousness can be found in many contemporary novels. Yet Woolf does something stranger than follow the thought processes of her central character. What is less often commented on is the way in which she moves between different consciousnesses. Narration allows sudden yet lucid shifts to other characters. We are given many streams of consciousness. This, I think, is what Cunningham finds hardest to replicate. You get a clue to this aspect of Woolf's method in the opening of *Mrs Dalloway*. The first three paragraphs have taken us into Clarissa's thoughts and memories, as she leaves her London house. 'She stiffened a little on the kerb, waiting for Durtnall's van to pass' (3). We could still be with her, but the next sentence tells us otherwise: 'A charming woman, Scrope Davis thought her (knowing her as one does know people who live next door to one in Westminster); a touch of the bird about her, of the jay, blue-green, light, vivacious, though she was over fifty, and grown very white since her illness.' With a small jolt we are in another mind. She is being seen by a neighbour, his thoughts variously banal (that complacent parenthesis) and whimsical (the way he pursues that birdlike notion). He knows of 'her illness', but we, at present, do not. What are we to suppose?

Woolf uses the very spaces of the city to move between different streams of consciousness. As characters cross each others' paths, their thoughts cross in front of us too. In *The Hours*, already split between three narrative strands, the narrative seems unsure whether it is willing to give us access to many characters' thoughts. The strand featuring Virginia Woolf imagines almost entirely her consciousness, but not entirely. When she joins her husband for breakfast, we slip into his head briefly. 'She may be the most intelligent woman in England, he thinks. Her books may be read for centuries' (33). In the strand from the 1940s we have the thoughts of Laura Brown without digression or descant. And in the present-day strand Cunningham toys with multiple streams of consciousness. Halfway through the novel he suddenly takes us into the mind of Clarissa Vaughan's friend Louis—'She looks older, Louis thinks...' (15)—of her daughter's lover, of her own partner. Yet it seems a passing experiment, a dabbling in variety. Richard kills himself, so the party planned for him is abandoned. In *Mrs Dalloway*, the final party is the occasion for allowing Woolf to vary constantly between different streams of consciousness. It would be difficult to match her narrative fluidity, as she manoeuvres us around the room, between the reflections of different characters.

> She had the simplest egotism, the most open desire to be thought first always, and Clarissa loved her for being still like that . . . The Prime Minister? Was it really? Ellie Henderson marvelled. What a thing to tell Edith. . . . Lord, lord, the snobbery of the English! thought Peter Walsh, standing in the corner. How they loved dressing up in gold lace and doing homage. (146)

With some of the dizziness of a party, we move from stream to stream of consciousness, overhearing, as it were, snatches of different characters' thoughts. Managing such glimpses of many minds is a difficult thing to imitate successfully.

9
Devices

NEAR the beginning of Daniel Defoe's novel *A Journal of the Plague Year* (1722)—on the third page in modern editions—the narrator, H.F., introduces evidence of the arrival of the Plague in London. Late in 1664 rumours of deaths from the deadly disease had begun to spread, he recalls, and it was observed that, in four central parishes, 'the ordinary Burials encreased in Number considerably' (3). He then sets out on the page a Bill of Mortality: that is, a table with the numbers of deaths recorded in particular parishes, week by week. Several of these tables appear at different places in the *Journal*. They are provided as if they were real documents, diligently transcribed by the author from official records. We now know that Defoe did draw on real Bills of Mortality for the period when composing the novel. The device of these statistical displays (which would have had a place in the section on 'Lists' below) helped create the documentary effect that persuaded many readers, for decades after Defoe's death, that the *Journal* was a true memoir rather than a work of fiction. Amongst the tricks and embellishments used by novelists that are discussed in this chapter, some are as material as Defoe's Bills of Mortality: forms of writing (letters, emails, newspaper articles) that are normally used for purposes other than fiction.

The letter has long been useful to novelists. I have taken examples from A. S. Byatt's *Possession*, where a correspondence is natural between the imagined Victorian writers. Such people did write copious letters; we do not. Yet it is worth observing that even as what Samuel Richardson would have called 'familiar' letter-writing (i.e. letters between friends or family members) becomes rarer and rarer, novelists go on using letters. Characters continue to write letters in novels as they might not outside novels. It is remarkable that more than half of the contemporary novels on which I have focused in this book print letters, there for the perusal of the reader as well as one or more of the characters in the novel. It is sometimes assumed that letters feature in eighteenth- and nineteenth-century novels because people in those days wrote so many of them. Yet novelists like Monica Ali and Jonathan Coe, Mark Haddon and Carol Shields, are just as ready to present letters written by their characters as Jane Austen was. The letter has, in truth, fictional uses, considered below, that have little to do with letters in real life. What is now a much more common form of written communication, the email, has, in contrast, only begun to be exploited by novelists. Perhaps these missives have a baldness and a lack of intimacy that robs them of the voltage that letters can possess. Their very informality is likely to make them less interesting than letters to a novelist. In the examples examined below, it is the potential for error and misdirection that creates special fictional possibilities for emails.

Novels have always used (or invented) documents from the 'real world'. One of the novels examined in this book, Mark Haddon's *The Curious Incident of the Dog in the Night-Time*, includes signs, advertisements, maps, timetables, the patterns of fabrics and, finally, part of an A level maths exam. All are copied for us by Haddon's autistic narrator, Christopher, an often uncomprehending recorder of a confusing world. Amongst the documents that most often find their way into novels are newspaper reports. I take examples from Margaret Atwood's *The Blind Assassin*, but several of the other novels examined in this book also use them. Invariably these invented newspaper articles provide information that we need, but also misrepresent a reality that only the readers of the novel will discover. The two sections that follow also deal with ways in which the material of an invented world seems to obtrude itself into a story. The first of these concerns the insertion of a picture, or rather of the description of a picture, into a text. *Ekphrasis*, as it is called, is an old device, much used in poetry and made, in Orhan Pamuk's *My Name Is Red*, to show to the mind's eye the mutual strangeness of Eastern and Western codes of representation. The second, 'Lists', looks at a device much more native to novels. Here is the world's stuff, merely collected, the raw material out of which some kind of narrative significance must be made.

Further devices discussed in this chapter are, we might say, ornamental. Before novels were invented, it was thought reasonable by teachers of rhetoric that writers might want to decorate their work with ornaments, and this ideal did not entirely disappear with the arrival of the Novel. There have been novels, for instance, where passages of natural description were provided not because they mattered to the story but because they might have pleased the reader (as perhaps they had already pleased the writer). Ann Radcliffe's *The Mysteries of Udolpho* was a famous example.

> To the east, a vista opened, that exhibited the Apennines in their darkest horrors; and the long perspective of retiring summits, rising over each other, their ridges clothed with pines, exhibited a stronger image of grandeur, than any that Emily had yet seen. The sun had just sunk below the top of the mountains she was descending, whose long shadow stretched athwart the valley, but his sloping rays, shooting through an opening of the cliffs, touched with a yellow gleam the summits of the forest, that hung upon the opposite steeps, and streamed in full splendour upon the towers and battlements of a castle, that spread its extensive ramparts along the brow of a precipice above. (vol. ii, ch. v, 226)

The novel has many such descriptions, which were supposed to provide the readers of the 1790s with the pleasures of 'the sublime', a fashionable aesthetic experience. They were not composed from observation or memory, for Radcliffe had not travelled to Italy or seen mountains, but from the reading of travel literature. They appealed to the genteel reader's knowledge of paintings and prints. But then natural description in fiction is seldom merely observational or circumstantial. In the discussion below we will see how it inevitably takes on narrative meaning. Equally, similes, which might purport merely to help you 'see' something in a novel, take on a special significance, as if they were diversions into an author's true purposes for his or her story. Novels are, in general, less comfortable with metaphor than with similes. The latter keep figurativeness at arm's length, never letting you forget that there is a real world to be compared to an imagined one.

The chapter ends with devices through which the shaping influence of the author can be felt: names and coincidences. The earliest English novel, *Robinson Crusoe*, begins with an explanation of the protagonist's name, which is a mere corruption of his 'real', German name. His social mobility is embodied in his adopted name. Ever since, naming has mattered a great deal in novels, often representing either the changeableness or the unchangingness of a character's social identity. Some of the different types of name that a novelist can use are explored below. Finally, the section entitled 'Coincidences' explores what is sometimes thought the last resort of the desperate writer. Coincidences can trouble us, but there are novels where they may please us. Take the way that in Evelyn Waugh's early novels you keep bumping into the same people in the most unlikely circumstances. In the last chapter of *Vile Bodies*, sardonically entitled 'Happy Ending', Adam Fenwick-Symes is surrounded by the mud and devastation of the Western Front in the First World War. Lost on 'the biggest battlefield in the history of the world' he bumps into 'the drunk Major', a character who has several times before cropped up in the novel and who has cheated Adam of the money that would have allowed him to marry Nina (185). The drunk Major, now a general, is not in the least taken aback to meet his former acquaintance. Invited to the General's car for a drink, Adam finds a young woman asleep. Naturally she is not new to us either. She is none other than Chastity, the girl of easy virtue who was being seasick in the novel's opening passage. We should no more be surprised than she has been by the extraordinary misadventures that she briefly relates. ('Then there was a lady at a party, and she sent me to Buenos Aires, and then when the war came she brought me back again, and I was with the soldiers training at Salisbury Plain . . .'; 188). These are the patterns of a world satirically observed. The coincidences show you that you cannot get away from certain types of person.

LETTERS

The novel, since its youth, has needed letters. Novels by Richardson, Smollett, Burney, and Laclos were written entirely in letters. Jane Austen's first version of what was to become *Sense and Sensibility* was, according to family tradition, an epistolary novel called 'Elinor and Marianne'.[1] Even after the epistolary convention was largely abandoned, letters, these strange documents, often both formal and revealing, remained important. Think about how Mr Collins's letter of self-introduction comically reveals him in *Pride and Prejudice*, or how Mr Knightley performs a practical criticism of Frank Churchill's letter of self-exculpation in *Emma*. In her novel *Possession*, letters interest A. S. Byatt for many of the same reasons that they have interested novelists in the past. They reveal the truth through gaps, through what is not said. The clandestine courtship of the two Victorian poets Randolph Ash and Christabel LaMotte happens in between the letters they write to each other, discovered more than a century later. The reader must infer the drama and bring the affair alive from hints. *Possession* is in fact a novel about letters: their discovery, their possession, the stories they tell. 'They wrote a lot, in those days,' says Toby, a lawyer dealing with 'the most ferocious wrangle about a correspondence between dead poets that someone's just discovered' (415).

Roland and Maud, the academic sleuths who unearth this correspondence, begin with the dull motives of scholars. But the old letters reanimate the past and foster their own romance. The key moments of the novel are the various discoveries of these letters (making Roland and Maud, incidentally, the luckiest academics alive). There they are in a doll's cot, in a shoebox, then finally in a grave. The past floods into the present and Byatt rediscovers a traditional resource. The novel literally gives us these epistolary relics, laid out on the page. As in earlier English novels, they show that entering into a correspondence can be dangerous, for it can fall into the wrong hands. Love letters from Ash are purloined by Christabel's jealous lady 'companion'. Corresponding also undermines the self possession of the writers themselves: the poets are drawn into love through writing letters to each other. Christabel admits that this becomes 'an Addiction'. 'That space of freedom', Ash calls their correspondence (193). 'And did you find—as I did—how curious, as well as natural, it was that we should be so shy with each other, when in a papery way we knew each other so much better,' he writes to her (191). Letters permit an intimacy impossible in speech. They are most charged with this potential when they belong to a world where codes of propriety are strongest.

It is hardly surprising, then, that Jane Austen uses them so often. In *Pride and Prejudice*, Mr Darcy can only share his confidences with Elizabeth Bennet by pressing a letter into her hand. In *Persuasion*, Captain Wentworth has to declare his love to Anne Elliot by letter, even though she is sitting in the same room as him. In novels, letters say things that cannot be spoken. In *Possession*, Christabel writes to Ellen Ash when her husband is dying to ask her to pass him—what else but a letter? It is never handed on. If readers have found this deeply academic novel moving, it is because of the letters that do not get read, or sometimes do not get sent. Randolph Ash's letter to heal his breach with LaMotte is found by his wife at the back of his desk and burned. LaMotte's letter to Ash telling him about their daughter is discovered in Ash's grave, where his widow placed it, and when it is read, Beatrice Nest, the desiccated academic researcher, weeps. 'I'm sorry to be so silly. It's just so terrible to think—he can't ever have read it, can he? She wrote all that for no one' (504).

Above all, letters combine revelation with mystery. They seem to give us immediate access to a person, yet must also be distrusted. Sometimes in *Possession* the distrust is obvious. We read the letters of Ash to his wife, Ellen, written while on a trip to north Yorkshire. They are full of local history and amateur geology, and apparent fondness. Yet we know he is there with his lover. The excitement of his prose, we see, is not what it must have seemed to Ellen. From eighteenth- and nineteenth-century fiction, Byatt has learnt that a letter is alive when it imagines its intended reader, the single person who will examine it. Her correspondents can even rebel against the very 'Victorian' styles that she has fabricated for them. Randolph Ash's letters turn into mockery of his own sombre religious scepticism and slowly his proprieties crumble. 'But I write like a sermon preacher,' scribbles Christabel, puncturing the Christina Rossetti-like pietism she has just been reproducing (166). Letters are where the heart cannot be stilled.

EMAIL

Given how large and ordinary a part they now play in our lives, it is surprising how emails have only slowly begun to feature in novels over the last decade. Philip Roth's *The Human Stain* was an early example of a mainstream novelist exploiting them. While Roth might seem an unlikely writer to be au fait with the implications of information technology, there is unlikely to be a more telling use of this peculiar form of communication (and miscommunication) than Delphine Roux's misdirected email in his novel. Roth seizes on what we all know from occasional news items and perhaps our own lives: the recklessness into which this all too easy means of expression can lead the person at the keyboard. Delphine, an ambitious, clever, lonely academic, sits at the computer in her office, long after every colleague has gone home. She is composing, for the classified section of the *New York Review of Books*, a lonely hearts advertisement. She is tapping at the keys and imagining the ways she might describe herself and the man she wants. In a long, gripping passage of free indirect speech, Roth lets us into her fevered thinking—her yearning for something better than her life.

She thinks about describing who she is.

> Youthful, petite, womanly, attractive, academically successful SWF French-born scholar, Parisian background, Yale Ph.D., Mass.-based, seeks . . . ? And now just lay it on the line. Do not hide from the truth of what you are and do not hide from the truth of what you seek. A stunning, brilliant, hyperorgasmic woman seeks . . . seeks . . . seeks specifically and uncompromisingly *what*? (273)

She thinks about the man she wants. 'Mature man with backbone. Unattached. Independent. Witty. Lively. Defiant. Forthright. Satirical spirit. Charm. Knowledge and love of great books.' She urges herself on. 'Mediterranean complexion. Green eyes preferred. Age unimportant, but must be intellectual.' She looks at all she has written and is amazed to see 'a Coleman Silk duplicate', a sketch of her arch-foe (277). Coleman Silk, her enemy in the faculty, is old school; she is feminist radical. He is a literary connoisseur, educated in the classics; she is an expert on French post-structuralist theory. Yet she finds she has replicated him in her description of her desired partner. In her 'distracted, turbulent, emotionally taxing state' she neglects to notice that she has addressed the ad that she has been composing not to the *New York Review of Books* but 'to the recipients of her previous communication': all the other members of her department. She also neglects to notice that she is hitting not the delete button (the composition is supposed to be 'only an experiment') but the send button.

In order to cover for her error, Delphine fakes a break-in and pins the blame on Coleman Silk. She manages to make it look as if he has tried to humiliate her with a fake email, sent from her machine, thus exploiting the uncertainty about the origin of this kind of message. It was this that recommended it to Michael Crichton, whose 1994 novel *Disclosure* is the earliest I know to use emails as a key element of plotting. Thomas Sander, an executive in a Seattle high-tech company, receives mysterious emails from 'A FRIEND' that help him defeat the schemes of his rival and former lover Meredith. Eventually, he triumphs over her, only to find out that the emailer was the woman who has now moved in as the company vice-president. He has won, but was being used as a pawn in her game. Crichton was, as ever, vaunting his familiarity with the latest technology. More than a decade later, it is old news, yet still not prominent in fiction.

Only in that category sometimes called 'humour' has it truly lodged. Allison Pearson's best-seller *I Don't Know How She Does It* (2002) is typical of the various strains of comic lifestyle fiction that use emails. The fund manager Kate Reddy exchanges emails with female colleagues with whom she hardly talks. 'On screen, though, we're in and out of each other's minds like old-fashioned neighbours' (20). For the popular novelist, such exchanges provide a formula for informality and irreverence that is a good deal easier than dialogue. 'How U? Me: Cystitis. Too much SX. xxxx,' emails Kate's friend Cindy. (Oddly, Pearson's emailers often use text messaging abbreviations, as do characters in Martin Amis's *Yellow Dog*—the sign of a novelist straining for modishness?) 'What is SX? Rings vague bell.' And so on. In this novel too the plot relies on an email going astray. By mistake Kate sends one of her revealing girlfriend missives to a client in New York, Jack Abelhammer of the Salinger Foundation. His interest triggered by the error, he is soon Kate's email admirer (thus absolving her, naturally, of any actual flirtation). As if she were a true Victorian, Pearson has her heroine feel the pull of extramarital dalliance without consummation. She will return to her marriage suitably refreshed.

Roth's episode brilliantly exploits this same comic, even farcical, potential of the email. In the same fix in a different kind of book, in a comedy, Delphine would be fortuitously extracted by providential authorial machinations. But Roth also makes us feel Delphine's fear and horror. He has even used that special property of email software: the ease with which a message is sent simultaneously to many recipients. Electronically, collegiate belonging is revealed to be Delphine's curse. And her fix is appropriate to a means of communication to which academics are addicted. She is an expert on words, yet she is too captivated by their powers to consider what she is actually doing with them.

NEWSPAPER ARTICLES

Novelists have always used documents apparently snatched from the real world as evidence of fiction's factuality. When a novelist gives us newspaper reports, however, he or she is probably writing against, or taking us behind, the official record of the times. This is certainly the case in Margaret Atwood's *The Blind Assassin*. The novel uses eighteen invented newspaper or magazine articles at various points. They are inserted without comment, as if without the knowledge of her narrator, Iris. From the first they draw attention to the gap between public and private truth. The opening chapter describes the suicide of Iris's sister Laura, who drives her car off a bridge. 'The bridge was being repaired: she went right through the Danger sign' (3). Two witnesses, both 'dependable people', report what they saw. 'They'd said Laura had turned the car sharply and deliberately.' A policeman tells Iris that the brakes might have failed. 'It wasn't the brakes, I thought. She had her reasons.' We know that there is a different truth, but not yet what it is. Next we get a report from the *Toronto Star*, 26 May 1945, on the inquest. This tells us some facts that it would be artificial for the narrator to tell us herself. Iris, we discover, is married to Richard Griffen, a 'prominent manufacturer' (6). More intriguingly, it tells us that she has given evidence at the inquest that her sister 'suffered from severe headaches affecting her vision'. Those two witnesses have now disappeared. Instead, there is 'the police view that a tire caught in an exposed streetcar track was a contributing factor'.

The use of the newspaper article is neat because it is not merely informative. The novel is much concerned with the power of Iris's husband to conceal things. We can already sense, in the incongruity of the narrative opening and the article, that some power has turned attention away from the truth of Laura's terrible act. What is the truth? And why has the narrator been complicit in the concealment? 'QUESTIONS RAISED IN CITY DEATH', runs the newspaper headline. By a dramatic irony, it refers not to our questions but to the questions of 'local ratepayers' about 'the state of the streetcar tracks on this stretch of roadway'. Atwood uses journalism artfully to let us know in advance where some of the narrative strands will be taken. A report on Richard's death in 1947, two years after Laura's, is given before we even meet him, so we will know that his ruthless pursuit of political advancement is doomed. Something about the article—his body is found 'after an unexplained absence of several days'—suggests another mystery (17). 'Police report no foul play is suspected', yet we must suspect that this death of a rich, successful man in his forties will have to be explained. Extracts of 'news' inform, while intimating that the truth is something very different. A feature from a high-school alumni magazine, dated 1998, is inserted early in the book to show us that, half a century after her death, Laura will be a famed novelist (39–40). A memorial prize in creative writing has been endowed in her name in the will of Richard's sister Winifred. As we read on, we will discover how deeply Laura and Winifred hated each other.

All the journalistic sources that the novel uses are local. The *Toronto Star* (a real paper) is the least parochial. Others range from *Mayfair*, chronicler of Toronto high society in the 1930s, to the *Port Ticonderoga Herald and Banner*. (Atwood apparently rewrote real society columns from the period.) The articles are often anxious to make the best of their information, and are occasionally euphemistic or boastful. They have an inadvertently comic local pride sometimes comparable to the invented newspaper articles used in another recent novel set in Canada, Annie Proulx's *The Shipping News* (1993). Proulx's novel has a newspaper reporter as its protagonist. Moving from upstate New York to the town of Killick-Claw, Newfoundland, with his daughters, he works on the shipping news for the local newspaper, whose variously gruesome or droll reports punctuate the novel. They celebrate the life and characters of the Newfoundland fishing community, yet cannot resist its disasters. The newspaper reports in *The Blind Assassin* have none of this buoyancy. In a novel that has provincial Canadian narrowness as its background, they reflect the obsessive respectability of Iris's husband and sister-in law. Yet some of the insertions do feel a little like pushes from the author. An extract from a Canadian newspaper in 1936, for instance, tells you of Richard's support for Franco and for the fascist regimes in Germany and Italy (437–8)—as if this cold, decorous sexual predator were not dislikable enough already. Later, another article, dated 1938, has him applauding the Munich accord between Neville Chamberlain and Hitler, which 'would put paid to the Depression and would usher in a new "golden era" of peace and prosperity' (555). Richard, we are to understand, puts the progress of commerce before everything else. It seems too clear what these newspaper articles are telling us. They work much better in Atwood's novel when they disguise the truth rather than proclaim it.

EKPHRASIS

Ekphrasis is the verbal representation of a visual representation—the description of an artwork. The undertaking is an old one: Homer's *Iliad* has a lengthy account of Achilles' elaborately embossed shield, which Hephaistos, the blacksmith of the gods, decorates with elaborate scenes of men, women, and deities. These are equally elaborately described in Homer's verse.[2] Ekphrasis is more common in poetry than in fiction, perhaps because a poem can formally re-create some of the properties of a work of art. Think of the enigmatic stillness conjured in Keats's 'Ode on a Grecian Urn' or the tricks of perspective in Auden's 'Musée des Beaux Arts'. But fiction uses it too. The rhetorical set-piece is taken to an entertaining extreme in Oscar Wilde's *The Picture of Dorian Gray*, where descriptions of the changing portrait measure pictorially the eponymous character's corruption. More intriguing and unsettling is the chapter called 'The Cleopatra' in Charlotte Bronte's *Villette*. Here Lucy Snowe, the narrator, visits an art gallery and views sardonically both a portrait of a fleshy seductress and the hypocritical bourgeoisie of Villette (Brontë's version of Brussels) who enjoy its near-pornographic allure.

> She was, indeed, extremely well fed: very much butcher's meat—to say nothing of bread, vegetables, and liquids—must she have consumed to attain that breadth and height, that wealth of muscle, that affluence of flesh . . . She had no business to lounge away the noon on a sofa. She ought likewise to have worn decent garments; a gown covering her properly, which was not the case: out of abundance of material—seven-and-twenty yards, I should say, of drapery—she managed to make inefficient raiment . . . (ch. xix, 250)

The ekphrasis—Lucy's description of the painting—is at once mocking and fascinated. The image of voluptuousness amuses and intrigues the puritanical, self-contained Lucy Snowe as only a strange opposite can. The ekphrasis requires us to see it through her eyes.

Ekphrasis is a trope native to Orhan Pamuk's *My Name Is Red* because it is a novel about painting. Most of his narrators are painters, all severally obsessed with the details of their own perfectionist art and with the examples offered to them by the great manuscript illuminators of Eastern tradition. They describe paintings—their own and those of others—and each ekphrasis tells us about the character who is describing the art-work. Ironically, the paintings themselves are not supposed to display the individuality of their creators. By a strict Islamic code of artistic devotion, each must strive to be impersonal. The memorable pictures that are described have been refined from other illuminations rather than copied from anything in life. The great miniature is an idea of something seen by Allah, not the realization of something seen by the artist. It transcends particularity. Many such miniatures are described in the course of the book. Usually they form sequences, ornamenting narratives whose calligraphy itself is supposed an art. There are pages that invite us to imagine these decorative tableaux.

> We watched Our Sultan's great-grandfather Sultan Selim the Grim, during the time he declared war on the ruler of the Dhulkadirids, erect the imperial tent along the banks of the Küskün river and hunt scurrying red-tailed black greyhounds, gazelle fawns with rumps in the air and frightened rabbits, before leaving a leopard lying in a pool of red blood, its spots blooming like flowers. (328)

Yet ekphrasis reverses the orthodoxy that a painting should not have its own life. The text of this novel is always wondering at pictures. Instead of humble accompaniments to a work celebrating the Sultan's power, they become objects of veneration.

Ekphrasis is also important to the plot and the solving of the novel's mystery. From sketches found in a murdered man's possession it becomes evident that the murderer was a miniaturist who painted a horse in a certain way. If Black, the novel's detective figure, can find evidence of this style elsewhere, he can identify the culprit. He scours the Sultan's art collection and we hunt with him through what, to a Western reader, will seem the strange, enamelled paintings that Pamuk describes. The scrutiny is given a sharper point by the fact that the true Islamic artist is supposed not to have any style of his own. 'Style' is the mark of individuality and therefore of failure. Style will catch the killer. Style is the conceit of the Western artist. Several memorable ekphrases are descriptions, through Ottoman eyes, of Venetian portraits. Enishte, the master of the miniaturists, describes seeing one of these on an embassy to Venice. He is bewildered by the painting of a plump-faced nobleman, his very possessions particularized. (The Sultan is so impressed that, secretly, he commands his best painters to paint him in a lifelike manner too.) There are comical fragments of Italian religious art as seen from the East. Rich men demand their very presence in the paintings they own: 'in a painting of the burial of St. Stephan, you'd suddenly see, ah yes, present among the tearful graveside mourners, the very prince who was giving you the tour—in a state of pure enthusiasm, exhilaration and conceit—of the paintings hanging on his palazzo walls' (130).

In ekphrasis, writing seems to confess its subordination to another form. Words give an impression of the picture; the picture gives an image of the world. Indeed, characters in Pamuk's novel are apt to imagine how their adventures and small tragedies would be made to seem better as paintings. Shekure, describing her first intimacy with the artist Black, naturally thinks of the perfect, emblematic illuminations she has seen. 'Let me describe for you how our embrace might've been depicted by the master miniaturist of Heart, if this tragic story of mine were one day recorded in a book' (179). Black imagines how his pursuit of Shekure might become a sequence of miniatures, bright 'in the illustrated pages of my mind' (236). The characters describe these pictures, in which the bewilderment of experience would become the serene scene of art. The intriguing problem for the characters, and the resource for the novel, is that history has offered them two incompatible kinds of art to dream of: the individual or the eternal. The different artistic codes embodied in the novel's ekphrases represent compelling, incompatible aspirations.

LISTS

Novels are often intrigued by the circumstantiality of life, which listing crudely renders. Some of the earliest novels, grasping at a world of ordinary facts and things, used lists. Defoe's fiction is full of them. Moll Flanders lists her possessions, excited by the possessing of them but also offering the catalogues as evidence of her truthfulness. Particularity is veracity. It is as if such lists formed the most elemental reality of which fiction is capable. Defoe's protagonists are tireless accumulators of things, and, narrating their own stories, their prose accumulates things too. Here is Robinson Crusoe recalling what he recovered from the ship that is wrecked on his island.

> . . . I found besides these Chests, a little Cask full of Liquor, of about twenty Gallons, which I got into my Boat, with much Difficulty; there were several Muskets in a Cabin, and a great Powder-horn, with about 4 Pounds of Powder in it; as for the Muskets, I had no occasion for them; so I left them, but took the Powder-horn: I took a Fire Shovel and Tongs, which I wanted extremely; as also two little Brass Kettles, a Copper Pot to make Chocolate, and a Gridiron; with this Cargo, and the Dog, I came away. (192)

There are many such lists in *Robinson Crusoe*, a novel whose 'hero' is a salvager. As a narrator, he wants to remember things, and give us the evidence that he can do so. Listing is a kind of realism.

Listing goes on being important for many novelists. In

Jonathan Franzen's *The Corrections* people accumulate things, and families especially accumulate things. The novel begins down in the basement of the Lambert family home where, over the years, stuff has been stashed. It is one of those places that all families have, where the flotsam of life washes in and collects. Down there, secretly, Enid Lambert hoards all sorts, 'the whole shuffled pathos of a refugee existence' (7):

> non-consecutive issues of *Good Housekeeping*, black-and-white snapshots of Enid in the 1940s, brown recipes on high-acid paper that called for wilted lettuce, the current month's telephone and gas bills, the detailed First Notice from the medical lab instructing co-payers to ignore subsequent billings for less than fifty dollars, a complimentary cruise ship photo of Enid and Alfred wearing leis and sipping beverages from hollow coconuts, and the only extant copies of two of their children's birth certificates, for example.

That 'for example' does it. These particulars are just a selection, the meaningful and meaningless jumbled together. Upstairs we get a different list of things: 'chairs and tables by Ethan Allen. Spode and Waterford in the breakfront. Obligatory ficuses, obligatory Norfolk pines. Fanned copies of *Architectural Digest* on a glass-topped coffee table', and more. From the beginning, this novel likes its lists. No wonder that it collects material possessions, we might think. This is America, where people love their things. But don't we all? The Lamberts are caught between insecure display (those odd elements of a Midwest suburban interior) and even more insecure concealment (Enid's hoard preserves covert memories and unachieved aspirations). Lists in this novel are often associated with Enid because she tries to gather evidence of what she would wish her family to be. Her hoarding is absurd, yet some of Franzen's lists—in their very miscellaneousness—do seem aptly, pathetically to represent a family history.

When Enid's son Chip is on the ropes, sacked for his 'inappropriate' relationship with one of his students and on the verge of eviction from his university apartment, his despair is comically caught by a long list of the ridiculous presents that his family have sent him. From his mother he receives a box marked 'Stocking Stuffers',

> a package of cough drops, a miniature second-grade school photo of himself in a tarnished brass frame, plastic bottles of shampoo and conditioner and hand lotion from a Hong Kong hotel where Enid and Alfred had stayed en route to China eleven years earlier, and two carved wooden elves with sentimentally exaggerated smiles and loops of silver string that penetrated their little craniums so they could be hung from a tree. (94)

The average madness of families is in the objects it gathers. As Christmas nears and Chip sinks into drunken self-pity, the 'gifts'—and the lists—accumulate around him. Much later in the novel, with another Christmas approaching, Enid is once more rummaging in her dresser drawers on Chip's behalf; Franzen gives us a catalogue of the bizarre things that she has available as presents.

> She rejected the vases in shopworn boxes from Hong Kong, the many matching bridge decks and score pads, the many thematic cocktail napkins, the really neat and really useless pen-and-pencil sets, the many travel alarm clocks that folded up or beeped in unusual ways, the shoe-horn with a telescoping handle, the inexplicably dull Korean steak knives, the cork-bottomed bronze coasters with locomotives engraved on their faces, the ceramic 5 × 7 picture frame with 'Memories' in glazed lavender script, the onyx turtle figurines from Mexico, and the cleverly boxed kit of ribbon and wrapping paper called the Gift of Giving. (546)

The paragraph fills with her surreal clutter. Here is the useless plunder of the world, evidence of needless purchase and travel.

It is as if the listing enacts all the accumulated delusions, the small pretensions, the inevitable disappointments of the Lamberts' family life. And it is not just Enid. Her well-off son Gary, an expert accumulator, often sees the world through lists.

When things are bad, he consoles himself with a list of nice things his wife has said to him over the years. Accused of having written a sexist film script, Chip ruefully lists in his head all its 'breast references' (31–2). When Enid's daughter Denise mounts a furious clear-up in the Lambert basement, the long list of things she throws away mimics her angry energy. They all live through lists. So there can be poignancy in a list, when it stands for the human attempt to hold onto something. Near the novel's end, returned home, Chip gets 'a gust of memory' and suddenly remembers the things that he packed, with his parents' help, when he left home to go to college (634). All the useless items on the list—including the chess set, the six-volume biography of Lincoln, the navy-blue blazer, the photo of his sister, the various bits of clothing chosen by his father to protect him from the cold of a New England winter—come back to him. Like the protagonist of a novel by Defoe, he checks the items off as evidence of the truth of his recollection. In their odd assortment, they tell us of Chip's proud and uncomprehending parents. He recalls them at this narrative moment, just as his sick, demented father calls for him from upstairs. Belatedly, the list seems full of pathos.

NATURAL DESCRIPTION

In Alan Hollinghurst's *The Spell*, gay thirty-something civil servant Alex is out cruising on Hampstead Heath and finds himself following 'a sympathetic-looking man', with 'a quickening sense that something important was being allowed to happen' (247). We are being led to what will prove a rudimentary and rapid sexual encounter. Yet the narrative takes time to look keenly about, even during the short pursuit. 'The chestnuts were already bare, but the oaks were thick with gold and withered green, and a half-denuded poplar stood in a reflecting pool of its own fallen leaves.' Arriving at the 'shadowy area of woodland' where other men have gathered, Alex cannot help noticing, like some off-duty botanist, that the paths are 'crackly with beech-mast'. Given the urgent chase that is being narrated, why should the narrator bother about these incidental details about the surroundings?

Because they are incidental. Natural description provides for the escape from self in a novel whose characters helplessly pursue self-gratification. Hollinghurst has gratified his own eye for nature by moving much of the action of his book to Dorset, where his narrative is sensitized to the strange effects of light and weather, and, in a trance-like summer, nature burgeons. We always see through the eyes of one of his characters, their observations of nature seemingly sharpened by their perplexities. Robin, overwhelmed by feelings of parental protectiveness towards his promiscuous son, drives in a strange fury and is 'half-smothered in a whiteness that brushed and lurched at the car, the ragged may tumbling into banks of cow-parsley, horse-chestnuts with their balconies of dropping candles' (62). Closely observed, nature in Hollinghurst's novel is seen with intensity at moments of uncertainty or difficulty. Robin, interrogating Justin about his ex-lover Alex, unaccountably starts noticing snail tracks on the coping of a wall 'that shone in the moonlight like chalked hearts and girlfriends' names' (123). Danny approaches Alex at an overgrown garden's end to tell him that their affair is over, and becomes suddenly hypersensitive to his surroundings. 'The grass was dry, and bleaching from the mid-August heat, and where Danny's hands trailed into it they found it dusty and sometimes sticky with secretions like bubbled spit' (238). Unhesitating about taking and then leaving this lover, he is weirdly scrupulous in his natural observations: 'underfoot there was a crackling, and he realised he was treading on tiny grey snails—and there were dozens of them clinging like seed-cases on the thicker stalks'.

If this were D. H. Lawrence, nature here would be objectifying the inner states of his characters, or alerting them to its primal fecundity. Here is the opening of chapter xi of *Women in*

Love: 'Meanwhile Ursula had wandered on from Willey Water along the course of the bright little stream. The afternoon was full of larks' singing. On the bright hill-sides was a subdued smoulder of gorse. A few forget-me-nots flowered by the water. There was a rousedness and a glancing everywhere' (127). She is about to meet Birkin, who will become her lover and eventually her husband. She wanders, but forces propel her. That 'subdued smoulder of gorse' is wonderfully exact, yet prepares us for the suppressed excitement when she sees Birkin, a few sentences later. The prose is 'roused' to notice these things. Only occasionally does *The Spell* make nature meaningful or symbolic in this way. As Alex drives West by night to join the other characters for a party at Robin's cottage, feeling 'romantically alone', he watches the countryside sweep past him (111). 'Moths, labouring through the dark on their own amorous callings, rushed to obliterate themselves on the beacon of the car.' This is almost too much—too much like a symbolic representation of the helpless 'amorousness' of the men in the novel. It is just saved from portentousness by allowing us to think Alex's reflection absurd (for it is he comparing himself and his acquaintances to self-destructively sex-crazed insects).

Elsewhere, the novel's observations of the effects of light at certain times of day or in certain weathers are meticulous rather than symbolic. When we see dusk in a garden where 'the flowers and bushes glowed with a brief intensity of colour against the neutral light', the narrative is suffused with a melancholy that the characters fend off (27). As Alex and his ex-lover Justin go for an awkwardly amicable walk, they find themselves in 'a rutted lane already mysterious in the early evening under thickly leaved hazels and oaks' (24). Their chat, however, stays superficial. Evening and dawn are the magical times. On the brink of a casual pairing, Alex notices that it is 'that time of day he loved, when the lowering sun struck right in among the trees and made every branch burn' (247). Discussing the break-up of his last relationship on a walk with Danny, his new partner,

Alex notices the changing light of evening. 'He loved this time of day, with its delicate atmosphere of reward' (168).

At the novel's end, characters, paired off anew, are back in Dorset. Through Alex's eyes we notice nature passing from summer, the hedges 'festooned with the soft swarming stars of traveller's joy, already turning grey and mothy' (256). We leave him and three other men on the edge of a cliff, looking out over the sea. 'For a minute or two they watched the inky zones of the sea-bed, as the small cloud-shadows sailed across them; then as the sun dropped westward, the surface of the sea turned quickly grey, and they saw the curling silver roads of the currents over it.' The satisfaction of the scene is in the description. We look with the four characters, but we also notice that the scrupulous business of natural description can be taken as a distraction from other thoughts—thoughts about how temporary these latest happy pairings might be.

SIMILES

A simile might promise to let us see something more clearly, but it also diverts us from what is being described. In fiction that purports to give us the exactly observed circumstances of domestic life a simile is often surprising, even disruptive. Jonathan Franzen's *The Corrections* likes to veer off from what it sees, following the whimsical or witty digressions that similes allow. The crickets that have colonized the workshop of the elderly patriarch Alfred Lambert 'scatter across the room like a handful of dropped marbles, some of them misfiring at crazy angles, others toppling over with the weight of their own copious protoplasm' (8–9). The young Chip Lambert, made to eat his supper, stares at a wad of beet leaves on his plate, 'like a wetly compressed bird in an eggshell, or an ancient corpse folded over in a bog' (303). On a suburban dawn, affluent, discontented Gary Lambert watches 'crows as they worked their way up the Hill, over Navajo Road and Shawnee Street, like local teenagers heading to the Wawa Food Market parking lot to smoke their cigarettes' (270).

Via Hemingway, American fiction gave us the ideal of spare, pared-down fictional prose, but there is also a peculiarly American art of fictional analogy. A new energy was given to the device in the twentieth century by Raymond Chandler. Think of Philip Marlowe, arriving at the opulent Sternwood mansion in *The Big Sleep* (1939) and observing the trees 'trimmed as carefully as poodle dogs' (ch. 1, 3), or describing how the plants in the conservatory 'smelled as overpowering as boiling alcohol under a blanket' (ch. 2, 6). Women attract especially figurative sallies. Carmen Sternwood has 'little sharp predatory teeth, as white as fresh orange pith and shiny as porcelain' (ch. 1, 4). Marlowe makes a woman in the bookstore 'as sore as an alderman with mumps' (ch. 4, 17). A crook's wife is 'so platinumed that her hair shone like a silver fruit bowl' (ch. 28, 135). Such similes are, we might say, worldly, the product of Marlowe's hard-bitten but droll intelligence. The discovery, or invention, of a likeness tells us how a person thinks. In *The Corrections*, simile takes us inside the odd thought processes of each one of five family members. When Enid confronts the fact that her daughter might have married the grim Emile because of her own insistence on wedlock, the similes proliferate. 'Like a toothbrush in the toilet bowl, like a dead cricket in a salad, like a diaper on the dinner table, this sickening conundrum confronted Enid: that it might actually have been preferable for Denise to go ahead and commit adultery' (139). For Alfred's sufferings from Parkinson's disease, we are given one of the book's many food analogies. 'It was as if when he lay in bed for a night certain humors pooled in the right or wrong places, like marinade around a flank steak' (381). This is how his thoughts turn.

In novels there is something bountiful, potentially self-indulgent, about similes, especially when as extended as Franzen's often are. Only certain novelists use them; others stay close to what can be observed. It is difficult to imagine, say, Jane Austen reaching out for ornamental analogies. Similes were first introduced to English fiction as a joke in the mock-epic analogies of Fielding. The heading for the sixth chapter of *Tom Jones*, for instance, actually proclaims, 'Mrs Deborah Is Introduced into the Parish with a Simile'. Mrs Deborah is Squire Allworthy's formidable housekeeper, and is about to begin her search for the unfortunate mother of the (presumably bastard) baby recently deposited on her master's doorstep.

> Not otherwise than when a kite, tremendous bird, is beheld by the feathered generation soaring aloft, and hovering over their heads, the amorous dove and every innocent little bird spread wide the alarm, and fly trembling to their hiding places; he proudly beats the air, conscious of his dignity, and meditates intended mischief.
>
> So when the approach of Mrs Deborah was proclaimed through the street, all the inhabitants ran trembling into their houses . . . (bk. I, ch. vi, 40–1)

It is the kind of analogy that Fielding might have learnt from Homer, but here put to comic purposes. Mrs Deborah is a bogus moral judge who really just enjoys petty power; the local villagers are wise from experience to her tyrannical ways. Fielding characteristically intervenes to explain his figure of speech, for otherwise 'the great beauty of the simile may possibly sleep these hundred years, till some future commentator shall take this work in hand'. The artifice of the simile is self-mockingly highlighted, an elaborate literary means for representing such ordinary and base human behaviour.

It was Dickens, a century later, who made the simile as much an element of fiction as it had been of epic poetry. There is a special quality to the Dickensian simile shared by many such devices in *The Connections*. It is usually introduced not by the word 'like' but by 'as if'. In *Great Expectations*, the lawyer Mr Jaggers never laughs but has 'great bright creaking boots' that make up for their owner's lack of human responsiveness: 'in poising himself on these boots, with his large head bent down and his eyebrows joined together, awaiting an answer, he sometimes caused the boots to creak, as if *they* laughed in a dry and suspicious way' (vol. ii, ch. v, 198). In the opening of *Bleak House*, there is as much mud in the London streets 'as if the waters had but newly retired from the face of the earth, and it would not be wonderful to meet a Megalosaurus, forty feet long or so, waddling like an elephantine lizard up Holborn Hill' (ch. 1, 1). Often the Dickensian analogy is a flight of the author's fancy, whose fantastic logic he seems to follow for its own pleasure. Here is part of his description of Dover and its fishy smells in *A Tale of Two Cities*: 'The air among the houses was of so strong a piscatory flavour that one might have supposed sick fish went up to be dipped in it, as sick people went down to be dipped in the sea' (ch. 4, 22). No one 'might have supposed' this, of course, until Dickens did, taking to some odd extreme the idea of this port as a place where land and sea interpenetrate. Franzen too likes his *as ifs*. In *The Connections*, when Alfred's mind begins to go, it is 'as if he were a damaged transistor radio which after a vigorous shaking might function loud and clear or spew nothing but a static laced with unconnected phrases, the odd strain of music' (381). Enid sees other elderly tourists cluster around a financial adviser 'as if the potential lucrativeness of Jim Crolius's advice might somehow decline with one's distance from him' (386). Such similes are flights of absurdity, evidently untrue yet, for a moment, true to a character's perceptions.

NAMES

In *Money*, Martin Amis first delighted in a world of absurd, self-advertising names. The crass, bright vulgarity of the 1980s is there in the names that his narrator, John Self, lists for us. There are the emporia at which his girlfriend spends his money: Chez Zeus, Goliath's, Amaryllis, Aphrodite, Romulus & Remus.

'It seems that the chick hangs out in Troy or Carthage' (152). He chooses whether to indulge his piggish appetites at restaurants paradoxically called The Breadline, Assisi's, The Mahatma. He lingers in nasty pubs nastily named the Blind Pig, the Fancy Rat, the Jack the Ripper. Every proclamation of individuality is really the sign of a trend. The times and the places (New York, Los Angeles, and 'Unlovely London') are also epitomized by the names of the characters. In America, the ad man and would-be film-maker Self meets cinema people whose names are the outcome of some linguistic cosmetic surgery. His producer is the smooth, tanned Fielding Goodney—a name designed to sound expensive. His star is to be the superannuated Lorne Guyland—a name styled for an out-of-date attempt at allure (or 'Long Island' in a funny voice). This is America, where you can make yourself anew, with a new name that is as perfect and improbable as you are. Here actors are called Christopher Meadowbrook or Day Lightbowne or Butch Beausoleil (a woman).

These labels of self-manufacture are variants on a traditional habit of comic fiction, which often toys with the idea that a character's name proclaims his or her nature. When Martin Amis sarcastically calls the über-yob in *London Fields* (1989) Keith Talent or the tabloid hack in *Yellow Dog* Clint Smoker, you can recall that Fielding named his birch-wielding pedagogue in *Tom Jones* Thwackum and the punitive magistrate in *Amelia* Jonathan Thrasher JP. These are the kinds of name that we expect from satire, where the fate of characters is to be not singular but representative. Amis's predecessor as a novelist of urban disgust, Tobias Smollett, will call an oily politician Cringer and a ridiculous artist Pallet. A bailiff is Vulture, a pawnbroker is Gripewell. Aristocrats are called Stately, Shrug, or Strutwell. The name is a sign of typicality. Such names are sometimes called 'cratylic': they advertise a property that is fixed, whether terrible or ludicrous. A character thus named must act out a characteristic, which is his inescapable identity.

The joke relies on the other characters in the novel not recognizing what his or her name announces.

Since *Money*, Amis has hardly been able to coin a name that is not a joke. In *Yellow Dog*, Clint Smoker's fellow hacks are called Jeff Strite, Bill Woyno, and Desmond Heaf. Perhaps it has become a facetious tic. Even novelists who do not specialize in caricatures or representative types use names with connotations. In Jane Austen novels, it is always likely that characters called, exotically, Olivia or Maria are headed for trouble. In George Eliot, women with names as flowery as Rosamund or Gwendolen are, you sense, going to suffer for their attractions. Even novelists who do not label their characters cratylically have been preoccupied with finding significant names for them. Henry James would record usable names (sometimes these were culled from births, marriages, and deaths announced in *The Times*). His notebooks are regularly punctuated by these lists of names, some items accompanied by explanatory comments. Here is a typical entry from 1891:

> *Names*. Beet—Beddington—Leander (surname)—Stormer—Luard —Void (name of a place) or *Voyd* would do for this.—Morn, or *Morne*—Facer—Funnel—Haddock—Windermere—Corner—Barringer—Jay—State—Vesey—Dacca—Ulic (Xtian name)—Brimble (or for a house)—Fade—Eily, the Irish name—good for a girl.[3]

Clearly he relished their suggestiveness and oddness, though it is hard to believe that he would have risked the semantic resonance of a place called Void (or even Voyd). And could a delicate Jamesian fiction have borne the absurdity of a character called Haddock? One of James's lists appears in Colm Tóibín's novel about Henry James, *The Master*. Here the great man looks over his own notebooks and wonders at the names he once collected while musing on the disastrous play *Guy Domville*—'names which could lie inert in his notebooks or could still be used; he could spend day after day giving life to them' (69). Tóibín implies that, for James, a name was a character's foothold on life, and therefore had to come first. Seemingly random, a name was the first fact from which other details could be elaborated, the germ of all possibilities.

Another novelist who collected potential names was Dickens. For him, more directly than for James, to get the names was to get the character. In the novelist's notes for *David Copperfield*, you can see David's intimidating stepfather going from Mr Harden to Murdle to Murden before he becomes, unforgettably, Mr Murdstone: hard and murderous. Just right. The simplification and hyperbole in the name are not credible in themselves, but are made so by the novel's evocation of a child's fears. Dickens's names are sometimes clearly cratylic (the frozen Sir Leicester Dedlock, the utilitarian Gradgrind) and sometimes more poetically so (the dwarfish devil Quilp, the lovably foolish Traddles, the vampire lawyer Vholes). Surely Dickens would have appreciated the name of John Self's dental hygienist Roger Frift (suggestive both of his high earnings and of breath whistling through teeth). In *Money*, characters brandish their names like boasts. At Fielding Goodney's exclusive New York tennis club, Self spots the leading players Chip Fournaki and Nick Karebenkian, as well as the women's world champion Sissy Skolimowsky. Even the names are muscled. His business partners are Terry Linex and Keith Carburton: matey yet threatening; oikish yet upwardly mobile. And John Self? He of course has the name of the very era.

COINCIDENCES

A coincidence in a novel can be the sign of a failed plot or it can be a carefully deployed literary device. We can mock rickety narratives for relying on coincidences, yet recognize that certain accomplished novelists insist on them. Some of the greatest works of fiction turn on coincidences that no jobbing novelist would dare perpetrate. In *Jane Eyre*, for instance, the heroine, fleeing Rochester's house in a kind of panic, travels blindly across England before collapsing unconscious at the door of an isolated house in an unknown place. The inhabitants who take her in turn out to be her long-lost cousins. Providence is evidently working in her life. And where would Dickens be without coincidences? In a densely plotted novel like *Bleak House* they alert us to the unexpected connections between apparently distant characters that the novel investigates. Elsewhere they can simply be satirically appropriate, as near the end of *David Copperfield* when David, on a prison tour, encounters the novel's two servile villains Uriah Heep and Steerforth's butler Littimer, who have ended up in adjacent cells. Improbably but naturally, the book's accomplished hypocrites have ended up next to each other as the jail's two model prisoners.

Novelists need to have the courage of their coincidences. Ruth Rendell's *Adam and Eve and Pinch Me* hinges on a coincidence—a concurrence of events without causal connection. Minty, 'haunted' by her supposedly dead lover Jock, gets an unexpected afternoon off work and goes to the cinema. Jeff, who in the guise of Jock has conned money out of her before faking his own death, also decides on a whim to go to a film. Both choose the Odeon at Marble Arch. Both choose *The House on Haunted Hill*: Jeff because it is the next film to begin, Minty because 'she quite liked the sound of it. Ghosts in a film weren't frightening when you had a real ghost of your own' (173). In the darkness, Minty sees 'Jock's ghost' and stabs 'it' to the heart with the kitchen knife that she always carries.

Rendell's London is a place of chance encounters (natural enough where people walk or travel by public transport). Some thrillers, dedicated to the logical unravelling of plot, try to banish coincidence. Rendell's, however, give a special attention to accidents and the malign-seeming unspooling of consequences. Chance sets in motion violent events for which we have already been prepared. Meanwhile, the reader alone can grasp what connects the fates of characters who have no natural affinity.

Unable themselves to see what brings them together, they glimpse only 'coincidence'. By another happenstance Natalie, the journalist who does a profile on Zillah, Jeff's wife, is herself his former lover. She sets out to research the full story of Jeff's confidence tricks and their consequences, but never quite gets to the truth. Visiting the street where Minty lives, Natalie notes the bench where the body of a female vagrant (murdered by Minty under the delusion that she was another vengeful 'ghost') was recently found. 'Something of a coincidence, she thought, that one of the murder victims had died within a stone's throw of where the other victim's girlfriend—or one of them—lived' (415). Of course, it is not a coincidence at all.

This is a nice example of how coincidence often works best in fiction, half-revealing to characters the unseen shape of things. Dickens is the master of this, using the very unease that a coincidence generates to indicate a disturbing hidden connection. Especially brilliant and audacious are the coincidences in *Great Expectations*. The most far-fetched—the fact that Magwitch, the convict whom Pip helped as a boy, is the father of Estella, the woman he loves—is inadvertently revealed by his friend Herbert Pocket. Herbert is chatting as he removes Pip's bandages (Pip has been badly burned trying to save Miss Havisham from her self-immolation). Herbert is telling him what he has found out from 'Provis' (Magwitch's identity on his return from Australia).

> 'You remember his breaking off here about some young woman that he had had great trouble with. — Did I hurt you?'
>
> I had started, but not under his touch. His words had given me a start. (vol. iii, ch. xi, 405)

As Herbert chats and unwittingly shows Pip the dark connections between the characters who have shaped his life, he sympathizes with his friend, who he thinks is flinching from the pain of his dressings being removed: '—there's a bandage off most charmingly, and now comes the cool one—makes you shrink at first, my poor dear fellow, don't it? But it will be comfortable presently.' But Pip in fact recoils from the coincidences that are being revealed to him, more evidence that all his 'great expectations' are 'encompassed by all this taint of prison and crime' (vol. ii, ch. xiv, 264). Dickens does not just use coincidences, he makes his protagonist notice them. They are indeed, to the narrator, unwarranted evidence of disturbing connections.

Rendell too is happy to draw attention to coincidences and thus to unsettle the reader. Sometimes, indeed, she cannot resist prodding us to recognize what Hardy, in *Tess of the d'Urbervilles*, called 'the ill-judged execution of the well-judged plan of things' (ch. v, 48). So, in a manner effective only on film, she tells you that two of her characters unknowingly pass each other on the road, as her plot fatally unfolds. As Jeff approaches the place where he will be killed, she wants us to see the chance choices that undo him. As he wonders which tube stop to get off at, his fate is about to be sealed. 'The seal was poised and it wavered above the hot fresh wax' (168). She cannot resist squeezing the cliché, insisting on the mere fortune that leads him to be in the same London cinema for the same showing of the same film as his murderer-to-be. She somehow cannot allow coincidence to do its worst, unhampered by this commentary.

Rendell's characters in *Adam and Eve and Pinch Me* never see the coincidences on which she dwells. The idea of a coincidence that is not perceived by the characters whom it affects often intrigues novelists. There is an excellent example in Andrea Levy's *Small Island*, though it requires some plot summary to see how peculiar it is. As a girl in Jamaica, Hortense loves her second cousin Michael Roberts. Near the beginning of the Second World War, he leaves for England to serve in the RAF. Some time later he is lost in action over France. Three years after the war Hortense comes to London with her new husband, Gilbert. They stay in a lodging house owned by a white woman,

Queenie, whom Gilbert met in strange circumstances when he was himself serving in the RAF. Stationed in the Midlands, he one day encountered an old man in a Lincolnshire lane, apparently 'soft in the head' (167). The man silently produced his address on a piece of paper and Gilbert led him to his home, an isolated farmhouse. There he met Queenie, the man's daughter-in-law, with whom he subsequently struck up a friendship. Gilbert finds her again when he returns to England. Meanwhile, in Queenie's narrative we find that Michael Roberts, Hortense's lost love, was her lodger for a couple of days during the war, and that on his last night they slept together. The coincidence becomes more significant near the end of the novel, when Queenie gives birth to a son who is black. Her husband, Bernard, attacks Gilbert. But he is not the father. 'Am I the only black man in this world?' (488). The true father, though, is just as strangely singled out from all other possibilities. We are told by Queenie, in one of the chapters she narrates herself, that it was the same Michael Roberts who survived being shot down and visited her again three years after the war.

There are two odd things about this coincidence. One is simply that it is not necessary. Queenie's fling with a black serviceman while her husband was in India did not have to be with Michael. Levy has deliberately arranged that this be so. The other peculiarity is that the coincidence is invisible to everyone except the reader. Unable to imagine how she and Bernard, a white couple, can bring up a black child in 1940s England, Queenie gives him away to Hortense. Told that his name is Michael, 'Hortense flinched' (517). Unlike Pip in *Great Expectations*, she flinches at a connection that she does not truly understand, the symptom of a coincidence that neither of the women actually recognizes. We have read Hortense's narrative, but Queenie knows nothing of it. *We* know why the name Michael matters to Hortense and why it matters to Queenie, and that both women have known the same man—but they will never recognize this. Wanting to keep her secrets, Queenie even lies to Gilbert about why the baby is called Michael, saying it was the name of her brother, killed in the war. So, without knowing it, Hortense becomes mother to the son of the person she first loved.

Does this coincidence worry us? It is certainly obtrusive. Is the novelist cheating in some way, pulling two strands of her story together like this? Opinions will differ, but it is clear that something considered is being done. The invisibility of the coincidence to all the characters is just what explains its use. They are connected in ways they cannot grasp and destined to make their gains out of what they imagine are their losses. The novel gives a shape to all these characters' disappointments through the key coincidence of Queenie's son being fathered by Hortense's one-time sweetheart. That is the providence of fiction. The coincidence is also appropriate to the novel's theme. The 'small island' of its title is either Jamaica or Britain. Both are 'small' by the limitations they place upon their inhabitants, but also because they make people live within restricted circles of acquaintance. As we say in the face of some of life's ordinary coincidences, it is a small world.

10
Literariness

LITERARINESS: it is a clumsy word, but a useful label for the ways in which novels display their attachment to other works of literature. Books remember other books. Listen to a reader describe a striking new novel and you are likely to hear comparison with other novels. Writers are themselves readers and often invite their own readers to hear, if they can, echoes from other books in their novels. In academic discussion, the commonest word for this has, for some time, been 'intertextuality', the first of the topics treated below. The relative novelty of the term has sometimes persuaded the unsuspecting that it names a new tendency of fiction. In fact, as I try to show, it is a new name for a variety of traditional techniques. Plagiarism, quotation, allusion, imitation, burlesque, parody: all of these are different versions of intertextuality, and it is worth seeing the distinctiveness of each.

It is also worth seeing that some novels rely a great deal more on their 'literariness' than others. With its quotations from Locke, Burton, and Ephraim Chambers's *Cyclopaedia*, to name but three, Laurence Sterne's *Tristram Shandy* is a work of learned wit, made partly from rummaging in libraries. In the wonderful, if dizzying, Florida University Press standard edition of the novel, the notes, which mostly explain allusions and identify sources, fill one of the three volumes, 572 pages in total. You could not annotate a novel by Dickens or Trollope so expansively. In a different way, the literariness of James Joyce's *Ulysses* (itself also full of quotations and allusions) is a matter of its very structure. The different parts of the novel are modelled on parts of Homer's *Odyssey*, and knowing this should shape our interpretation of what is self-consciously a modern epic. Here one literary work provides the very skeleton for another. We must be careful, of course, what 'literary' means. Daniel Defoe's biblical tags or Nick Hornby's allusions to pop lyrics also belong amongst the literary material that is seizable by fiction.

We have got used to the idea that texts might be pieced together from pieces of other texts—that original writing might be more like an activity of recombination than of creation. Yet reaching for other literary works can be a sign of anxiety, a symptom of some kind of inferiority complex. When Samuel Richardson composed his great tragic novel *Clarissa*, he used, without acknowledgement, a book called *The Art of English Poetry* (1702), compiled by Edward Bysshe. This was an anthology of choice extracts from English poetry and drama. A former apprentice, now the self-made proprietor of a printing company, Richardson was deeply worried that his writing would be looked down on by educated readers. He went to Bysshe for the apt quotations that he could give to his clever, literate characters (especially his villain, Robert Lovelace). His search was not entirely foolish, for literary quotation is an appropriate habit for the brilliantly created Lovelace. Cultured and histrionic, he naturally sees himself as a dramatic character, a troubled poet, or even Milton's Satan.

Some contemporary novels still include highlighted fragments from other books. One reason for this might be that a surprising number of contemporary novels feature academic characters or situations. The novels discussed under 'Epigrams' and 'Quotation', Donna Tartt's *The Secret History* and J. M. Coetzee's *Disgrace*, take place at least partly in universities and feature teachers and students of literature. They also quote from other writers—in Tartt's case from Greek and Latin—because the Novel as a genre has always been interested in negotiating with older and higher genres of literature. Coetzee's novel carries with it a rueful awareness of the inapplicability of the literature that its protagonist carries in his head. Indeed, I argue below that Coetzee makes a point of the inappropriateness of the quotations that he neatly stitches into his narrative. Comparably, the *symbolism* in Muriel Spark's *Aiding and Abetting*, highlighted for us by means of biblical or liturgical quotation, is made utterly incongruous. There is a kind of mischievous scandal about the misapplication of religious texts in the minds of her characters.

The last section of this chapter looks at how novels with novelists as their protagonists allude to the fiction written by their own characters. This has been a possibility ever since David Copperfield followed his author in a career of novel-writing. Very few novels, however, go to the lengths of Margaret Atwood's *The Blind Assassin* and actually create quoted passages. Atwood puts these to ingenious use within her own novel, though we will see that there are problems in quoting from a book that does not exist. Most of all, perhaps, there is the difficulty that the extracts she uses fit her purpose too well. When one book reaches out to take part of another, there should be resistance as well as readiness, a sense of how far the fragment has been transported to make it serve a new use.

INTERTEXTUALITY

'Shall we for ever make new books, as apothecaries make new mixtures, by pouring only out of one vessel into another?' This is the narrator's complaint asked in Laurence Sterne's *Tristram Shandy* (vol. v, ch. i, 283). Except that it is plagiarized from Robert Burton's *Anatomy of Melancholy* (1621), one of Sterne's favourite books. Burton mocked writers who 'lard their leane bookes with the fat of others Workes', even as he conceded that all writers 'skim off the Creame of other mens Wits'.[1] These days we like to admire judicious larceny. The scholars who first discovered Sterne's 'borrowings' were shocked at his thieving.[2] Today's academics, in contrast, revel in his novel's intertextuality. Coined by the French critic Julia Kristeva in the 1960s, 'intertextuality' is one of those rare terms of literary theory that has migrated into the mainstream media. It was once the word with which theorists declared that any piece of writing referred to other pieces of writing, rather than to any world beyond texts. Now it is shorthand for almost any kind of allusiveness or imitation.

Michael Cunningham's *The Hours* represents a special kind of intertextuality, where one work proceeds as a homage to one other particular work. It is inspired by, and follows some of the patterns of, Virginia Woolf's *Mrs Dalloway*. This devoted fidelity is rare. Perhaps the most successful example of recent years is Jane Smiley's *A Thousand Acres* (1992), which closely follows *King Lear*. The readers of the first edition will have had to discern the source for themselves: the realization will have come like a shaft of light. Later readers are likely to have picked up a paperback edition festooned in recommendations from reviewers, one or two of which mention Shakespeare's play. Awareness of the source certainly makes a difference to the way you read Smiley's novel. You know where her story of an Iowa farmer and his three daughters is heading. You will be curious not so much about what is going to happen as how the novelist is going to find parallels for each significant part of her source story. Smiley's reliance on a pre-existing work is appropriate as she is writing a family tragedy. She wants us to sense the inevitability of discord and disaster from the moment that Laurence Cook relinquishes his responsibility for the family farm. Her variation on Shakespeare's version of events (itself, of course, borrowed and adapted) is to give the narrative to one of the 'bad' sisters, Ginny. Her modern Lear turns out to deserve the angry resentment of two of his daughters, for he has sexually abused them as children. Only the chilly, proper Caroline, Smiley's unsympathetic Cordelia figure, who goes off to be a lawyer while her sisters stay with the farm, refuses to believe her father's malignity.

Smiley has chosen as her source a work that is widely known and, importantly, widely studied in schools. It would be interesting to know what proportion of the tens of thousands who have bought *The Hours* have already read *Mrs Dalloway*. For those, surely the minority, who have done so, Cunningham inserts traces of intertextuality in its smaller varieties, like simple quotation. His fictionalized Virginia Woolf, approaching a breakdown, leaves her Richmond home one evening, without telling her husband, and walks to the station. 'She will go, she thinks, to London; she will simply go to London' (167). She is running away, from her marriage and her demons. 'What a lark! What a plunge!' To catch her thoughts, the novelist lifts these famous exclamations from the opening paragraph of *Mrs Dalloway* (see Chapter 8 above). Yet the girlish jollity of Clarissa Dalloway's interior monologue, on a fresh morning in June on the day of a party, is exactly inappropriate here, with her creator on the edge of desperation. The incongruity is there for the well-read reader to recognize, though the sense that the exclamations have been inserted for just this purpose is problematic. Woolf's interior world is made subordinate to the novelist's display of his purposes.

Then there is allusion. The dying Richard tells Clarissa that he has been hearing Furies singing to him in a foreign language. 'I believe it may have been Greek. Archaic Greek' (59). The reader of *Mrs Dalloway* recalls the shell-shocked Septimus Warren Smith, returned from the trenches of the First World War. In Woolf's novel he sits in Regent's Park and hears sparrows singing 'in voices prolonged and piercing in Greek words, from trees in the meadow of life beyond a river where the dead walk, how there is no death' (21). He will kill himself before the end of the book, as Richard will before the end of *The Hours*. Unlike the first readers of *Mrs Dalloway*, Cunningham's reader might know from biography about Woolf's own delusions—the 'voices' she heard in her bouts of madness.[3] Yet the allusion seems little more than a congratulatory gesture from the novelist to the special reader who knows any of this. Cunningham also uses what was called in the seventeenth and eighteenth centuries 'imitation': the making contemporary of some esteemed original—a translation that is an updating. Clarissa Vaughan's walk through Manhattan is meant to evoke Clarissa Dalloway's shopping trip in London's West End and to let us see how Woolf has given a model for the pleasures of urban pedestrianism. It follows the drift of her thoughts and catches the delight of life's particular textures.

> And then, thought Clarissa Dalloway, what a morning—fresh as if issued to children on a beach . . . in the triumph and the jingle and the strange high singing of some aeroplane overhead was what she loved; life; London; this moment of June. (*Mrs Dalloway*, 4)

> The vestibule door opens onto a June morning so fine and scrubbed Clarissa pauses at the threshold as she would at the edge of a pool, watching the turquoise water lapping at the tiles, the liquid nets of sun wavering in the blue depths. . . . What a thrill, what a shock, to be alive on a morning in June, prosperous, almost scandalously privileged, with a simple errand to run. (*The Hours*, 9–10)

To those who know the original the updated version offers the pleasure of recognizing its admiring correspondences, but *The Hours* presents such readers with parody too. In Woolf's novel, Clarissa Dalloway's daughter Elizabeth is attached to the frighteningly feminist (and crudely named) Doris Kilman. She despises Mrs Dalloway's easy ways and easy life. 'Fool! Simpleton! You who have known neither sorrow nor pleasure, who have trifled your life away! And there arose in her an overmastering desire to overcome her; to unmask her' (106). In *The Hours*, Clarissa Vaughan's daughter Julia has an older lover (also balefully named), Mary Krull. She is a 'stern and rigorous' New York lesbian, disdainful of Clarissa's Bloomsbury-style civilities.

'*Fool*, Mary thinks, though she struggles to remain charitable or, at least, serene. No, screw charity. Anything's better than queers of the old school, dressed to pass, bourgeois to the bone, living like husband and wife' (160). Here the parallel is bathetic rather than evocative, a comic modernizing of Woolf's slice of consciousness. Various are the forms of intertextuality that *The Hours* uses. It lets us see how many different ways one work may draw on another—how many different literary techniques intertextuality bundles together, sometimes indiscriminately.

EPIGRAMS

Epigrams have an overlooked role in the history of the Novel. Frequently they appear at the head of a novel, conventionally on a page between the title page and the opening of the narrative (see Chapter 1). However, some novels have epigrams sewn into the very fabric of the narrative. Henry Fielding has an epigram on the title page of *Tom Jones* that is a provoking joke about the status of the Novel, which puts old literary material to 'low' modern uses. He also inserts Greek and Latin epigrams into the narrative itself, providing rough-and-ready translations for the unlettered reader. Partridge, the incompetent schoolmaster, has good reason to muse on a tag from Ovid's *Amores* as he watches his jealous wife drive Jenny Jones from their house.

> Mr Partridge had profited too much by experience to interpose in a matter of this nature. He therefore had recourse to his usual recipe of patience; for, though he was not a great adept in Latin, he remembered and well understood the advice contained in these words:
>
> —*Leve fit, quod bene fertur onus.*
>
> In English: 'A burden becomes lightest when it is well borne.' (bk. II, ch. iii, 74)

The terrifying Mrs Partridge must be left to act out her tempest. The noble Latin is put to an application both apt and comically incongruous. Epigrams are a novel's connections to a world to which it cannot belong, so they often take on a rueful tone.

A modern example of a novel laced with epigrams is Donna Tartt's *The Secret History*. Many are in Latin or Greek: ancient-sounding fragments of wisdom. Tartt's characters are, after all, students of ancient Greek at a small American university. Indeed, they are the only students of Greek at this university. They are preoccupied with the world of the ancient Greeks—its beauty, its mysteries, its eloquence. Epigrams mark their affiliation—and that of the novel—with this 'other' world (they allow themselves to use Latin as well). There is something ridiculous and affected about it. '*Salve amice*,' one of them greets another (484). '*Khairei!*' exclaims Henry, the most addicted to Greekishness, when he realizes that it is his teacher Julian on the phone. But then they are undergraduates, earnest and self-regarding and able to treat solemnly what others would find ridiculous. The twist is that this shared code of ancient phrases and lore allows them to become murderers. The narrator's favourite epigram tells us of the very connection between these ancient fragments of wisdom and the violence to which the characters are drawn. '*Χαλεπὰ τὰ καλά. Beauty is harsh*.' (In ancient Greek, the word for 'beauty' echoes the very sound of 'harsh'.) It is 'about the first sentence that I ever learned in Greek', says Richard, Tartt's narrator (612). He and his murderous friends like to speak in other tongues. Greek seals them off effectively from their peers, but they flourish quotations from French and Italian too, as if their American English were somewhere to escape from. They have been brought together by their strange but charismatic teacher Julian, who likes to begin a Greek class by declaring, 'I hope we're all ready to leave the phenomenal world, and enter into the sublime?' (38). Greek is the language of the beyond, the primal, the more-than-human. It is the language of heroes and gods.

Epigrams insert into a world of ordinary discourse something stranger and better. The five other students in Julian's highly selective class, which Richard manages to join, seem to him other-worldly, '*sic oculos, sic ille manus, sic ora ferebat*' (32). He translates for the uninitiated: 'such eyes, such hands, such looks'. The Latin epigram has a special gravity (*O tempora, O mores*). It is a piece of the eternal. Think of Boswell recording Samuel Johnson's impatience with an eloquent English memorial on a tomb: 'Dr Johnson said, the inscription should have been in Latin, as every thing intended to be universal and permanent, should be.'[4] Even the clichés that occur to Richard are ancient. *In extremis* he has thoughts like '*amor vincit omnia*', '*requiescat in pace*', or '*et tu, Brute*'. Latin is the language of stability—the truth *sub specie aeternitatis*. '*Nihil sub sole novum*, I thought, as I walked down the hall to my room. Any action, in the fullness of time, sinks to nothingness.' (333) 'Nothing new under the sun', says the Latin. And, like some eternal piece of marble, the epigram stands for what it means. A good maxim, as Nietzsche remarked, 'is too hard for the teeth of time and is not eaten up by all the centuries'.[5] His own piece of wisdom demonstrates this well enough, being adapted without acknowledgement from Sir Thomas Browne's *Religio Medici* (1643), where the Bible is described as the only work 'too hard for the teeth of time'.[6] This kind of truth is like something unearthed.

QUOTATION

Quotation is a difficult art, easily feeling like pretension or condescension. People who use quotations are often irritating. Are they asking to be admired? Are they pretending to appeal to some common knowledge, while in fact flourishing their superiority? What good reasons would a novelist have for using formulations borrowed from elsewhere, not invented but purloined? J. M. Coetzee's *Disgrace* is fearlessly full of quotations, most of them literary, but knows very well what can go wrong with brandishing them. When the protagonist, the academic

David Lurie, is trying to seduce a student thirty years younger than himself, he tries a beguiling quotation on her. '"From fairest creatures we desire increase," he says, "that thereby beauty's rose may never die"' (16). No sooner has he spoken the opening lines from the first of Shakespeare's Sonnets than he knows that they have fallen flat.[7] 'Not a good move.' He knows immediately that in the girl's eyes he is no longer a potential lover. 'He has become a teacher again, man of the book, guardian of the culture-hoard.' She leaves.

Novels with academics as their protagonists (like those of David Lodge or Malcolm Bradbury) often scatter quotations. *Disgrace* has whole passages of Wordsworth and Byron that Lurie offers to his surly students (and to us) for elucidation. We know that the Romantic poetry should carry passion, should invigorate, but we know too that the lecturer is hearing the students' unresponsiveness. Outside the lecture room, however, Coetzee's quotations, though marked off by italics or by incongruous diction, are unattributed. We must trace them ourselves. You can sense what he is up to on the novel's first page. We are being told of the protagonist's regular appointments with Soraya, a prostitute. 'In the desert of the week Thursday has become an oasis of *luxe et volupté*' (1). Luxury and sensual delight? The italicization and the fact that the words are in French signal that there is a quotation here. The source is a lyric by Charles Baudelaire, 'L'Invitation au voyage', published in his 1857 collection *Les Fleurs du mal.* In it the poet dreams languorously of some state in which all appetites would be satisfied. The refrain is repeated three times,

> Là, tout n'est qu'ordre et beauté,
> Luxe, calme et volupté.[8]

Baudelaire's poem is an opium-tinged reverie and the quotation captures a self-indulgent contentment. What better words could there be for this condition than those of a French decadent poet?

Yet quotations in this novel are often inappropriate as well as fitting, and so it is in this case. Symbolist lyricism is, we might think, wishful when attached to David Lurie's pragmatic commercial arrangement, made through a company called Discreet Escorts. Near the end of the book, Lurie daydreams of the women he has known. 'Like leaves blown on the wind, pell-mell, they pass before him. *A fair field full of folk*: hundreds of lives all tangled with his. He holds his breath, willing the vision to continue' (192). Again the italics, as well as the alliteration and unusual diction, signal a quotation. It is a sweet-sounding phrase, and obviously taken from somewhere in Lurie's literary memory. In fact, it is from the opening of William Langland's fourteenth-century poem *Piers Plowman.* The narrator, lying down to sleep 'on a May mornynge' by a stream in the Malvern Hills, dreams of all the world's human variety. In between the tower on the hill and the dark dungeon is the place of this world, and there are the world's people.

> A fair feeld ful of folk found I ther bitwene—
> Of alle manere of men, the meene and the riche,
> Werchynge and wandrynge as the world asketh.[9]

It is as if, for a moment, the memories of a sensualist become like those of a religious poet; both are, after all, enjoying a 'vision'. Then events return him and us to a present in which his urges are far more basic.

The novel uses bits of Virgil and Verdi, Goethe and Hardy, because they supply the words on which its protagonist relies. In reaching for fitting quotations the narrative gives us a sharp sense of his thoughts. When he sees his daughter growing from youthful beauty to plainness, we get two pained lines from a song by François Villon (65). When he pities himself for being unable to forget the girl who has denounced him, we get a regretful fragment of late Yeats (190). He thinks of the feral dogs whom he helps to put down and a piece of *Jude the*

Obscure returns upon him: 'The dogs are brought to the clinic because they are unwanted: *because we are too menny*' (146)—the infamous line from the note left by Little Father Time before he kills his siblings and himself binds humans and dogs, equally disgraced. When his daughter Lucy proposes giving her land to her black neighbour Petrus, throwing herself on his mercy, 'with nothing', Lurie says, 'Like a dog' (205). When she agrees with his judgement, is she also recognizing the quotation from the end of Kafka's *The Trial*—the thought in K.'s head as he is murdered (see Chapter 11)? Here is a universal story of humiliation, of powerlessness. Quotation is eternal verity, but also embodies the character's rueful hope that he might dignify his story, alchemically transform it into something better—even something more tragic or melancholy—than it is. One day an academic editor will identify all the novel's quotations on behalf of toiling students; for now, we must find the sources ourselves. Quotation gives us elemental sentiments, clichés made sublime. The novel has taken words from a better world: what oft was thought but ne'er so well expressed. Quotation gives Coetzee's disgraced protagonist something, however incongruous, to cling to.

SYMBOLISM

Symbolism in a novel is risky because it presses meaning on the reader. It gestures beyond events to their greater significance, detecting what is essential or eternal in the particular. Muriel Spark, an avowedly Roman Catholic writer, is happy with the risk, echoing in her fiction biblical and liturgical texts. Indeed, in her novel *Aiding and Abetting* she recognizes and exploits this very sense of symbolism's excessiveness, its claim to transcend the literal. You can spot the symbols because the characters themselves draw attention to them. Spark's Lord Lucan is preoccupied with how much his children's nanny bled when, mistaking her for his wife, he bludgeoned her to death. Sitting in a Paris restaurant with Hildegard, his shrink, he muses on the religious significance of blood. 'They say it is purifying' (44). He is eating his perennial meal, smoked salmon followed by lamb chops. '"It is said we are washed in the Blood of the Lamb," he said, sticking his knife into lamb chop number three. "I sang in the school choir."' In that last statement the dull murderer bathetically explains why this Christian symbolism should pop into his head: a dimly recalled religious ritual from schooldays. The Blood of the Lamb is the sacrificial blood of Christ, shed to redeem men from their sins. *Agnus Dei qui tollis peccata mundi*. 'Could he be a religious maniac?' thinks Hildegard, the bogus psychiatrist, in an attempt at psychological insight. No, it is rather that Spark's characters live amongst symbols that they dumbly recognize but whose efficacy they do not grasp.

Hiding up in a Scottish hotel, Lucan finds, after another dish of lamb chops, that the echo of the symbolism lingers. '"We are washed in the Blood of the Lamb." He looked warily over his shoulder at this thought' (49). 'Warily' is a classic Spark adverb: this character is not feeling guilty, but recalling the language of religious sacrifice suddenly reminds him that he is a man pursued. He is unsettled, evidently, but not in the way that he should be. He is certainly not up to acknowledging the sacramental logic of the symbolism. Spark's is a kind of anti-symbolism, drawing attention to religious truths—of salvation or damnation, of sin and penitence—that her characters manage to avoid facing. And this despite the ubiquity in *Aiding and Abetting* of religious forms and practices (though invariably parodied or emptied of belief). Hildegard has made her way to affluence by pretending to be a stigmatic with miraculous powers, conning money out of gullible Catholics. Lucan has posed as a defrocked priest. Both have hidden from the law in religious communities. One of Lucan's aiders and abetters is a monk, Ambrose, a model religious performer who had 'no fear of any but the most shallow pitfalls' (95). In the novel's key coincidence, Lucan is recommended to Hildegard by Brother Heinrich, in whose 'prayer-hostel' he lodged (63). Heinrich was, years earlier, the theological student with whom Hildegard concocted her stigmatic scam.

'She made blood-money' (121), and blood is the novel's dominant symbol. Yet everyone thinks it is just some sticky substance. 'As Hildegard knew from her own experience as a stigmatic fraud, blood, once let loose, gets all over the place' (140). Her story also is 'dripping in blood' (142). It sounds as though she is thinking of blood's power to represent violence, destiny, guilt, consanguinity, or sacrifice. But in fact she is thinking literally. Lucan cannot get over all the blood he spilt. 'I will never forget the blood that flowed in such quantity from that girl' (42). Continually he echoes Lady Macbeth's 'who would have thought the old man to have had so much blood in him?' Lady Macbeth says this as she sleepwalks, her question a measure of her guilty horror at her own deeds. Lucan speaks in mere puzzlement. 'There must be something about the lower orders, they bleed so.' Symbols obtrude, but Spark's characters fail to be stopped short. In an ironic conclusion we are shown what happens when symbolism is not properly understood. Lucan and his double, Walker, end up in Kanzia, in central Africa, where they are to tutor the chief's sons. The chief assumes they are Christians, men who, as he tells his henchman, 'worship the Lamb' (206). 'They wash in the blood of the lamb . . . They say it makes them white.' Their new employers have their own version of the symbolic rite of Communion. Lucan is killed at the behest of the chief, and then he is cooked and eaten by all the male children of the tribe. *Hoc est corpus*.

NOVELS WITHIN NOVELS

Plenty of novels feature novelists, but few give even a line of the novels that the characters are supposed to write. Take Reta Winters, narrator of Carole Shields's *Unless*. She has written 'a light novel' with a happy ending and a jokey title, *My Thyme Is Up* (14). In the course of *Unless* she is writing a sequel whose characters and development divert her, and us, from her family troubles. Yet though we are given extracts from 'reviews' of Reta's fiction, we do not get even a sentence from what she writes. Further back, there is Nicholas Jenkins, the narrator of Anthony Powell's *roman-fleuve A Dance to the Music of Time*. By the fourth volume of this sequence, *At Lady Molly's* (1957), we find out that he is a published novelist, when he tells us with a characteristic nonchalance, 'I was then at the time of life when one has written a couple of novels' (16). Yet we never taste his writing, however consistently we might see all events and characters through his eyes. Powell is happy, in this same volume, to invent an imagined entry from Pepys's diary, describing a visit to a grand house in which some of his characters now live. He gives us nothing of his protagonist's fiction, however. It is important to both Shields and Powell that the protagonists have had success with their own novels. Yet these fictional fiction-makers are so much the alter egos of the actual novelists that, one imagines, they would hardly be able to write in a different way from Shields or Powell themselves.

It is rare for a novel actually to provide specimens of a fictional novel contained within it, though it is a trick sometimes played by formally self-conscious novelists. An influential pioneer in this respect was Doris Lessing in *The Golden Notebook* (1962). Its heroine, Anna Wulf, is herself a novelist, and records in four notebooks (Black, Red, Yellow, and Blue) different, apparently contradictory, aspects of her life. In the Yellow Notebook she writes the beginnings of a new novel. 'The yellow notebook looked like the manuscript of a novel, for it was called *The Shadow of the Third*. It certainly began like a novel' (148). It appears to elaborate a fictional version of her own hopes and disappointments in love. It is interleaved, though, with Anna's commentary on what she is writing ('I see another theme, of which I was not conscious when I began it. The theme is, naivety . . .'; 182). Readily it gives way to Anna's reflections on the difficulties of writing. The novel cannot be satisfactory, and the Yellow Notebook becomes a series of sketches for possible stories. The destiny of the novel within a novel is to enact the failure of one kind of self-expression.

There have been several more recent examples of the technique. In *Everything Is Illuminated*, Jonathan Safran Foer gives us sections from a fictional account of a Ukrainian Jewish community through the centuries. It is written by a character called 'Jonathan Safran Foer' and is subjected to a sceptical commentary, within the book, by his Ukrainian translator. I suggest in Chapter 4 that this narrative experiment is defensive, distancing the author from the presumptuousness of knowing the history that he imagines. We might infer defensiveness in another example, A. S. Byatt's *Babel Tower* (1996), which includes extracts of a sexually sadistic Arthurian romance, *Babbletower*, written by one of its characters, Jude Mason. Byatt's novel, set in the 1960s, includes a court case in which *Babbletower* is prosecuted for obscenity. Much concerned, like other Byatt novels, with literary judgement, it is not surprising that it includes this fictional fiction. Pastiche (see Chapter 8) has always been her inclination. Pastiche is also the purpose of Stephen King in his novel *Misery* (1987). The novelist Paul Sheldon, immobilized after a car accident, is held captive by a demented fan, Annie Wilkes. She makes him write a new novel in which Misery, a beloved character killed off in an earlier book, is to be brought back to life. We are given the opening chapters of this, which is a parody of a Stephen King horror novel, or rather, of what a literary snob might imagine one to be. It seems the author's joke against detractors. As with Byatt's *Babbletower*, King's novel within a novel is printed in a different font. In this case it imitates the print of the old typewriter that Sheldon has to use, complete with the inked-in characters where the typewriter key has not worked.

In Margaret Atwood's *The Blind Assassin*, the novel within a novel is neither merely trick nor joke. It has a real narrative function. *The Blind Assassin* is not just the title of Atwood's book, it is also the title of a novel written by one of its characters. Atwood's narrator, Iris, has told us of her sister Laura's suicide in the book's opening chapter; soon we find out from an interpolated newspaper clipping that Laura 'made her posthumous debut as a novelist' two years later (17). Iris arranged the publication of the work of fiction that Laura apparently left behind at her death. Iris's account of her life with her sister is interleaved with extracts from this novel. Immediately after the report of Laura's death, we are given the novel's opening under the heading 'The Blind Assassin. *By Laura Chase. Reingold, Jaynes & Moreau, New York, 1947*'. In the extract a woman intently examines a photograph of herself and a young man.

> She's preserved this photo carefully, because it's almost all she has left of him. It's black and white, taken by one of those boxy, cumbersome flash cameras from before the war, with their accordion-pleat nozzles and their well-made leather cases that looked like muzzles, with straps and intricate buckles. The photo is of the two of them together, her and this man, on a picnic. *Picnic* is written on the back, in pencil—not his name or hers, just *picnic*. She knows the names, she doesn't need to write them down. (7)

Further extracts follow, without commentary or explanation, throughout the novel. They tell of the secret meetings between the two unnamed lovers. She is married, he is a political activist, perhaps on the run from the police. Like Iris's own narrative, it is set in the 1930s (he goes to fight in Spain; later he is killed in the Second World War) and presumably in Canada, but it is stripped of almost all specific markers of time and place. The lovers meet, they make love (though this is never described), they tell each other stories, and then they part. The style, as in the fragment above, is undemonstrative, spare, even blank. Facts are enumerated down to incidental details of decor in the rooms in which the lovers meet, but feelings are left implicit.

Why are we given this novel within a novel? Some of Atwood's own characters misconstrue its purposes. Iris's daughter Aimee radically misinterprets the novel to fit her own resentment. 'She said it was obvious: her real mother was Laura, and her real father was that man, the one in *The Blind Assassin*' (531). Without a father, and furious at her mother, Aimee reads to fulfil her angry fantasy. Near the end of Atwood's novel Iris tells us that Laura's book caused an 'uproar' amongst 'the pulpit-thumpers and local biddies' in her small town (622). 'Innuendo began to flow' and all the speculation about the 'true' story behind the novel helped ruin her husband, Richard. It emerged that, after sexually abusing Laura, he had had her confined in a 'clinic' and finally had apparently driven her to kill herself. The novel was her indirect testimony, and its success was her revenge on him. His career in politics ruined, he commits suicide, though this is covered up. 'He was found with the book at his elbow, however' (624).

Yet we are reading this book too and, if we are shrewd, coming to different conclusions from those two frantic interpreters. Near her story's end Iris tells us the truth about Laura's novel. 'But you must have known that for some time' (626). It should not spoil the book for any first-time reader if I say that, by this stage, he or she should not be surprised by what is revealed. For the clever thing is that the significance of the novel within a novel—what it tells us about Iris and Laura—has slowly become evident. Different readers will realize at different points. Fiction, we see, is taken from life, but not in the way that any reader within the novel realizes. So this novel within a novel has an important narrative role. The role is complicated by a further story that the lovers in the novel-within-a-novel tell each other. This is a fantasy tale—part Arabian Nights and part science fiction—that is an allegory of love's vicissitudes. The only problem is that the snatches of the 'novel' that Atwood invents serve her purposes almost too well. They are given their resonance by our growing understanding that they fictionalize a part of Iris's life about which she cannot tell us directly. If one was to extract them from the novel where they belong, they would be lifeless. It is difficult to imagine that these blank-toned episodes could actually be parts of the successful book that the plot requires. They work beautifully, yet they are not like extracts from any publishable novel.

11
Ending

WHEN William Godwin, now best known for being the father of Mary Shelley, set out to compose his novel *Caleb Williams*, he wrote the ending first. Recalling the process of composition in 1832, he described how he 'invented first the third volume of my tale, then the second, and last of all the first'.[1] He believed that 'carrying back my invention from the ultimate conclusion to the first commencement' would ensure 'an entire unity of plot'. The ending would not only provide a fitting climax, it would prove the novelist's point. Godwin had a political message about the ways in which 'the spirit and character of the government intrudes itself into every rank of society' (preface, 1). As an indication that the story was a parable of the state of the nation, he called it *Things As They Are* (its title was only changed by Godwin more than thirty years later). He knew that his demonstration of his political argument would be strongest at his novel's end—that there would be his *conclusion*: his final judgement.

It is no accident that our feelings about how a narrative satisfies, or fails to satisfy, us are often concentrated on its ending. Here, in the ending of it, promises are to be kept, questions answered, uncertainties resolved. Many readers will know how, as the sense of an impending ending becomes strong, the last pages of a novel take on a special intensity. It is impossible not to be influenced by what Jane Austen, nearing the very end of *Northanger Abbey*, admits to her readers is 'the tell-tale compression of the pages before them' (vol. ii, ch. xvi, 203). Readers and characters are 'all hastening together to perfect felicity'. If plot is all, we might now read with increasing speed, avid to find how it will be worked out. Or we might slow ourselves to relish a conclusion for which we have long prepared. It is not surprising that novelists worry about their endings. Godwin himself did so. In manuscript, he had an ending in which his hero and narrator, wrongly imprisoned by his aristocratic foe Falkland, senses that he has been poisoned. As we reach the end of his account, he is growing weaker and weaker. This was the version that he wrote first of all. Yet, having written the rest of the novel, Godwin then had second thoughts. He wrote a new ending. In the published version, there is a trial at which Caleb vindicates himself, only to feel appalled at seeing Falkland, who was once his friend, finally crushed. Now at least truth triumphs, a fitting conclusion in that his great work of political theory, *An Enquiry concerning Political Justice*, had argued that truth, if demonstrated rationally, was irresistible.

Ending the novel is not the same as completing it. Franz Kafka never finished *The Trial*, but he did end it. Early in the process of the novel's composition he completed both its opening and its final chapters. Perhaps 'chapter' is the wrong word, for the sections that he wrote, though given schematic titles, were unnumbered and were kept in separate files, as if self-contained units. Several sections exist only as incomplete drafts, usually excluded from published versions. Kafka gave no indication of the order in which these sections should be arranged, and experts still argue over this. He never finished the novel and he instructed his executor, Max Brod, to destroy it after his death, along with the rest of his unpublished writings. Unfinished it might be, but its sense of an ending is indubitable. The protagonist, Joseph K., is taken from his lodgings at night by two state functionaries, marched out into the countryside, and killed. The novel ends with the double twist of a knife in his heart and one of the most memorable concluding sentences in the history of fiction. '"Wie ein Hund!" sagte er, es war, als sollte die Scham ihn überleben.'[2] '"Like a dog!" he said. It was as if the shame would outlive him.' Kafka may not have known for certain what he wanted to put in or take out, but he knew where the logic of his book must finally take him. This sense that an ending must fulfil what has come before is deep within all novel readers.

We can feel the importance of endings in recorded instances of novelists, like Godwin, changing their minds about how to finish their novels. The only manuscript fragment that we have of one of Austen's finished novels is the original ending that she wrote to *Persuasion*. Here she had Captain Wentworth deputed by Admiral Croft to ask Anne Elliot if she was indeed engaged to Mr Elliot, so that the Admiral would know to relinquish Kellynch Hall to the happy couple. Anne's denial immediately produces Wentworth's declaration of his feelings. Compared to the dramatically elaborate scene that Austen eventually substituted, with Wentworth overhearing the conversation between Anne and Captain Harville about the constancy of men's and women's feelings, it seems merely efficient. Her second thought, to have Anne and Wentworth crowded by other characters, unable to communicate directly, produced one of the great endings in English fiction. Yet she did not change her mind about what was to happen. For Austen the questions were about means; she was perfectly decided about what end (the marriage of lovers who have rediscovered their love) she would bring about. In other cases the change of mind is more radical. Dickens wrote two endings for *Great Expectations*, according to his friend and biographer John Forster, after being advised by his fellow novelist Bulwer Lytton: 'upon Bulwer Lytton objecting to a close that should leave Pip a solitary man, Dickens substituted what now stands'.[3] In the published version, Pip revisits the place where Satis House once stood and meets Estella there, still beautiful, but with a 'saddened softened light' in her eyes (vol. iii, ch. xx, 483). Estella says that they 'will continue friends apart', but in the next sentence, the last of the novel, Pip says that in the evening's 'broad expanse of tranquil light . . . I saw the shadow of no parting from her' (484). It is something like a happy ending, though ambiguous still. Dickens was true enough to the sadness of his book not to engineer anything like a betrothal. Yet this resembles rather more closely the conventional ending of a Victorian novel than what he first wrote. The proof of the original ending survives. In this version Pip tells us that, after the death of her first husband, the brutal Bentley Drummle, Estella has married 'a Shropshire doctor'.[4] Pip, in the company of Joe and Biddy's young son, meets her again in Piccadilly: 'the lady and I looked sadly enough on one another'. The sadness is made sharper by her false assumption that the boy is Pip's son, and by his not disabusing her. Pip, we see, has lost his chance to be a father. He says that he was 'very glad afterwards to have had the interview', for it assures him that suffering has softened her and 'given her a heart to understand what my heart used to be'. And there we finish.

At the end of novels, debts must be paid, marriages arranged. In Dickens's first thoughts, Pip's paying off his debts excluded him from marriage, that usual end for a hero or heroine. He has travelled back to the 'marsh country' of his childhood in order to propose to Biddy, but arrives on the very day of her wedding to Joe. Once Biddy would have had him, but his vain 'expectations' led him away. Forster thought the first version 'more consistent with the drift, as well as natural working out, of the tale'. Bulwer Lytton, however, was surely right that Dickens had written an ending that would have disappointed many of his readers. When they end their novels, novelists are likely to think of their readers' expectations. Henry James, a pioneer of inconclusive endings, thinks of responses to the ending of *The Portrait of a Lady* when he lays out a close plan of its narrative in his note-books. He proposes to end the novel with Isabel starting out for Italy to return to her cruel husband, whom she does not love.

> The obvious criticism of course will be that it is not finished—that I have not seen the heroine to the end of her situation—that I have left her *en l'air*.—This is both true and false. The *whole* of anything

is never told; you can only take what groups together. What I have done has that unity.[5]

That 'obvious' marks James's awareness of the pressure upon the novelist to provide the required sense of an ending. In the first section of this chapter, I discuss the ending of a novel, Carol Shields's *Unless*, whose novelist narrator has this pressure put on her by her publisher. We might no longer expect an ending to be as studiously tied up as that of a novel by Dickens or Trollope, but we need to feel we have reached a conclusion, that 'loose ends' have not been left. The reader's appetite for an ending is just what a novelist can exploit pleasingly in the provision of a 'twist' at the end, or a false ending (see below).

For endings have different phases. There are cases when a reader will feel that he or she has reached the 'real' ending long before the final few pages. An extreme and early example is Samuel Richardson's *Pamela*. The frightening yet engrossing pursuit of the resourcefully virtuous heroine by her predatory master, Mr B., ends with him falling in love with her and marrying her. By page 275 of the modern World's Classics edition, Pamela is safely betrothed to him. Yet there are still well over 200 pages to go, filled with Pamela's moralistic reflections about the joys and duties of married life. To Richardson, this part of the novel was essential to his didactic purposes, but most readers will think that the story is over. Novels have ways of formalizing this sense of narrative taken up beyond the end of a story, and the last two sections of this chapter reflect on our need for proper conclusions by examining these. As even Jane Austen, the provider of emphatically 'closed' endings, recognized (see 'The Postscript', below), the most satisfying endings still leave us wanting to know more.

THE DENOUEMENT

Every novel ends, but not every novel has a denouement. The word is from the French for 'unknotting' and refers to the resolving or untying of a story's complications. Denouements occur in novels where the novelist has created problems that have to be solved, mysteries that have to be cleared up. A denouement is not just a conclusion, it is also an explanation, belatedly providing information that has previously been held back. So the word has also come to refer to the part of a narrative that comes after some climax or crisis. The main part of the story has ended, but there are still conclusions to be traced and consequences described. In George Eliot's novel *Adam Bede*, for example, the climax is the planned hanging of the servant girl Hetty Sorrel, who has been condemned to death for the supposed murder of her illegitimate baby. Eliot builds up to this climax, giving us a highly wrought dialogue on the eve of execution between Hetty and her cousin the Methodist preacher Dinah Morris. When Hetty is reprieved on the very scaffold, we might say that the narrative has reached and passed its final crisis. But there is still explaining to be done, still nine chapters to come. Hetty is sentenced to be transported. Arthur Donnithorne, the well-born father of Hetty's baby, is dispatched abroad. Adam Bede himself, who has always hopelessly loved Hetty, is to be made to love Dinah, and to marry her.

Denouements are necessary to our satisfaction, yet can seem imposed from outside. Thus novels with complicated plots will sometimes invent a character whose only role is providentially to arrive to reveal the schemes of the villainous and the true parentage of the virtuous. Fielding's *Tom Jones* and Dickens's *Nicholas Nickleby* (1838–9) are notable examples. In *Tom Jones* the crucial unravelling involves not just the revealing of the villainous Blifil's scheming against the virtuous Tom, but also the revelation of Tom's true parents. First Mrs Waters, formerly Jenny Jones, arrives to tell Squire Allworthy, and the reader, that she is not Tom's mother, but that his father was a character whom we have never met: Mr Summer, the scholarly son of one of Allworthy's friends, who once stayed for a while in his house, and died young. Very belatedly, for otherwise there could have been no novel, the lawyer Dowling then arrives 'in the utmost haste' as the agent of the denouement. At last he delivers the message with which Bridget Allworthy entrusted him on her deathbed, many hundreds of pages earlier. 'Tell my brother Mr Jones is his nephew.—He is my son' (bk. XVIII, ch. viii, 840). (The message never arrived because Allworthy was ill and Blifil intercepted it.) Now, finally, all can be resolved. Comparably, in *Nicholas Nickleby* Dickens brings in after some sixty chapters a character, Brooker, who has played no part in the story so far but is now revealed to be a former confederate of Ralph Nickleby. His role is to tell us of Ralph's past, and of the secret at the novel's heart: that Smike, the backward, brutalized boy whom Nicholas has befriended and saved from the sadistic schoolmaster Squeers, is in fact Ralph's son, his only child. That boy 'is now in his grave' (ch. 60, 737). Appalled, Ralph throws the table lamp to the ground and is gone. The end is in sight.

So often in a novel, someone must arrive with an explanation. We need—the narrator needs—an explanation in Carol Shields's *Unless*, which has bleakly imagined a problem without any evident solution. How will Shields untie her tight knot? The story is a contemporary nightmare common in news stories: the beloved child who, for reasons beyond understanding, chooses to become an implacable outcast. In *Unless*, Norah, the daughter of the narrator, Reta, squats on a Toronto street corner, a sign round her neck saying merely GOODNESS, impervious to friends and family. She is beyond blandishment or persuasion, silent and frightening. The life of her family goes on, but under the shadow of her withdrawal. Why has this happened? How can it all end? *Unless* frets a good deal about its need for a denouement. As often when Shields wants to comment on her own novel, she has her narrator, Reta, worry about the novel that she is writing, *Thyme in Bloom*. She is contemplating the last couple of chapters. 'Then the dénouement, which will contain a twist that is certain to challenge any reader's good will, but I'm determined to go through with it' (237). Hers is a romantic and comic novel, and she must decide how to leave her two fictional lovers. She pictures a reader whom she would like to surprise, but must also gratify.

Arthur, Reta's ingratiating but bullying editor, worried about whether his author will give her novel a reader-pleasing denouement, declares piously, 'the form will complete itself in the only way it can' (241). He is himself an affected literary critic, dignifying his attempts to rewrite Reta's book with theoretical ruminations when she talks of her plans to write the final chapter.

> 'Ah yes, the final chapter. The all-important final chapter.'
>
> 'The most difficult chapter in a way.'
>
> 'I absolutely agree, It's critical. What is a novelist to do? Provide closure for the reader? Or open the narrative to the ether?'
>
> 'You mean—'
>
> 'I think of the final chapter as the kiln. You've made the pot, Reta, the clay is still malleable, but the ending will harden your words into something enduring and beautiful. Or else beautiful and ethereal.' (277)

Yet the satire here seems like a diversion from a challenge that Shields herself faces. Reta ruefully tells us that, in her novel, nothing is left unresolved. 'Everything is neatly wrapped up at the end, since tidy conclusions are a convention of comic fiction, as we all know' (317). She does what is expected.

Shields too is under pressure to explain. You might say that her novel could have left Norah to her psychosis. In life, she might have stayed on the street, or been taken into psychiatric care, or simply gone on being 'a problem' into an indefinite future. But novels must take a shape and achieve the sense of an ending. In the final chapter of *Unless* ('Not Yet') we find out—

because Reta has now found out—that there is a precise narrative explanation for Norah's withdrawal. There was an original trauma. She was a passer-by when a Muslim woman, a political protester, set herself on fire at that same Toronto street corner. It was an event in the television news that passed by us early in the novel. Norah saw the woman die and badly burned herself in a vain attempt to save her. This was what drove her into her own stunned, silent protest against the world. By chance, the evidence of what Norah saw and did was preserved on CCTV footage, given to the police, in the end seen by her family. If it had not been so, her affliction would have remained a mystery; 'unless, unless, all this would have been lost' (315). The narrator notices how fortunate is the explanation.

So the novel ends with a solution. On the last page, 'Norah is recovering at home, awakening atom by atom' (320). We are back (as if in Dickens) to the family hearth. Yet there is something awkward about the denouement. 'We know now, Norah,' says the narrator. 'You can put this behind you. You are allowed to forget' (315). Can we believe this confidence, the settlement of all the narrator's previous doubts? Here the knowledge of events, such as is traditionally allowed to a reader at the end of a novel, is conflated with a knowledge of what must have been going through Norah's mind. But these two kinds of knowledge are not the same. Does the author, we may wonder, quite believe in her own unknotting?

THE FALSE ENDING

Certain narratives please us by providing twists at their endings. On TV and in the cinema, we are used to thrillers that end by showing that we have been under some misapprehension for much of the preceding story. One way in which such surprise is engineered is by the use of what can be called the *false ending*: an apparent conclusion that is provided only in order to be unsettled by the true ending. A. S. Byatt's *Possession* is a neat example of this. Its first, false ending solves the novel's central mystery and provides a romantic consummation. The final numbered chapter is headed by a fragment of Ash's poetry that is all about our appetite for endings.

> We are driven
> By endings as by hunger. We *must know*
> How it comes out, the shape o' the whole . . . (476)

We duly get this shape. The long-lost letters of the Victorian poet Christabel LaMotte have been unearthed from the grave of her fellow poet, and secret lover, Randolph Ash. A final letter makes clear that she gave birth to his daughter, May, who was brought up by Christabel's sister as her own child. When she grew up, May married happily and had her own child; she would never know her true parentage. Ash never read this letter, which was placed unopened in the grave by his widow. His child is revealed (in Byatt's most stretched coincidence) to be the great-great-great-grandmother of Maud, one of the novel's academic detectives. Roland and Maud, long kept tantalizingly apart, are finally allowed to sleep together, with the implication that this coupling is for ever: 'I'll take care of you, Maud' (507). There is some awkwardness here. Byatt's phrasing is stilted, mock-decorous—'Roland finally, to use an outdated phrase, entered and took possession of all her white coolness that grew warm against him'—but the end has been reached.

Yet then there is the 'Postscript', the true ending, undoing some of the conclusions that the reader, and the novel's leading characters, thought had been reached. Dated '1868', it reveals information never to be known to modern-day researchers. 'There are things which happen and leave no discernible trace . . . This is how it was' (508). On a beautiful day in May, a gentleman 'with an ashplant in his hand' met a child playing in a meadow. They talked and played. She gave him a lock of her hair. He said he was a poet and gave her a message for her 'aunt', saying he was 'looking for the Belle Dame Sans Merci' but would now 'not disturb her' (510). The child got into a game with her brothers on her way home and the message was never delivered.

So Ash did know. He even met his daughter. It is her plait of hair that Roland and Maud discover in Ash's grave, not (as the sleuths suppose, and will go on supposing) Christabel's. The past is, we see, not discoverable after all. What is most important might be just what leaves 'no discernible trace'. The neat and poignant adjustment is made possible by the 'false ending' carefully arranged on the preceding pages. We see how every present-day character in the novel is doomed to misunderstand the past, especially those who know most about it. Ash's meeting with his daughter, his only child, is an encounter of which no one except him will ever know. The Postscript that shows this is composed in a dreamlike, florid language, loaded with literary allusions. 'There was a meadow full of young hay, and all the summer flowers in great abundance. Blue cornflowers, scarlet poppies, gold buttercups, a veil of speedwells, an intricate carpet of daisies where the grass was shorter . . .' (508). Its tone of pastoral make-believe has seemed unconvincing to some. What has passed without comment, however, is a psychological contradiction that is the consequence of Byatt's narrative ingenuity. We can well believe that, if Ash was earlier able to track Christabel down to her remote hiding place in Brittany, where she retired to conceal her pregnancy and then have her baby, he would certainly find her in Lincolnshire. She is, after all, living with her titled sister. But why, at the end of his happy encounter with his unknowing daughter, is he so casual with that message for her 'aunt'? All too clearly this leaves the possibility of the message failing to get through. May, after all, is 7 or 8 years old. (The 2002 film of *Possession*, as if worried about his carelessness, makes him give her a letter for Christabel, and then shows this being dropped and lost.) Christabel dies racked with guilt at concealing from Ash his daughter's very existence. The Postscript implies that her lover has, in effect, condemned her to this bitter self-reproach. Yet clearly it is not part of the book's redemptive purpose that he should have done so. Why did he not find some reliable method of letting Christabel know that he knew? What about the excellent Victorian postal system? Of course, proper communication would not have allowed Byatt her deft reversal of expectations. The novelist's beautifully performed trick has its price.

EPILOGUE

Until the twentieth century it was common for plays, especially comedies, to have epilogues. (*Epilogue* means in Greek 'a speech added on'.) One of the actors would step forward out of the play's true ending to comment, often wittily, on its events and absurdities. The audience would be asked for its indulgence. Done well, it was, and still can be, a way of confirming a bond between performer and spectator. In a novel, an epilogue can look like the novelist distrusting the reader, as if unwilling to let him or her draw their own inferences from the novel's conclusion. It is hard to find the earliest novel with a declared 'epilogue', but this formal after-story became a feature of fiction in the mid-nineteenth century. Herman Melville's *Moby-Dick* (1851) has a brilliant little example. The whaling ship the *Pequod* has been sunk by the great white whale in an extraordinary final scene. The crew is lost. But then there is an epilogue. '*The drama's done. Why then does any one step forth?*' (625). Melville reminds us of stage convention, as Ishmael tells us how he was providentially saved. If he had not been, of course, the story could not have been told, for the novel has been narrated in the first person by Ishmael. In heightened language this epilogue implies that Ishmael has been spared in order to tell his tale. '*The unharming sharks, they glided by as if with padlocks on their mouths; the savage sea-hawks sailed with sheathed beaks.*' On the second day, after the destruction of Ishmael's ship and all his shipmates, '*the devious-cruising*

Rachel', a ship encountered earlier searching for one of its own missing whale boats, returns to find him, '*another orphan*'.

Some great English Victorian novels also have epilogues. The epilogue of George Eliot's *Adam Bede* takes us forward by more than seven years to show the appropriate fates of its chief characters. Adam, the artisan hero, has prospered and is now owner of the timber-yard where he was once but an employee. Dinah, the good woman whom he married, has been rewarded with beautiful children. We meet them again as they talk of Arthur Donnithorne, the rakish young squire who has just returned from abroad. Adam has just been to meet him. He has been punished with illness as well as the pains of exile. Adam reports that 'his colour's changed, and he looks sadly' (538). We gather from a passing remark by Adam's brother Seth that the young woman whom Arthur seduced, Hetty Sorrel, 'the poor wanderer', has died even as she was returning from Australia. Eliot's moral scheme is secure, rewards and punishments effected, but it is done with characteristic skill. The conversation through which we hear of characters' fates also dramatizes the mixed contentment and sadness of Adam and Dinah at the end of it all.

Slightly later than *Adam Bede*, Wilkie Collins's *The Moonstone* has an epilogue that satisfyingly brings his narrative full circle. The mystery of the Moonstone's theft has been solved. In the epilogue we hear how this fabulous diamond is restored to the Indian idol from which it was first taken in the novel's Prologue (see Chapter 1). In keeping with the curse, mentioned in that Prologue, on anyone who might take it from where it belongs, the Moonstone returns to 'the god of the Moon' (466). Later detective fiction also uses epilogues. Most of Colin Dexter's Inspector Morse novels, for instance, have them. In the calm after the denouement accounts are settled and Morse himself is pictured rueful and solitary, a melancholy figure until another murder can animate him again. Here is the very end of *The Dead of Jericho* (1981).

> And what of Morse? He still walks to his local most evenings, and would appear to take most of his calories in liquid form, for no one has seen him buying cans of food in the Summertown supermarkets. In mid-December he was invited to another party in North Oxford; and as he waited in the buffet queue his eyes caressed the slim and curving bottom of the woman just in front of him as she leant across the table. But he said nothing; and after eating his meal alone, he found an easy excuse to slip away, and walked home alone. (302)

Morse cannot be allowed to consummate his urges, for he must preserve his solitary restiveness (note the awkward repetition of the word 'alone') for the next whodunnit.

The epilogue has come to seem a rather old-fashioned device, perhaps partly because it was common in creaky American TV dramas of the 1960s. When Anne Patchett's *Bel Canto* settles its accounts with a final chapter labelled 'Epilogue', it risks appearing to manipulate its readers' sympathies. The novel has had its catastrophe—its disastrous resolution. Its leading characters, guests at a diplomatic party, are held hostage for most of its duration. The siege gives us a drama of romance, comedy, and daydreaming, but is abruptly concluded when troops storm in. 'At the sound of the shot, it seemed the man with the gun divided, first into two and then four, eight, sixteen, thirty-two, sixty-four' (311). There are soldiers everywhere. 'With every loud pop more came.' Several of the characters whom we have come to know are killed in this assault. The violence and finality is convincing, the narrative taking on the numbed surprise of the characters. In the chapter's final sentence, Mr Hosokawa the opera enthusiast and Carmen the revolutionary are killed, the former trying to save the latter. 'One shot fixed them together in a pairing no one had considered before: Carmen and Mr. Hosokawa, her head just to the left of his as if she was looking over his shoulder' (313). We are left in a state of shock.

But then we have an 'epilogue'. It is six months later and two former hostages are getting married. The tragic conclusion is behind us, and now we have an ending that is conventional in comedy. The odd thing is that the bride and groom—Roxanne, the opera singer who was performing when guerrillas stormed the building, and Gen, the translator who was one of her fellow hostages—each had a brief, secret affair during the siege. Their lovers were those two characters who died in its final moments. Patchett's epilogue seems too clearly designed to rescue something from her tale. The bereaved partners must marry each other. The epilogue here, as elsewhere in fiction, risks persuading the reader that the author feels uneasy about the ending that has already been provided. After the conclusion of a fable, an epilogue is a proper summary, where the moral might be gracefully pointed. At the end of a novel, however, it should be different. A novel is too much like life, we might think, to be reducible to a moral. Its epilogue is more like an afterthought, something that could not be got into the story. Why then does Patchett need hers? She wants to believe that her characters have truly been transformed by their strange experience, that they have been redeemed by the events that she has plotted. Her epilogue is there because she wants the reader to believe this too.

THE POSTSCRIPT

Some narrative conventions first developed by novelists are now more familiar from film and television. One of these, used in the final chapter of John le Carré's *The Constant Gardener*, is the *postscript*. A story has been brought to its conclusion and the credits are ready to roll. Now, however, extra footage informs you what happened—after the story's end, perhaps years later—to some of the characters you have encountered. A postscript differs from an epilogue, which presents some representative episode from a future time. Postscripts, in contrast, feature brief summaries of future events—in films, often a few sentences on the screen. They are favoured by narratives that purport to be based on 'real' people and events (which can be seen to spill over, therefore, beyond any artificially imposed ending). The postscript is schematic, succinct, often didactic. In fiction, it has sharp lessons and ironies to display.

In the final chapter of *The Constant Gardener*, we leave le Carré's hero, Justin Quayle, in the African bush, on the trail of his wife's killers, to be told 'a chapter of events' in the months that follow. We get given the peculiar fate of each secondary character. Sandy Woodrow is rewarded for dealing diplomatically with Tessa Quayle's murder by being made High Commissioner. The Foreign Office 'Africa Tsar' Sir Bernard Pellegrin, who has made sure that her findings about the murderous research practices of a large pharmaceutical company are 'buried', gets a senior post with the very company that she was investigating. Kenny Curtiss, the entrepreneur whose company was testing the new drug on Africans, is made a Lord. Rob and Lesley, the police officers doggedly investigating Tessa's death, leave the police service. Yet the villains of the piece do not quite escape. Le Carré cannot bring himself merely to invalidate his hero's sleuthing. Quayle has ensured that inconvenient documents become public, and the novel's postscript includes rumblings in press and Parliament about a conspiracy behind Tessa's murder. The Foreign Secretary is embarrassed by questions on the floor of the House. Only the string of legal petitions and cross-petitions disarms protest, ensuring that 'the case would run for years' (553). There is a twist of chronology in this. For the postscript also tells us of 'the unhappy passing of Justin Quayle' (550). 'Deranged by despair and grief, he had taken his own life at the very spot where his wife Tessa had been murdered only weeks before.' This is the final, official account—but not the truth. For now the narrative shifts back in time to show us what really happened, what has been hushed up in that summary. Quayle has, of course, been murdered.

In le Carré's postscript, poetic injustice seems to be the point. His is a sardonic use of a convention that is almost as old as the Novel itself. Perhaps the earliest example is in Samuel Richardson's *Clarissa*, completed in 1748. After reaching his tragic conclusion—agonizingly foreseen by attentive readers for the preceding seven volumes—Richardson signs off with the death of the villain Lovelace, destroyer of his heroine, Clarissa. He then appends a postscript (though it is labelled 'Conclusion'), detailing the fates of all the other characters. Clarissa's tyrannical brother makes an unhappy marriage and is gnawed by guilt at his treatment of Clarissa. Her spiteful sister marries 'a man of quality' who turns out to be a libertine. Everyone gets his or her deserts. The prostitute who helped Lovelace trick Clarissa duly dies of 'a fever and surfeit got by a debauch'. Clarissa's loyal governess finds that her financial investments multiply in value. The device is both elaborate and clumsy, forcing on us the author's concern that his novel be exemplary. Yet it caters to the reader's desire that characters not be forgotten: that, at the end, everyone be accounted for.

The Novel is a genre that would have us believe that its characters might have a life beyond its pages. Jane Austen used to enjoy discussing with her family the after-fates of Elizabeth and Darcy, Emma, Mr Woodhouse, and Mr Knightley. According to Austen's nephew James-Edward Austen-Leigh, his aunt told the family that 'Miss Steele never succeeded in catching the Doctor; that Kitty Bennet was satisfactorily married to a clergyman near Pemberley, while Mary obtained nothing higher than one of her uncle Philips's clerks, and was content to be a star in the society of Meryton.'[6] Mr Woodhouse would die two years after Emma's marriage, allowing her to move to Donwell (and perhaps retrospectively justifying his hypochondria), while the sensitive Jane Fairfax would apparently have only nine or ten years of married life with Frank Churchill before her death. Sometimes with a little more subtlety, the contents of a postscript could be contained within the ending of Victorian novels. A famous example is the final section of George Eliot's *Middlemarch*, entitled 'Finale', which records the fitting destinies of its main characters years beyond the novel's proper conclusion.

Some readers will feel that, as much as Richardson, le Carré has designs on us with his postscript. His is a political point: ordinary citizens and newspaper readers will never be told the kind of story found in his novel. His voice comes through with sarcastic directness. 'The permanent government of England, on which her transient politicians spin and posture like so many table dancers, had once more done its duty' (551). Yet the postscript is also offered as a form of verisimilitude. In the real world of multinational skulduggery and Foreign Office complicity, things continue. Foreign Office wheels keep turning; businessmen and diplomats leave one scheme only to turn up elsewhere. The bureaucrats who really run the country do not recognize the significance of any one person's story. Our protagonist reaches the end of his road, but the bigger narrative continues. The novelist makes a shapely tale, but in life there are no proper endings.

Notes

INTRODUCTION

1. The anecdote is told by Brontë's publisher, George Murray Smith. I take it from Rebecca Fraser, *The Brontës: Charlotte Brontë and Her Family* (Crown Publishers, 1988), 349.
2. His own account is quoted in Juliet Barker, *The Brontës* (1994; Phoenix, 1999), 535.

CHAPTER 1

1. See Samuel Richardson, *Pamela*, ed. T. Keymer and A. Wakely (Oxford World's Classics, 2001), 5. The World's Classics paperback is the only British edition of the first edition of the novel.
2. Anthony Trollope, *An Autobiography*, ed. Michael Sadleir and Frederick Page, introd. P. D. Edwards (Oxford World's Classics, 1999), ch. xii, p. 234.
3. Graham Greene, *Stamboul Train* (Bodley Head, 1974), p. x.
4. *Devotions upon Emergent Occasions*, XVII.
5. Gerard Genette, *Paratexts: Thresholds of Interpretation*, trans. Jane E. Lewin (Cambridge University Press, 1997), 160.
6. I owe this to Edgar Wright's annotations to his Oxford World's Classics edition of *Mary Barton* (1998). We now know that Gaskell had another son who died, in about 1839. It may be that he is the other one of the two ghostly beings mentioned in the epigraph. See Jenny Uglow, *Elizabeth Gaskell* (Faber, 1993), 126, 154–5.

CHAPTER 2

1. Henry James, *The Ambassadors*, New York edition, xxi (Scribner's, 1909; repr. 1937), p. xvii.
2. Ibid., p. xix.
3. Letter, 3 Mar. 1911. See *Henry James: A Life in Letters*, ed. Philip Horne (Penguin, 1999), 500.
4. David Lodge, *Consciousness and the Novel* (Penguin, 2002), 86.
5. Wayne C. Booth, *The Rhetoric of Fiction* (University of Chicago Press, 1961); see 158–9.
6. T. S. Eliot, *The Waste Land*, I: 'The Burial of the Dead', line 76.
7. Lodge, *Consciousness and the Novel*, 46.

CHAPTER 3

1. L. C. Knights, 'How Many Children Had Lady Macbeth?' (1933), in *'Hamlet' and Other Shakespearean Essays* (Cambridge University Press, 1979), 285.
2. Mieke Bal, *Narratology: Introduction to the Theory of Narrative*, trans. Christine van Boheemen (University of Toronto Press, 1985), 80.
3. Anthony Trollope, *An Autobiography*, ed. Michael Sadleir and Frederick Page, introd. P. D. Edwards (Oxford World's Classics, 1999), ch. xxii, p. 229.
4. John Bayley, *The Characters of Love: A Study in the Literature of Personality* (Constable, 1960), 33.
5. *Boswell's London Journal*, ed. Frederick A. Pottle (Yale University Press, 1992), 47.
6. *New York Review of Books*, 11/11 (19 Dec. 1968).
7. Ibid.
8. In Arthur Conan Doyle, *The Adventures of Sherlock Holmes and the Memoirs of Sherlock Holmes* (Penguin, 2001), 490.

CHAPTER 4

1. Alastair Fowler, *Kinds of Literature: An Introduction to the Theory of Genres and Modes* (1982; Oxford University Press, 1987), 20.
2. Ibid. 31.

3. See Charles Dickens, *Household Words*, 14 Sept. 1850; repr. in *Charles Dickens: Selected Journalism 1850–1870*, ed. David Pascoe (Penguin, 1997), 269–76.
4. Godwin gave this account in his preface to the 1832 edition of his novel *Fleetwood*. It is reproduced as an appendix to David McCracken's Oxford World's Classics edition of *Caleb Williams* (1998). This passage is on p. 337.
5. William Congreve, Preface to *Incognita* (1692), in Paul Salzman (ed.), *An Anthology of Seventeenth-Century Fiction* (Oxford World's Classics, 1991), 474.

CHAPTER 5

1. Hardy published his rejoinder in the *Athenaeum*, 30 Nov. 1878. I owe my knowledge of his article to Raymond Chapman, *Forms of Speech in Victorian Fiction* (Longman, 1994), 54, from which I take my quotations.
2. Letter to W. S. Williams, 27 Sept. 1850, in *The Letters of Charlotte Brontë*, ed. Margaret Smith, 3 vols. (Oxford University Press, 1995–2004), ii. 479.
3. See Wayne C. Booth, *The Rhetoric of Fiction* (University of Chicago Press, 1961), 2.
4. David Lodge, *Consciousness and the Novel* (Penguin, 2003), 173.
5. David Lodge, *The Art of Fiction* (Penguin, 1992), 170.
6. See Kingsley Amis, *The King's English: A Guide to Modern Usage* (HarperCollins, 1997), 72–4.

CHAPTER 6

1. Anthony Trollope, *An Autobiography*, ed. Michael Sadleir and Frederick Page, introd. P. D. Edwards (Oxford World's Classics, 1999), ch. xii, p. 232.
2. From an interview with Tom LeClair quoted in Tony Tanner, 'Afterthoughts on Don DeLillo's *Underworld*', *Raritan*, 17/4 (Spring 1998), 56.

CHAPTER 7

1. In Pat Rogers (ed.), *Defoe: The Critical Heritage* (Routledge & Kegan Paul, 1972), 118.
2. Graham Greene, Introduction to *The Heart of the Matter* (Bodley Head, 1971), p. vii.
3. BBC Books, 1989.
4. Letter to Sarah Orne Jewett, 5 Oct. 1901, in *Henry James: A Life in Letters*, ed. Philip Horne (Penguin, 1999), 360.

CHAPTER 8

1. Jonathan Swift, 'Apophthegms and Maxims', in Angus Ross and David Woolley (eds.), *The Oxford Authors: Jonathan Swift* (Oxford University Press, 1984), 183.
2. I. A. Richards, *Practical Criticism* (Routledge, 1982), 182.
3. Ian Watt, *The Rise of the Novel* (Penguin, 1979), 31.
4. Albert C. Baugh and Thomas Cable, *A History of the English Language* (1951; Routledge, 2002), 244.
5. Letter to Anna Austen, 28 Sept. 1814, in *Jane Austen's Letters*, ed. Deirdre Le Faye (1995; Oxford University Press, 1997).
6. Letter to William Leon Mead, 27 Mar. 1899, in *Henry James: A Life in Letters*, ed. Philip Horne (Penguin, 1999), 315.
7. Quoted in Marjorie Donker and George M. Muldrow, *Dictionary of Literary-Rhetorical Conventions of the English Renaissance* (Greenwood Press, 1982), 58.
8. John Lennard, *But I Digress* (Oxford University Press, 1991), 141.
9. Walter Scott, *Chronicles of the Canongate*, ed. Claire Lamont (Edinburgh University Press, 2000), 9.

CHAPTER 9

1. See Deirdre Le Faye and W. and R. A. Austen-Leigh, *Jane Austen: A Family Record* (G. K. Hall, 1989), 83.
2. See Homer, *The Iliad*, trans. Richmond Lattimore (1951; University of Chicago Press, 1961), 18. 478–607.
3. *The Complete Notebooks of Henry James*, ed. Leon Edel and Lyall H. Powers (Oxford University Press, 1987), 57.

CHAPTER 10

1. Robert Burton, 'Democritus Junior to the Reader', in Burton, *The Anatomy of Melancholy*, ed. Thomas C. Faulkner, Nicolas K. Kiessling, and Rhonda L. Blair (Oxford University Press, 1989), i. 9.
2. See Alan B. Howes, *Yorick and the Critics* (Archon Books, 1971), ch. 4.
3. See Julia Briggs, *Virginia Woolf: An Inner Life* (Allen Lane, 2005), 147.
4. Samuel Johnson and James Boswell, *A Journey to the Western Islands of Scotland and The Journal of a Tour to the Hebrides* (Penguin, 1984), 245.
5. Friedrich Nietzsche, *Mixed Opinions and Maxims*, aphorism 168, in *Sämtliche Werke. Kritische Studienausgabe*, ed. Giorgio Colli and Mazzino Montinari (de Gruyter, 1980), ii. 446. The same thought is repeated in his *Twilight of the Idols*, trans. R. J. Hollingdale (Penguin, 1968), sect. 51, p. 104.
6. Sir Thomas Browne, *Religio Medici* (1643), ed. L. C. Martin (Oxford University Press, 1964), sects. 23, 24.
7. Coetzee was probably himself quoting from memory, for the lines in the novel contain a slight misquotation: 'may' for what is 'might' in the original.
8. Charles Baudelaire, 'L'Invitation au voyage', in Baudelaire, *Les Fleurs du mal*, ed. Claude Pichois (Gallimard, 1996).
9. *The Vision of Piers Plowman*, ed. A. V. C. Schmidt (Dent, 1978), 1.

CHAPTER 11

1. He wrote this in the preface to a new edition of his novel *Fleetwood*. It is reproduced as an appendix to the Oxford World's Classics edition of *Caleb Williams*, ed. David McCracken (1998), 337.
2. *Der Proceß* (S. Fischer, 1990), 312.
3. John Forster, *The Life of Charles Dickens*, 2 vols. (1871–3; Chapman Hall, 1911), ii. 324.
4. The original ending was first printed in Forster's *Life*. It is reprinted as an appendix to the Penguin Classics edition (1996), 508–9, from which I quote.

5. *The Complete Notebooks of Henry James*, ed. Leon Edel and Lyall H. Powers (Oxford University Press, 1987), 15.
6. Deirdre Le Faye and W. and R. A. Austen-Leigh, *Jane Austen: A Family Record* (G. K. Hall, 1989), 216.

Select Bibliography

NOVELS

ACKROYD, PETER, *Hawksmoor* (Penguin, 1993).

—— *The House of Mr Dee* (Penguin, 1994).

ALCOTT, LOUISA M., *Little Women*, ed. Valerie Anderson (Oxford World's Classics, 1998).

AMIS, KINGSLEY, *Lucky Jim*, introd. David Lodge (Penguin, 1992).

AMIS, MARTIN, *The Information* (Flamingo, 1995).

—— *Success* (Vintage, 2004).

—— *Yellow Dog* (Vintage, 2004).

AUSTEN, JANE, *Emma*, ed. James Kinsley, introd. Adela Pinch (Oxford World's Classics, 2003).

—— *Jane Austen's Letters*, ed. Deidre Le Faye (Oxford University Press, 1997).

—— *Mansfield Park*, ed. James Kinsley, introd. Marilyn Butler (Oxford World's Classics, 1990).

—— *Northanger Abbey*, ed. John Davie, introd. Terry Castle (Oxford World's Classics, 1990).

—— *Persuasion*, ed. Gillian Beer (Penguin, 2003).

—— *Pride and Prejudice*, ed. Fiona Stafford (Oxford World's Classics, 2004).

—— *Sense and Sensibility*, ed. James Kinsley, introd. Margaret Anne Doody (Oxford World's Classics, 1990).

BANVILLE, JOHN, *Doctor Copernicus* (Picador, 1999).

—— *Kepler* (Granada, 1983).

—— *The Untouchable* (Picador, 1997).

BRADBURY, MALCOLM, *To the Hermitage* (Picador, 2001).

BRONTË, CHARLOTTE, *Jane Eyre*, ed. Michael Mason (Penguin, 1996).

BRONTË, CHARLOTTE, *Villette*, ed. Mark Lilly (Penguin, 1979).

BRONTË, EMILY, *Wuthering Heights*, ed. Ian Jack (Oxford World's Classics, 1983).

BRUNTON, MARY, *Self-Control* (Pandora, 1986).

BURNEY, FANNY, *Evelina*, ed. Edward A. Bloom (Oxford World's Classics, 1982).

BYATT, A. S., *Babel Tower* (Vintage, 1997).

CALVINO, ITALO, *If on a Winter's Night a Traveller* (Vintage, 1998).

CHANDLER, RAYMOND, *The Big Sleep*, in *Three Novels* (Penguin, 1993).

COE, JONATHAN, *The Closed Circle* (Penguin, 2004).

—— *The House of Sleep* (Penguin, 1998).

COLLINS, WILKIE, *The Moonstone*, ed. John Sutherland (Oxford World's Classics, 1999).

—— *The Woman in White*, ed. John Sutherland (Oxford World's Classics, 1999).

CONAN DOYLE, ARTHUR, *The Adventures of Sherlock Holmes and the Memoirs of Sherlock Holmes* (Penguin, 2001).

CONRAD, JOSEPH, *Heart of Darkness*, ed. Robert Hampson (Penguin, 1995).

—— *Nostromo*, ed. K. Carabine (Oxford World's Classics, 1994).

—— *The Secret Agent*, ed. Roger Tennant (Oxford World's Classics, 1983).

COVENTRY, FRANCIS, *The History of Pompey the Little*, ed. R. A. Day (Oxford University Press, 1974).

CRICHTON, MICHAEL, *Disclosure* (Arrow, 1994).

DE BERNIÈRES, LOUIS, *Birds Without Wings* (Secker & Warburg, 2004).

—— *Captain Corelli's Mandolin* (Minerva, 1995).

DEFOE, DANIEL, *A Journal of the Plague Year*, ed. Louis Landa, introd. David Roberts (Oxford World's Classics, 1990).

—— *Moll Flanders*, ed. G. A. Starr (Oxford World's Classics, 1990).

—— *Robinson Crusoe*, ed. J. Donald Crowley (Oxford World's Classics, 1983).

—— *Roxana*, ed. John Mullan (Oxford World's Classics, 1996).

DEXTER, COLIN, *The Dead of Jericho* (Pan, 1982).

DICKENS, CHARLES, *Bleak House*, ed. Stephen Gill (Oxford World's Classics, 1998).

—— *David Copperfield*, ed. Nina Burgis, introd. Andrew Sanders (Oxford World's Classics, 1999).

—— *Dombey and Son*, ed. Alan Horsman, introd. Dennis Walder (Oxford World's Classics, 2001).

—— *Great Expectations*, ed. Charlotte Mitchell and David Trotter (Penguin, 1996).

—— *Nicholas Nickleby*, ed. Mark Ford (Penguin, 2003).

—— *The Old Curiosity Shop*, ed. Elizabeth M. Brennan (Oxford World's Classics, 1999).

—— *Oliver Twist*, ed. Kathleen Tillotson (Oxford World's Classics, 1982).

—— *Our Mutual Friend*, ed. Adrian Poole (Penguin, 1997).

—— *The Pickwick Papers*, ed. James Kinsley, rev. Kathleen Tillotson (Oxford World's Classics, 1998).

—— *A Tale of Two Cities*, ed. Richard Maxwell (Penguin, 2000).

EASTON ELLIS, BRETT, *American Psycho* (Picador, 1991).

EDGEWORTH, MARIA, *Belinda*, ed. Kathryn Kirkpatrick (Oxford World's Classics, 1999).

ELIOT, GEORGE, *Adam Bede*, ed. Valentine Cunningham (Oxford World's Classics, 1998).

—— *Daniel Deronda*, ed. Graham Handley (Oxford World's Classics, 1988).

—— *Middlemarch*, ed. Rosemary Ashton (Penguin, 1994).

—— *Romola*, ed. Dorothea Barrett (Penguin, 1996).

ELLROY, JAMES, *LA Confidential* (Arrow, 1994).

FAULKNER, WILLIAM, *As I Lay Dying* (Vintage, 2004).

FIELDING, HENRY, *Joseph Andrews*, ed. D. Brooks-Davies and Martin C. Battestin, introd. Thomas Keymer (Oxford World's Classics, 1999).

—— *Tom Jones*, ed. John Bender and Simon Stern (Oxford World's Classics, 1996).

FITZGERALD, F. SCOTT, *The Great Gatsby*, introd. Tony Tanner (Penguin, 2000).

—— *Tender Is the Night*, ed. Richard Godden (Penguin, 1975).

FLEMING, IAN, *Dr No* (Penguin, 2002).

—— *Goldfinger* (Penguin, 2004).

—— *The Spy Who Loved Me* (Penguin, 2002).

FLEMING, IAN, *Thunderball* (Penguin, 2002).

FODEN, GILES, *The Last King of Scotland* (Faber, 1998).

FORD, FORD MADOX, *The Good Soldier*, ed. David Bradshaw (Penguin, 2002).

FORSTER, E. M., *A Room With a View*, ed. Oliver Stallybrass (Penguin, 2000).

GARNER, ALAN, *Red Shift* (CollinsVoyager, 2002).

GASKELL, ELIZABETH, *Mary Barton*, ed. Edgar Wright (Oxford World's Classics, 1998).

—— *Wives and Daughters*, ed. Pam Morris (Penguin, 1996).

GODWIN, WILLIAM, *Caleb Williams*, ed. David McCracken (Oxford World's Classics, 1998).

GOLDING, WILLIAM, *Lord of the Flies* (Faber, 1996).

GOLDSMITH, OLIVER, *The Vicar of Wakefield*, ed. Arthur Friedman (Oxford World's Classics, 1999).

GREENE, GRAHAM, *The Heart of the Matter* (Bodley Head, 1971).

—— *Stamboul Train* (Bodley Head, 1974).

HARDY, THOMAS, *Far from the Madding Crowd*, ed. Rosemarie Morgan and Shannon Russell (Penguin, 2000).

—— *Tess of the d'Urbervilles*, ed. Juliet Grindle and Simon Gatrell, introd. Penny Boumelha (Oxford World's Classics, 2005).

—— *Under the Greenwood Tree*, ed. Simon Gatrell (Oxford World's Classics, 1999).

HARTLEY, L. P., *The Go-Between*, ed. Douglas Brooks-Davies (Penguin, 2000).

HEMINGWAY, ERNEST, *In Our Time* (Scribner, 1986).

HEYER, GEORGETTE, *An Infamous Army* (Arrow, 2004).

HIGHSMITH, PATRICIA, *The Talented Mr Ripley* (Vintage, 1999).

HOLLINGHURST, ALAN, *The Folding Star* (Vintage, 1995).

—— *The Line of Beauty* (Picador, 2004).

JAMES, HENRY, *The Ambassadors*, New York edn., xxi (Scribner's 1909; repr. 1937).

—— *The Aspern Papers and The Turn of the Screw*, ed. Anthony Curtis (Penguin, 1985).

—— *The Awkward Age*, ed. Vivien Jones (Oxford World's Classics, 1999).

—— *The Portrait of a Lady*, ed. Nicola Bradbury (Oxford World's Classics, 1998).

JOHNSTONE, CHARLES, *Chrysal; or, The Adventures of a Guinea* (1760–5).

JOYCE, JAMES, *A Portrait of the Artist as a Young Man*, ed. Jeri Johnson (Oxford World's Classics, 2000).

—— *Ulysses* (Penguin, 1992).

KAFKA, FRANZ, *The Trial* (Penguin, 1994).

—— *Der Proceß* (S. Fischer, 1990).

LANCHESTER, JOHN, *The Debt to Pleasure* (Picador, 1997).

LAWRENCE, D. H., *Women in Love*, ed. David Bradshaw (Oxford World's Classics, 1998).

LE CARRÉ, JOHN, *Tinker, Tailor, Soldier, Spy* (Sceptre, 1999).

LESSING, DORIS, *The Golden Notebook* (McGraw-Hill, 1963).

LEWIS, MATTHEW, *The Monk*, ed. Howard Anderson (Oxford World's Classics, 1973).

LODGE, DAVID, *Author, Author* (Secker & Warburg, 2004).

—— *Small World* (Penguin, 1985).

LOTT, TIM, *Rumours of a Hurricane* (Penguin, 2003).

MCEWAN, IAN, *The Cement Garden* (Vintage, 1997).

MANKEL, HENNING, *One Step Behind* (Vintage, 2000).

MELVILLE, HERMAN, *Moby-Dick*, ed. Andrew Delbanco and Tom Quirk (Penguin, 1992).

NABOKOV, VLADIMIR, *Lolita* (Penguin, 2000).

O'BRIAN, PATRICK, *The Yellow Admiral* (HarperCollins, 2003).

ORWELL, GEORGE, *Nineteen Eighty-Four* (Penguin, 2000).

PEARS, IAIN, *The Dream of Scipio* (Vintage, 2003).

—— *An Instance of the Fingerpost* (Vintage, 1998).

PEARSON, ALLISON, *I Don't Know How She Does It* (Vintage, 2003).

POWELL, ANTHONY, *A Dance to the Music of Time*, 12 vols. (Arrow, 2005).

PROULX, E. ANNIE, *The Shipping News* (Fourth Estate, 1994).

PROUST, MARCEL, *Remembrance of Things Past*, trans. C. K. Scott-Moncrieff, rev. Terence Kilmartin (Penguin, 1983).

RADCLIFFE, ANN, *The Mysteries of Udolpho*, ed. B. Dobrée, introd. Terry Castle (Oxford World's Classics, 1998).

RENDELL, RUTH, *The Bridesmaid* (Arrow, 1990).

RENDELL, RUTH (as Barbara Vine), *The Brimstone Wedding* (Penguin, 1996).
—— *The Crocodile Bird* (Arrow, 1994).
—— *Going Wrong* (Arrow, 1991).
—— *The Keys to the Street* (Arrow, 1997).
—— *The Killing Doll* (Arrow, 1985).
RICHARDSON, SAMUEL, *Clarissa*, ed. Angus Ross (Penguin, 1986).
—— *Pamela*, ed. T. Keymer and A. Wakely (Oxford World's Classics, 2001).
—— *Sir Charles Grandison*, ed. Jocelyn Harris (Oxford World's Classics, 1986).
ROTH, PHILIP, *American Pastoral* (Vintage, 2005).
—— *The Ghost Writer* (Vintage International, 1995).
—— *My Life as a Man* (Vintage International, 1993).
—— *Zuckerman Unbound*, in *Zuckerman Bound: A Trilogy and Epilogue* (Vintage, 1998).
RUSHDIE, SALMAN, *Midnight's Children* (Picador, 1982).
SALINGER, J. D., *The Catcher in the Rye* (Penguin, 1994).
SCOTT, WALTER, *Chronicles of the Canongate*, ed. Claire Lamont (Edinburgh University Press, 2000).
—— *The Heart of Midlothian*, ed. Claire Lamont (Oxford World's Classics, 1982).
—— *Ivanhoe*, ed. Graham Tulloch (Penguin, 2000).
—— *Old Mortality*, ed. Angus Calder (Penguin, 1985).
SMILEY, JANE, *A Thousand Acres* (Harper Perennial, 2004).
SMOLLETT, TOBIAS, *The Adventures of Peregrine Pickle*, ed. James L. Clifford (Oxford University Press, 1969).
—— *The Expedition of Humphry Clinker*, ed. Lewis M. Knapp, rev. Paul-Gabriel Bouce (Oxford World's Classics, 1998).
SPARK, MURIEL, *The Finishing School* (Penguin, 2005).
STERNE, LAURENCE, *The Life and Opinions of Tristram Shandy, Gentleman*, ed. Melvyn New and Joan New (Penguin, 1997).
—— *The Life and Opinions of Tristram Shandy, Gentleman*, i and ii: *The Text*, ed. Melvyn New and Joan New, iii: *The Notes*, by Melvyn New, Richard A. Davies, and W. G. Day (University Presses of Florida, 1978, 1984).
—— *A Sentimental Journey*, ed. Paul Goring (Penguin, 2001).

TARTT, DONNA, *The Little Friend* (Bloomsbury, 2003).

THACKERAY, WILLIAM MAKEPEACE, *The History of Henry Esmond, Esq.*, ed. Donald Hawes (Oxford World's Classics, 1991).

—— *Vanity Fair*, ed. John Sutherland (Oxford World's Classics, 1983).

TÓIBÍN, COLM, *The Master* (Picador, 2005).

TOLSTOY, LEO, *Anna Karenin*, trans. Rosemary Edmonds (Penguin, 1978).

TREMAIN, ROSE, *Music and Silence* (Vintage, 2000).

TREVOR, WILLIAM, *A Bit on the Side* (Penguin, 2005).

TROLLOPE, ANTHONY, *Is He Popenjoy?*, ed. John Sutherland (Oxford World's Classics, 1986).

—— *The Way We Live Now*, ed. John Sutherland (Oxford World's Classics, 1999).

TWAIN, MARK, *The Adventures of Huckleberry Finn*, ed. Peter Coveney (Penguin, 1985).

VIDAL, GORE, *Lincoln* (Abacus, 1994).

WALKER, ALICE, *The Color Purple* (Phoenix, 2004).

WALPOLE, HORACE, *The Castle of Otranto* ed. Michael Gamer (Penguin, 2001).

WAUGH, EVELYN, *Brideshead Revisited* (Penguin, 2000).

—— *A Handful of Dust*, ed. Robert Murray Davis (Penguin, 2000).

—— *Vile Bodies*, ed. Richard Jacobs (Penguin, 2000).

WOOLF, VIRGINIA, *Mrs Dalloway*, ed. David Bradshaw (Oxford World's Classics, 2000).

—— *To the Lighthouse*, ed. Margaret Drabble (Oxford World's Classics, 2000).

OTHER WORKS

AMIS, KINGSLEY, *The King's English: A Guide to Modern Usage* (HarperCollins, 1997).

AUSTEN, JANE, *Jane Austen's Letters*, ed. Deidre Le Faye (Oxford University Press, 1997).

BAL, MIEKE, *Narratology: Introduction to the Theory of Narrative*, trans. Christine van Boheemen (University of Toronto Press, 1985).

BARKER, JULIET, *The Brontës* (Phoenix, 1999).

BAUDELAIRE, CHARLES, *Les Fleurs du mal*, ed. Claude Pichois (Gallimard, 1996).

BAUGH, ALBERT C., and THOMAS CABLE, *A History of the English Language* (Routledge, 2002).

BAYLEY, JOHN, *The Characters of Love: A Study in the Literature of Personality* (Constable, 1960).

BOOTH, WAYNE C., *The Rhetoric of Fiction* (University of Chicago Press, 1961).

BOSWELL, JAMES, *Boswell's London Journal*, ed. Frederick A. Pottle (Yale University Press, 1992).

BRIGGS, JULIA, *Virginia Woolf: An Inner Life* (Allen Lane, 2005).

BRONTË, CHARLOTTE, *The Letters of Charlotte Brontë*, ed. Margaret Smith, 3 vols. (Oxford University Press, 1995–2004).

BROWNE, SIR THOMAS, *Religio Medici*, ed. L. C. Martin (Oxford University Press, 1964).

BURTON, ROBERT, *The Anatomy of Melancholy*, ed. Thomas C. Faulkner, Nicolas K. Kiessling, and Rhonda L. Blair (Oxford University Press, 1989).

CHAPMAN, RAYMOND, *Forms of Speech in Victorian Fiction* (Longman, 1994).

DICKENS, CHARLES, *Selected Journalism 1850–1870*, ed. David Pascoe (Penguin, 1997).

DONKER, MARJORIE, and GEORGE M. MULDROW, *Dictionary of Literary-Rhetorical Conventions of the English Renaissance* (Greenwood Press, 1982).

ELIOT, T. S., *Selected Poems* (1954; repr. Faber, 2002).

FORSTER, JOHN, *The Life of Charles Dickens*, 2 vols. (Chapman Hall, 1911).

FOWLER, ALASTAIR, *Kinds of Literature: An Introduction to the Theory of Genres and Modes* (Oxford University Press, 1987).

FRASER, REBECCA, *The Brontës: Charlotte Brontë and Her Family* (Crown Publishers, 1988).

GENETTE, GERARD, *Paratexts: Thresholds of Interpretation*, trans. Jane E. Lewin (Cambridge University Press, 1997).

HOMER, *The Iliad*, trans. Richmond Lattimore (University of Chicago Press, 1961).

—— *The Odyssey*, trans. Robert Fitzgerald (1961; Harvill, 1988).

HOWES, ALAN B., *Yorick and the Critics* (Archon Books, 1971).

JAMES, HENRY, *The Complete Notebooks of Henry James*, ed. Leon Edel and Lyall H. Powers (Oxford University Press, 1987).

—— *Henry James: A Life in Letters*, ed. Philip Horne (Penguin, 1999).

JOHNSON, SAMUEL, and JAMES BOSWELL, *A Journey to the Western Islands of Scotland and The Journal of a Tour to the Hebrides* (Penguin, 1984).

KNIGHTS, L. C., 'How Many Children Had Lady Macbeth?' (1933), in *'Hamlet' and Other Shakespearean Essays* (Cambridge University Press, 1979).

LE FAYE, DEIRDRE, and W. and R. A. AUSTEN-LEIGH, *Jane Austen: A Family Record* (G. K. Hall, 1989).

LENNARD, JOHN, *But I Digress* (Oxford University Press, 1991).

LODGE, DAVID, *The Art of Fiction* (Penguin, 1992).

—— *Consciousness and the Novel* (Penguin, 2003).

NIETZSCHE, FRIEDRICH, *Mixed Opinions and Maxims*, in *Sämtliche Werke. Kritische Studienausgabe*, ed. Giorgio Colli and Mazzino Montinari (de Gruyter, 1980).

RICHARDS, I. A., *Practical Criticism* (Routledge, 1982).

ROGERS, PAT (ed.), *Defoe: The Critical Heritage* (Routledge & Kegan Paul, 1972).

ROSS, ANGUS and DAVID WOOLLEY (eds), *The Oxford Authors: Jonathan Swift* (Oxford University Press, 1984).

SALZMAN, PAUL (ed.), *An Anthology of Seventeenth-Century Fiction* (Oxford World's Classics, 1991).

SUTHERLAND, JOHN, *Victorian Novelists and Publishers* (University of Chicago Press, 1978).

TENNYSON, ALFRED, LORD, *Tennyson: A Selected Edition*, ed. Christopher Ricks (Longman, 1989).

TROLLOPE, ANTHONY, *An Autobiography*, ed. Michael Sadleir and Frederick Page, introd. P. D. Edwards (Oxford World's Classics, 1999).

UGLOW, JENNY, *Elizabeth Gaskell* (Faber, 1993).

The Vision of Piers Plowman, ed. A. V. C. Schmidt (Dent, 1978).

WATT, IAN, *The Rise of the Novel* (Penguin, 1979).

Index

The main entries on given topics or works are indicated in bold type.